Families and Children with Special Needs

Professional and Family Partnerships

● ● ● ● ● ● ● ● ● ● ● ● ● ● ● ○ ○

Tom E. C. Smith
University of Arkansas

Barbara C. Gartin
University of Arkansas

Nikki L. Murdick
Saint Louis University

Alan Hilton
*Special Education Local Plan Area,
San Luis Obispo County, California*

PEARSON

Merrill
Prentice Hall

Upper Saddle River, New Jersey
Columbus, Ohio

Library of Congress Cataloging-in-Publication Data

Families and children with special needs: professional and family partnerships / Tom E.
C. Smith .. [et al.].—1st ed.
   p. cm.
   Includes bibliographical references and index.
   ISBN 0-13-570003-5
   1. Children with disabilities—United States—Family relationships. 2. Special
education—United States—Parent participation. 3. Children with disabilities—Services
for—United States. I. Smith, Tom E. C.

HQ773.6.F357 2006
371.9'04—dc22

2004066193

Vice President and Executive Publisher: Jeffery W. Johnston
Acquisitions Editor: Allyson P Sharp
Editorial Assistant: Kathleen S. Burk
Production Editor: Sheryl Glicker Langner
Production Coordination: Jolynn Feller, Carlisle Publishers Services, Inc.
Design Coordinator: Diane C. Lorenzo
Photo Coordinator: Maria B. Vonada
Cover Designer: Jason Moore
Cover image: Corbis
Production Manager: Laura Messerly
Director of Marketing: Ann Castel Davis
Marketing Manager: Autumn Purdy
Marketing Coordinator: Brian Mounts

This book was set in Novarese Book by Carlisle Communications, Ltd. It was printed and bound by Courier
Stoughton, Inc. The cover was printed by Courier Stoughton, Inc.

Photo Credits:
Tim Cairns/Merrill, p. 1; Ken Karp/PH College, p. 19; Anthony Magnacca/.Merrill, pp. 39, 79; Barbara Schwartz/
Merrill, p. 55; Andy Brunk/Merrill, p. 103; Tom Watson/Merrill, p. 135; Scott Cunningham/Merrill, pp. 161, 205;
Anne Vega/Merrill, pp. 183, 219.

Pearson Prentice Hall™ is a trademark of Pearson Education, Inc.
Pearson® is a registered trademark of Pearson plc
Prentice Hall® is a registered trademark of Pearson Education, Inc.
Merrill® is a registered trademark of Pearson Education, Inc.

Pearson Education Ltd.
Pearson Education Singapore Pte. Ltd.
Pearson Education Canada, Ltd.
Pearson Education—Japan

Pearson Education Australia Pty. Limited
Pearson Education North Asia Ltd.
Pearson Educación de Mexico, S.A. de C.V.
Pearson Education Malaysia Pte. Ltd.

10 9 8 7 6 5 4 3 2 1
ISBN: 0-13-570003-5

To our children, spouses, and the special individuals who
share our lives, and who help make us a family.
Specifically, to:

Debi
Alex
Suni
Jake

Ed
Meredith

Mike
Jason
Lynn

Jason
Tyson
Zachary

Educator Learning Center: An Invaluable Online Resource

Merrill Education and the Association for Supervision and Curriculum Development (ASCD) invite you to take advantage of a new online resource, one that provides access to the top research and proven strategies associated with ASCD and Merrill— the Educator Learning Center. At **www.educatorlearningcenter.com**, you will find resources that will enhance your students' understanding of course topics and of current educational issues, in addition to being invaluable for further research.

HOW THE EDUCATOR LEARNING CENTER WILL HELP YOUR STUDENTS BECOME BETTER TEACHERS

With the combined resources of Merrill Education and ASCD, you and your students will find a wealth of tools and materials to better prepare them for the classroom.

Research

- More than 600 articles from the ASCD journal *Educational Leadership* discuss everyday issues faced by practicing teachers.
- A direct link on the site to Research Navigator™ gives students access to many of the leading education journals, as well as extensive content detailing the research process.
- Excerpts from Merrill Education texts give your students insights on important topics of instructional methods diverse populations, assessment, classroom management, technology, and refining classroom practice.

Classroom Practice

- Hundreds of lesson plans and teaching strategies are categorized by content area and age range.
- Case studies and classroom video footage provide virtual field experience for student reflection.
- Computer simulations and other electronic tools keep your students abreast of today's classrooms and current technologies.

LOOK INTO THE VALUE OF EDUCATOR LEARNING CENTER YOURSELF

A four-month subscription to Educator Learning Center is $25 but is **FREE** when packaged with any Merrill Education text. In order for your students to have access to this site, you must use this special value-pack ISBN number **WHEN** placing your textbook order with the bookstore: 0-13-155249-X. Your students will then receive a copy of the text packaged with a free ASCD pincode. To preview the value of this website to you and your students, please go to **www.educatorlearningcenter.com** and click on "Demo."

Preface

Although the definitions of families differ from source to source, most dictionaries generally define families as parents and children; a group of individuals living together in a supportive manner; or groups of individuals genetically related. Partnerships, on the other hand, are often defined as persons having a joint interest or a group of individuals having an association.

On the surface, the process of developing effective partnerships between families and school professionals seems easy. Invite family members to the school; sit down and get to know each other; discuss issues about the child; make important decisions about the child. However, as anyone who has worked in schools knows, developing effective partnerships between families and school professionals is not easy. They are not easy to develop; and they are not easy to maintain. Effective, collaborative partnerships between professionals and family members are worth the effort and should always be pursued.

Although parent–professional partnerships are important for all children, they are especially critical for children with special needs. Since the mid-1970s, educators have been required by federal and state laws to secure meaningful involvement of family members in the educational programs for children with special needs. They must be involved in every step of the special education process, from referral to annual reviews and reevaluations. Schools can choose to involve parents, or *really* involve parents. Having family members sitting around a table and signing forms is not real involvement. *Real* involvement means that family members are involved in the discussions about their child and decisions affecting their child. They are "at the table" as equal if not senior partners in the education of their children. Gone are the days when professional educators made decisions about children in isolation because they felt like they knew what was in the best interest of the child. We in the business of providing services to children with special needs and their families have finally come to realize that without family involvement, real involvement, our efforts will not be as successful as they could be. We have finally begun to realize that we are not the helpers and providers, we are the supporters and collaborators. Together, school professionals and family members can make a difference in the lives of children with special needs.

This text provides an overview of families and how effective parent–professional partnerships can be developed and maintained. It provides a practical approach to parent–professional partnerships. Even though there are several texts on the market that focus on families and children with disabilities, this text offers several advantages and features not available in other books. First, this book is written from a very practical approach. Although research is provided to support various concepts and interventions, the primary focus of this text is on practical applications. Teachers must not only know the composition of families and why it is important to involve families, but also must know specific steps to include them and maximize their involvement. This text provides such steps.

Examples of parent–professional partnerships, through real-life scenarios, are provided throughout the book to give the reader an idea about how real situations between schools and families develop, and how to work with family members in the best interest of the child. Many of these scenarios can be used as a basis for discussions about what actions could be taken to effectively deal with the issues presented. Each chapter provides specific teacher tips that give down-to-earth, practical suggestions for school professionals when working with families. Finally, standards and principles from the Council for Exceptional Children (CEC), Interstate New Teacher Assessment and Support Consortium (INTASC), and Praxis (Special Education Knowledge-Based Core Principles) are referenced in the margins to reflect the connection between content in this text and the standards and principles of these organizations. A complete list of these principles and standards is located in the Appendix in the back of this book. This text will provide students with a strong foundation for understanding families and ways to develop strong parent–professional partnerships to facilitate the education of children with special needs.

We would like to thank all those who have been involved in this project, especially our families who have put up with the time we have spent away from them, either physically or mentally, while preparing this book. We also want to thank all those at Merrill/Prentice Hall who have been resolute in their support and patience as we labored to put this manuscript together. We especially want to thank Ann Davis, who originally signed the book, and Allyson Sharp, who took over and helped guide us through the final stages.

We also want to thank those who provided formal reviews of the book. Their comments and positive critiques had a very positive impact on the final product: Robert Ortiz, California State University, Fullerton; Kenneth M. Coffey, Mississippi State University; Greg Conderman, Northern Illinois University; Alec F. Peck, Boston College; Melanie Jephson, Stephen F. Austin State University; James A. Siders, The University of Southern Mississippi; Ellen Williams, Bowling Green State University; David W. Anderson, Bethel College; Abigail Baxter, University of South Alabama; Jane B. Pemberton, University of North Texas; Kimberly Fields, Albany State University; and Kimberly Callicott, Texas A&M University.

Finally, we want to thank all professionals and family members who strive to work together to improve the lives of children and adolescents with special needs. Through their tireless efforts, the lives of individuals are changed daily.

Discover the Merrill Education Resources for Special Education Website

Technology is a constantly growing and changing aspect of our field that is creating a need for new content and resources. To address this emerging need, Merrill Education has developed an online learning environment for students, teachers, and professors alike to complement our products—the *Merrill Education Resources for Special Education* website. This content-rich website provides additional resources specific to this book's topic and will help you—professors, classroom teachers, and students—augment your teaching, learning, and professional development.

Our goal is to build on and enhance what our products already offer. For this reason, the content for our user-friendly website is organized by topic and provides teachers, professors, and students with a variety of meaningful resources all in one location. With this website, we bring together the best of what Merrill has to offer: text resources, video clips, web links, tutorials, and a wide variety of information on topics of interest to general and special educators alike.

Rich content, applications, and competencies further enhance the learning process. The *Merrill Education Resources for Special Education* website includes:

RESOURCES FOR THE PROFESSOR—

- The **Syllabus Manager**™, an online syllabus creation and management tool, enables instructors to create and revise a syllabus with an easy, step-by-step process. Students can access your syllabus and any changes you make during the course of your class from any computer with Internet access. To access this tailored syllabus, students will just need the URL of the website and the password assigned to the syllabus. By clicking on the date, the student can see a list of activities, assignments, and readings due for that particular class.

- In addition to the **Syllabus Manager**™ and its benefits just listed, professors also have access to all of the wonderful resources that students have access to on the site.

RESOURCES FOR THE STUDENT–

- Video clips specific to each topic, with questions to help you evaluate the content and make crucial theory-to-practice connections.
- Thought-provoking critical analysis questions that students can answer and turn in for evaluation or that can serve as basis for class discussions and lectures.
- Access to a wide variety of resources related to classroom strategies and methods, including lesson planning and classroom management.
- Information on all the most current relevant topics related to special and general education, including CEC and Praxis standards, IEPs, portfolios, and professional development.
- Extensive web resources and overviews on each topic addressed on the website.
- A message board with discussion starters where students can respond to class discussion topics, post questions and responses, or ask questions about assignments.
- A search feature to help access specific information quickly.

To take advantage of these and other resources, please visit the *Merrill Education Resources for Special Education* website at

http://www.prenhall.com/smith

Brief Contents

Contents

CHAPTER 4
Working with Families: Understanding Family Factors   55

CHAPTER 5
Working with Families: Respecting Diverse Backgrounds   79

CHAPTER 6
Working with Families: Communicating to Overcome
Challenges and Develop Solutions   103

CHAPTER 7
Working with Families: The Legal Bases
for Family Involvement   135

CHAPTER 11
Working with Families: Understanding Transitioning and the Transition Process   219

Note: *Every effort has been made to provide accurate and current Internet information in this book. However, the Internet and information posted on it are constantly changing, and it is inevitable that some of the Internet addresses listed in this textbook will change.*

CHAPTER 1
Family and School Partnerships

Objectives

After reading this chapter, you will:

- Understand the philosophy that guides special education
- Understand how various issues, such as school organization and neighborhood schools, have impacted family and school partnerships
- Know how laws, in addition to IDEA, are expanding supports for students with learning problems

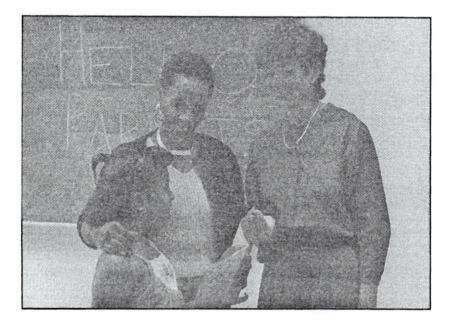

- Understand the trend and rationale behind the inclusion movement
- Know how the roles of school staff have changed and will continue to change
- Understand changes that have occurred in family structure and function
- Know the importance of family empowerment and the role of schools in achieving family empowerment

Family-school partnerships can be characterized by a collaborative relationship between family members and school professionals who focus on the needs of children and their families. Although such partnerships have been found to be extremely helpful in educating children with special needs, the future of such partnerships will be influenced over the next decade by a multitude of factors, such as changing structures of the schools, changes in the delivery of services, changes in training of teachers, the expansion of diversity in the country, changes in family expectations, and an increase in family empowerment. These factors will certainly continue to affect how educational professionals and families of children with disabilities relate, interact, and form partnerships. Understanding these changes and their possible impact will help predict the future of family-school partnerships. These factors are briefly described in this chapter and then expanded in subsequent chapters in this text.

CHANGES AND FUTURE IMPLICATIONS IN THE STRUCTURE OF THE SCHOOLS

INTASC 10

School and Community Involvement

Over the past two to three decades, there have been notable changes in the philosophy and focus of the field of special education that have resulted in special education becoming an integral part of public education in the United States. Since 1975 when Public Law 94-142 became law, the role of families has changed significantly in a positive direction. Bennett, Lee, and Lueke (1998) pointed out that in the past professionals based their role with children having disabilities and their families on a pathological perspective and the development of a therapeutic relationship with the children and their families. Now, educators are beginning to see their role as a builder of family partnerships rather than someone who provides help to the family. This shift has been demonstrated by changes in both terminology and practice in family-school interactions.

CEC 10

Collaboration

CEC 9

Professional and Ethical Practices

Philosophy

The philosophy that guides the special education perspective of families has changed dramatically as knowledge concerning effective pedagogy has increased. Since the enactment of P.L. 94-142, special educators have increased their efforts to involve families of children with disabilities to the fullest extent in the education of their children and to assure parents and students their due-process rights. This change in philosophy can be demonstrated by examining the changes in the terminology, or language, used in the field.

TEACHER TIP 1.1

Teachers need to develop a thorough understanding of the philosophy underlying family involvement in the education of children with disabilities.

In the 1997 amendments to the Individuals with Disabilities Education Act (IDEA), formerly P.L. 94-142, several language changes were incorporated that indicate this changing philosophy. These changes were maintained in the 2004 reauthorization of IDEA. These include the use of the term *disabilities* rather than *handicapped* and the use of "people-first" language emphasizing that individuals with disabilities are, indeed, "people," just like other individuals. In addition to the changes in legal and professional terminology, there have also been changes in research publications, professional journals, and textbooks. Table 1.1 lists in chronological order a sample list of textbooks focusing on working with families. A review of these titles demonstrates the changes in terminology and the shift from professionals "helping" families to "including" family members as partners. The table also shows how textbooks have shifted from terms like *handicapped child* to *child with a disability*, from *parents* to *families*, and from *working with* or *counseling* to *partnerships*. Read the scenario in Box 1.1. Reflect on how the language used indicates a positive approach to working with families of children with disabilities.

PRAXIS 2

Legal and Societal Issues

CEC 9

Professional and Ethical Practices

Table 1.1 Sample of textbooks relating to working with families.

Date Published	Author	Title
1968	Barsch	The parent of the handicapped child: The study of childrearing practices
1979	Seligman	Strategies for helping parents of handicapped children
1979	Heward, Darding, & Rossett	Working with parents of handicapped children
1980	Featherstone	A difference in the family
1981	Marion	Educators, parents, exceptional children
1983	Buscaglia	The disabled and their parents: A counseling challenge
1985	Gargiulo	Working with parents of exceptional children
1986	Steward	Counseling parents of exceptional children
1986	Gallagher & Vietze	Families of handicapped persons
1986	Fewell & Vadasy	Families of handicapped children: Needs and supports across the lifespan
1986	Karpel	Family resources: The hidden partner in family therapy

(continued)

Table 1.1 *Continued*

Date Published	Author	Title
1990	Turnbull & Turnbull	Families, professionals, and exceptionality
1991	Gartner, Lipsky, & Turnbull	Supporting families with children with disabilities
1995	Berger	Parents as partners in education
2000	Lambie	Family systems within educational contexts
2001	O'Shea, O'Shea, Algozzine, & Hammitte	Families and teachers of individuals with disabilities: Collaborative orientations and responsive practices
2001	Turnbull & Turnbull	Families, professionals, and exceptionality: Collaborating for empowerment

Box 1.1

Ms. Bilox is Mattie's third-grade teacher. Ms. Bilox believes that Mattie may have mental retardation, since she is more than 1 year behind her peers in reading and other academic subjects and has difficulties with basic concepts understood by all of her peers. During Mattie's first 3 years of school, she continued to fall further and further behind. The district Mattie attends does not encourage referral for special education until third grade. Now that Mattie is in the third grade, Ms. Bilox is ready to make a referral, and arranges for a conference with Mattie's parents.

At the conference, held after school one day, Ms. Bilox begins by saying: "Thank you for coming to this meeting so we can discuss some of my concerns about your daughter. I have reason to believe that she may have a disability that is causing her to have problems. I want to work with you and Mattie to ensure that she does well in my class."

Mattie's mother asks: "What do you think Mattie's problems could be?"

Ms. Bilox responds: "Well, I really do not know what the problems could be, but as a result of teaching for several years, I do think that there may be some factors that are causing her to have problems. There may be a variety of things causing her problems, so I would like for you to consider referring her for some testing. This testing will help us better understand Mattie's problems and will give us a better chance for helping her do well in school."

School Organization

Another change during the 1990s that affected family-school partnerships was the shift of many management functions in schools from the school district level to the individual, or local, school. The decentralization in control and authority to a principal and local management team includes the transfer of many administrative functions related to services for children with disabilities. The building principal is now charged with the supervision of special education teachers and special education programs in his or her building. The decentralization movement recommends the establishment of advisory councils or site councils to guide the direction of the school. This change is a positive step toward the inclusion of families in the decision making and control of their local schools, and coincides with the mandates of P.L. 94-142 and IDEA to include families in decisions about their children with disabilities.

The decentralization of school management along with IDEA resulted in many students being educated in their neighborhood school who had previously been denied educational services or served in other facilities. Although students without disabilities routinely received an education in their neighborhood schools, many students with disabilities began receiving such services at local schools only with the passage of legislation and shift in philosophy. As a result, many families of students with disabilities became involved with the educational programs of their children in their neighborhood.

CEC 1

Foundations

CEC 9

Professional and Ethical Practices

Neighborhood Schools

Along with the shift to serving children with disabilities in local, neighborhood schools came the increased responsibility of building administrators for decision making concerning this group of students and their families. In the past, these decisions were often made and scrutinized by district-level administrators. Now, the responsibility for interaction with families and supervision of special education personnel at the district level has shifted to the school level. Thus, the principal now has a major role in this process. Improved understanding of the needs of children with disabilities by principals should have positive implications for family-school partnerships.

INTASC 10

School and Community Involvement

Family-school partnerships have the potential to greatly enhance education for children with disabilities. There are, however, emerging challenges to the effective implementation of family-school partnerships. Two of these potential threats to home-school partnerships are (1) the need to provide specialized services to a growing number of students and (2) an impending teacher shortage.

Specialized Services

The expansion of specialized services will also impact family-professional partnerships. There appears to be a trend to expand the support services to students beyond those traditionally qualifying for special education. For example, Section 504 requires individualized adaptations for students with disabilities, using the broad definitions of disability from the Rehabilitation Act of 1973 (Smith & Patton, 1998). Although this is a positive trend in serving all students with special needs, it results in general classroom teachers having to provide different services to a wider variety of students. Because Section 504 requires schools to involve family members in decision making, this law will expand the need for positive family-school partnerships.

CEC 10

Collaboration

INTASC 10

School and Community Involvement

TEACHER TIP 1.2

Learn about Section 504 of the Rehabilitation Act and how it impacts the relationship between schools and families of children with disabilities. Understand the differences between 504 and IDEA.

Additionally, there are many other students and families who have special needs but cannot qualify for services under IDEA or Section 504. These children are often considered at risk for failure. As diversity in American schools grows, the number of these students also grows (Garmon, 2004). With the recent push by the federal government and many state legislatures to require students to meet special academic standards, schools are faced with providing necessary academic programs and supports to ensure that these students are academically successful. The 2004 re-authorization of IDEA allows schools to use up to 15% of their IDEA funds on programs for this group of children. Even though this results in an excellent opportunity for many students, too often there are no requirements in these instances to ensure that family involvement is enhanced or assured or that due-process protections are made available.

Teacher Shortages

For a variety of reasons, the United States is faced with an impending teacher shortage in all instructional areas. One reason is the upcoming retirement of many teachers from the baby-boom generation. Currently, approximately one-fourth of the teachers in this country are over 50 years old, meaning that over the next decade retirements will increase (Haselkorn & Calkins, 2000). In addition to retirements, teacher attrition is a major factor in teacher shortages (Harrell, Leavell, van Tassel, & McKee, 2004). These factors will have a significant impact on all areas of education, but especially special education, which has already experienced teacher shortages for several years (U.S. Department of Education, 2001).

Another factor related to teacher shortages is that the need for teachers is increasing. Silvestri (1995) has projected that in the year 2005 the United States will need between 545,000 and 648,000 special education teachers. This projection, when compared to the 1994–1995 number of employed teachers, suggests an increase of between 41 to 67%. Even conservatively these figures mean there will be well over 100,000 new special education positions by the year 2005.

As a result, fully trained special education teachers and other specialists will become increasingly difficult to find. The *Twenty-Fourth Annual Report to Congress on the Implementation of the Individuals with Disabilities Act* (U.S. Department of Education, 2002) noted, "In 43% of the states, shortages of teachers and related service providers contributed to a failure to provide needed special education services" (p. IV–47). The *Twenty-Third Annual Report to Congress on the Implementation of the Individuals with Disabilities Act* (U.S. Department of Education, 2001) noted that for school year 1999–2000, there were more than 12,000 unfilled special education positions or positions filled by substitutes because of the lack of certified special education teachers.

The shortage of teachers may negatively impact family-school partnerships in the future. If a large number of teachers untrained in special education are used to fill the open positions in special education, then the teachers may not possess the knowledge or skill in developing or maintaining effective partnerships. Training is critical if family-school partnerships are to achieve their potential for success. Employing untrained, unqualified special education teachers will only exacerbate problems in the development of family-school partnerships.

CHANGES AND FUTURE IMPLICATIONS IN THE DELIVERY OF SERVICES

The growth of family-school partnerships will be closely related to issues and changes in the structure of public schools and the delivery of special education services. Patterns of service delivery will continue to be directly tied to the ability of the states and local communities to fund special education programs at an appropriate level. Therefore, funding will impact family-school relationships because it will be related to more appropriate services, increased opportunities for interaction, and higher family satisfaction.

Comprehensive Services

Comprehensive services, required by IDEA and Section 504, include early intervention for preschool children, helping families of preschool children secure needed services, long-range planning, appropriate programming for school-age students, and transition services. This wide array of mandated services provides children and their families with services needed to meet both the child's and the family's needs.

CEC 1

Foundations

TEACHER TIP 1.3

Know the most recent changes made to IDEA. New reauthorizations of the law occur every 5 to 7 years, the most recent being in 2004; make sure that you are aware of any changes that are made in new versions of the law.

Although not fully achieved, significant progress has been made toward making comprehensive services more accessible to families. Along with improved accessibility, the requirements of IDEA obligate joint planning among agencies involved in meeting the needs of students with disabilities and their families. This legal support signifies a potential for similar future legislation, and thus continued progress in accessible family-centered service delivery.

Inclusive Service Delivery

The inclusion of students with disabilities in general education settings has become the primary focus of services for students with disabilities (Smith, Polloway, Patton, & Dowdy, 2004). Successful inclusion of students requires a comprehensive effort on behalf of school professionals and family members. Inclusion, as a trend, appears to be gaining momentum for all students with disabilities, just as it did for students with mild disabilities. The *Twenty-Fourth Annual Report to Congress on the Implementation of the Individuals with Disabilities Act* (U.S. Department of Education, 2002) stated that in 1999–2000, 96% of students with disabilities were served in regular school buildings. The report noted that the number of students served outside the regular classroom for less than

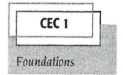

CEC 1

Foundations

21% of the school day increased 87.1%, while the number of students served in separate facilities dropped significantly. If this trend continues, the nature of special education will continue to change, including the way school personnel and families work together to develop and implement effective educational programs. As more students with special needs receive services in inclusive settings, the family-school partnership will expand to include both special and general education teachers.

Even though families of children with disabilities usually favor inclusive programs for their children, many families have raised legitimate concerns (Smith et al., 2004). These concerns include:

- Harassment from nondisabled children
- Inadequately prepared general classroom teachers
- Lack of special education support
- Inappropriate curriculum

Regardless of the specific reasons why some family members and professionals do not support inclusion, the trend appears to be continuing.

Professional Training

Several barriers to successful inclusion include:

- Many general education teachers have received little training in the area of educating students with disabilities.
- Many general education teachers have not received training in how to appropriately involve parents and families in the child's educational program.
- Many general education teachers feel that they lack the time to involve families of students with disabilities.

As a result of these training issues, family-school partnerships may be adversely impacted.

CEC 10

Collaboration

In 1975, P.L. 94-142 required the schools to involve families in the education of their children. Although family involvement was viewed in the literature as being critically important and a best practice as early as 1980, teacher-training institutions often included information and training in family involvement only as an elective course. This is changing slowly, and now university courses focusing on families are often required. Additionally, the content or focus of these courses has become more reflective of the need for the development of cooperative relationships and family involvement. See Table 1.2 for a general description of different approaches for working with families, past and future.

CEC 3

Individual Learning Differences

There is a growing awareness that family involvement is a critical component of the education of students with disabilities (Smith et al., 2004). Family involvement is considered a "best practice" and, therefore, an essential component in the training of special educators (Hilton & Henderson, 1993; Hilton & Ringlaben, 1998; Kraft, 2001). The Council for Exceptional Children (CEC) recognizes the importance of this training area and includes it as an integral component of the CEC Standards for Training Special Education Professionals (CEC, 2001, see Table 1.3 for CEC Standards).

Table 1.2 Approaches for working with families, past and future.

General Concerns	Past View	Direction of Future View
Role of Professional	Counselor/therapist	Facilitator
Role of the Family	Receiver of services and "help" for the child	Co-participant in developing and ensuring services for the child and family
Knowledge Base	Generalizable between disability groups/families	Few predictions, unique families
Composition	Two parents and child	Diversity of makeup
View of the Child	Child-centered	Child as a component
Impact of the Family	Negative factor	Veritable impact
View of the Family	Deficit model	Strengths and supports
Grieving	Loss of the perfect child	Multidimensional model

Table 1.3 Council for Exceptional Children (CEC) Standards.

Knowledge

1. Roles of individuals with exceptional learning needs, families, and school and community personnel in planning of an individualized program.
2. Concerns of families of individuals with exceptional learning needs and strategies to help address these concerns.
3. Culturally responsive factors that promote effective communication and collaboration with individuals with exceptional learning needs, families, school personnel, and community members.

Skills

1. Collaborate with families and others in assessment of individuals with exceptional learning needs.
2. Foster respectful and beneficial relationships between families and professionals.
3. Assist individuals with exceptional learning needs and their families in becoming active participants in the educational team.
4. Plan and conduct collaborative conferences with individuals with exceptional learning needs and their families.
5. Communicate effectively with families of individuals with exceptional learning needs from diverse backgrounds.

TEACHER TIP 1.4

Become familiar with the CEC Standards for Training Special Education Professionals. Because the CEC is the primary professional organization of special educators, all practitioners should be well aware of its standards.

CEC 10

Collaboration

INTASC 10

School and Community Involvement

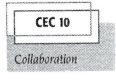

CEC 10

Collaboration

INTASC 10

School and Community Involvement

Role Changes for Special Educators

Changes in the way services are provided to students with disabilities and families resulted in the need to change the responsibilities of special education professionals. Prior to the changes already discussed, special education professionals were primarily teachers of children with disabilities, often in self-contained classrooms. They infrequently interacted with general educators and often had limited contact with families. IDEA, the inclusion movement, and parents' demands to play a more important role in the education of their children resulted in major changes.

Changes in the role of special education professionals can be grouped into two major areas: changes in relationship with general educators and changes in relationship with family members. The changes in the relationship between special education professionals and general educators focus on providing supports for general classroom teachers who are serving students with disabilities, and providing supports for students with disabilities included in general education settings. Providing supports for teachers can occur through a collaborative-consultative role, co-teacher, or member of a teacher-assistance team (Helmstetter, Curry, Brennan, & Sampson-Saul, 1998; Smith et al., 2004). In inclusive settings, special education teachers may find themselves primarily supporting general education teachers and, therefore, indirectly supporting students with disabilities (Smith et al., 2004).

The second major change in the role of special education professionals is their relationship with family members. As a result of IDEA and Section 504, special education professionals must make a significant effort to include family members in educational decision-making for children with disabilities. This includes notice and consent. Special educators, as a result, find themselves as partners, often the junior partner, in efforts to educate students with disabilities. As a result, the amount of contact with both general education teachers and families will increase significantly. Further, communication with general education teachers and families, essential in building partnerships, must be expanded (Williams & Cartledge, 1997). Families have already frequently identified increased reporting of progress as an area of desired improvement in home-school interactions (Bennett et al., 1998; Lange, Ysseldyke, & Lehr, 1997). If inclusion continues to expand, the need for increased reporting will grow.

Although the need for professionals to work closely with families has been recognized, educators often fall short in implementing practices that would lead to strong family involvement (Bennett, Deluca, & Bruns, 1997). Additionally, a few school professionals actually view family involvement as unnecessary, often time-consuming without any benefits, unnecessary, or as an "add on" to their jobs (Hilton & Henderson, 1993).

Obviously, because of the increased need for educators to be trained in working with families, changes in preparation and training of school personnel emphasizing family involvement and family-school partnerships are essential (Bennett et al., 1997; Hilton & Henderson, 1993; Horwath, 1998). Without such preparation, it is not likely that educators will take advantage of the opportunities offered by strong family-school partnerships.

TEACHER TIP 1.5

Seek training in areas of family involvement in which you feel less than adequate. For example, if many of your parents do not attend IEP meetings, request staff development that will give you suggestions for increasing involvement.

CHANGES AND FUTURE IMPLICATIONS IN THE ROLE AND EXPECTATIONS OF THE FAMILY

Changes in the cultural makeup and the population of schools have impacted educational practices, and indirectly, teacher preparation. These changes have also impacted service delivery and our view of diversity and of children and families who exhibit diverse characteristics (Sparks, 1998).

Cultural Diversity

Over the past 25 years, cultural and racial composition in the United States has become increasingly more complex. From 1972 until 2000, the number of racial/ethnic minority students increased 17% (*Condition of Education*, 2003). Obviously, this diversity extends to the families who are served by schools. Unfortunately, in many cases educational systems and individual educators have been slow to recognize these changes and have continued to interact with families using outdated, traditional models or stereotypes (Cartledge, Kea, & Ida, 2000; Linan-Thompson & Jean, 1997; Sparks, 1998). The challenge for the future is to include diversity issues in the teacher education curriculum. "Teacher education programs are endeavoring to find effective ways of raising the multicultural awareness and sensitivity of prospective teachers" (Garmon, 2004, p. 210), and to encourage the recognition and valuing of diverse families in the educational process.

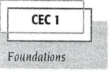

PRAXIS 1

Understanding Exceptionalities

CEC 1

Foundations

Family Differences

Over the past 10 years, research has also helped professionals develop a better understanding of how to effectively work with families of students with disabilities. One important finding of recent research is that families differ greatly. For example, Palmer, Borthwick-Duffy, and Widaman (1998) pointed out that ". . . it cannot be assumed that all parents whose children demonstrate significant cognitive disabilities, or any other characteristic, share the same values regarding the school's role or curricular emphasis" (p. 280). School personnel must avoid sweeping generalizations about any group of people, including children with disabilities and their families. Determining appropriate programs for children with disabilities and their families must be done on an individual basis. In order to develop programs that can meet the needs of children and their families, school personnel must be trained to collaborate with families in order to identify and address the needs of the individual family and to develop appropriate educational programs.

Family involvement in developing intervention programs is now accepted not only as the best practice but also as an ethical responsibility. For example, in the area of assistive technology, it is now recognized that not only do families need to be involved in the selection process, but also professionals must be sensitive to the impact the selection of technology has on family routines, preferences, and acceptance (Hourcade, Parette, & Huer, 1997). In the future, services cannot be solely determined based on the characteristics of a particular child but must also take the characteristics and wishes of the family into consideration.

Family Empowerment

A transition from providing services to children and their families to building collaborative relationships between families and schools must occur. Families must be empowered to assume the role of equal partners with school personnel (Smith et al., 2004). Horwath (1998) believes that family empowerment comes about as a natural consequence of collaboration with schools. As parents become better trained and more experienced in accessing educational services, collaborative activities should increase. Empowerment is also present when families are confident that they have the information and problem-solving skills to deal with challenging situations (Dunlap, 1999; Thompson et al., 1997) Therefore, school personnel should expand parent-training programs and support groups to provide information and training to all parents. Additionally, schools need to expand the roles available for collaboration, thereby allowing for more opportunities and experiences in the role of partner for both parents and school personnel Read the scenario in Box 1.2 and reflect on the positive nature of the interactions.

TEACHER TIP 1.6

Focus efforts on empowering families. Even though empowered families may result in more involvement than you may wish, an empowered family can provide supports and direction for children with disabilities long after they exit public schools.

INTASC 10

School and Community Involvement

CEC 9

Professional and Ethical Practices

Box 1.2

Ms. San is a fifth-grade teacher; one of her students, Michael, has been referred for special education and diagnosed as having emotional disabilities. Ms. San is meeting with Michael's parents to communicate with them about his problems and possible interventions. Ms. San notes "I am so glad that we will be working together to help Michael become as successful as possible. I want you to know that this needs to be a true team effort if Michael is going to achieve as well as he is capable. He is a very bright child and should be able to be very successful, regardless of his disability.

"There are several opportunities that might be of interest to you that will enable us to work together more successfully with Michael. The district is offering team training next Saturday. This will be a full day of training that will help us learn to work as a team better. I will be attending and it would be helpful if one or both of you could also attend so that we can learn together how best to function as a team.

"I want you to always feel free to express your opinions about Michael and about the program we develop for him. If you cannot be at an IEP meeting, please feel free to give me your thoughts at any time. After all, you know Michael much better than any of us at the school; we must be able to address his problems together."

Legislation mandating services for preschool students with disabilities, P.L. 99-457, resulted in greater family-school partnerships because of the requirements of the law. In the future, it is likely that many of the positive aspects found in early childhood programs relating to family-school partnerships will be incorporated into the K–12 system. Some of this will come by way of effective practices being implemented by caring professionals, some will be achieved through legal mandates, and some will result from family members empowered in preschool programs who exercise their rights in the K–12 arena.

CEC 1

Foundations

Expectations

Changes in federal and state legislation in the area of early childhood education have changed the expectations of parents of children being served in these programs. The Individual Family Service Plan (IFSP), for example, takes into consideration the needs of the entire family, not just the child with a disability. This in and of itself expands the focus from the child to the child and family.

In early childhood programs, teachers often have daily contact with family members of children receiving services in these programs. Even though school personnel have contact with families in grades K–12, the number and extent of the interactions usually declines as the child gets older. Additionally, in the delivery of services to families with children in early childhood programs, a high degree of interagency cooperation is usually achieved, something often not occurring in programs for older children. These two factors contribute to increasing parental expectations in the areas of communication and cooperation from parents who have participated in early intervention services. As students with disabilities "grow up" in the special education system, parents who are both experienced and trained will expect to play a greater role in educational programs for their children. Moreover, parents will expect school personnel to be more focused on, and desirous of, family involvement.

Mediation and Litigation

The 2004 IDEA amendments require states to offer mediation, with the hope that this option would enable family members and school personnel to work through problems and arrive at decisions mutually acceptable to both parties (Smith et al., 2004). If mediation is not selected, or if the difficulties are not resolved, then the parents or school may request a hearing. Prior to the hearing, the school shall convene a resolution session in which members of the IEP team and the parents attempt to resolve the dispute. This meeting is held unless both parties agree to waive it. If the meeting results in a resolution, this agreement is written up as legally binding. The resolution session is new under the 2004 amendments to IDEA. If either party is not satisfied with the outcome of the hearing, a civil lawsuit may be filed in state or federal court. Although hearing officers' decisions are considered sound, in nearly half of all cases appealed to courts, the courts have reversed the hearing officer's decision. This fact has led to a feeling that there is a strong possibility that the courts may reverse or make significant changes in hearing officers' decisions, the result being an encouragement of litigation (Newcomer & Zirkel, 1999). In fact, although litigation in education has declined over the past two decades, litigation in special education has increased dramatically (Newcomer & Zirkel, 1999).

In the future, schools should recognize that parents now see the court as a useful tool in compelling the school to provide a "free appropriate public education" for their child. Because as a society we are becoming more litigious, schools should recognize that their treatment of children with disabilities and their families might have direct consequences, including defending their actions in a court of law.

Skill Development

As the level of expectations held by families entering the K–12 educational system has increased, so have the skills and knowledge of these families. Educators are increasingly encountering families who are better prepared to identify, delineate, and advocate for the needs of their children. More families have participated in parent-training programs, with the result being parents with both knowledge and motivation to become more involved in the educational programs for their children. For these families, professionals can expect to focus on providing additional parent training designed to expand skills in the areas of self-advocacy, political advocacy, and grassroots organization.

TEACHER TIP 1.7

Work with families to provide training that will enhance their skills as primary supports for children with disabilities. Find out what training is needed and help offer such training.

The power of family expectations has led in part to the current trend of including all students with disabilities in general education classes. The challenge, to effectively include students with disabilities, is a prime example of families entering the system with both high expectations and the skills needed to participate in changing the educational system. In the future, these challenges will continue; and educators must continue to evolve to be effective partners with parents.

THE IDEAL

When looking at the future of family-school partnerships, it helps to develop an "ideal" vision of such partnerships. The following are suggested components of a model for ideal family-school partnerships:

PRAXIS 2

Legal and Societal Issues

- Highly trained empathetic general and special education teachers who view family involvement as a high priority in the education of students with disabilities
- Districts with the financial resources to support family involvement activities
- Positions in school districts to provide training, support, and assistance to families in need
- Families who view high levels of involvement with the schools as essential to the education of their children
- Available and accessible resources in the community and from other agencies that help train and support children, families, and schools
- Nonadversarial interactions between families and schools for the planning and implementation of educational programs for all students with disabilities

TEACHER TIP 1.8

Learn what is the ideal level of family involvement and work to secure such involvement from all families in your school.

In the ideal situation, the above components would exist. The result would be true partnerships between families and schools. Until that time, professionals must continue to work with families to bring us closer to that ideal. There are and will continue to be barriers to effective family-school partnerships. Only with the strong desire to build such partnerships among family members and school personnel will such an ideal be realized.

SUMMARY

The future of family-school partnerships and family involvement in the schools is not clear. It is unclear in part because legislative policymakers routinely change laws and regulations that impact on family involvement. Although family-school partnerships are viewed by most professionals and policymakers as essential to the education of students with disabilities, it has not garnered the level of funding necessary for wider implementation.

From a historical standpoint, family involvement and the concept of family-school partnerships in special education have evolved over the past 30 years. This evolution has paralleled changes in the field of special education from legal, philosophical, and practical views. As views have changed, the role of the family has grown in importance in the educational process. As service models have been altered, so has the role of the professional in reference to family interaction. Moreover, as the role of professionals has changed, so has the emphasis on family involvement as a legal requirement in the provision of public education.

The movement to increase family-school partnerships will continue to be refined in the future. As inclusion becomes more widespread, and as professionals continue to understand the importance of family involvement, family-school partnerships will become even more important. Thus, this chapter provides a brief summary of the issues involved when families and school professionals work together to meet the needs of children with special needs. Subsequent chapters will expand on the characteristics of families of students with special needs and the successful implementation of professional family-school partnerships.

QUESTIONS FOR DISCUSSION

1. Describe how the changing philosophy of special education has impacted on family involvement. Have the changes been good or bad? Why?

2. Inclusion has been the basis of the special education service delivery model for the past several years. How are family-school partnerships different within an inclusive model compared to the historical segregated, special services model? Should parents be more or less involved in an inclusive model?

3. Describe your "ideal" family-school partnership. What makes your partnership ideal, and how could you facilitate the development of such an ideal partnership?

REFERENCES

Bennett, T., Deluca, D., & Bruns, D. (1997). Putting inclusion into practice: Perspectives of teachers and parents. *Exceptional Children, 64,* 115–131.

Bennett, T., Lee, H., & Lueke, B. (1998). Expectations and concerns: What mothers and fathers say about inclusion. *Education and Training in Mental Retardation and Developmental Disabilities, 33,* 108–122.

Cartledge, G., Kea, C. D., & Ida, D. J. (2000). Anticipating differences—Celebrating strengths. *Teaching Exceptional Children, 32,* 30–37.

Condition of education. (2003). National Center for Education Statistics. Washington, DC: NCES.

Council for Exceptional Children. (2001). *What every special educator must know. The international standards for preparation and licensure of special educators* (4th ed.). Reston, VA: Author.

Dunlap, K. M. (1999). *Family empowerment: One outcome of parental participation in cooperative pre-school education.* New York: Garland.

Garmon, M. A. (2004). Changing preservice teachers' attitudes/beliefs about diversity. *Journal of Teacher Education, 55,* 201–213.

Harrell, P., Leavell, A., van Tassel, F., & McKee, K. (2004). No teacher left behind: Results of a five-year study of teacher attrition. *Action in Teacher Education*, 26, 47–59.

Haselkorn, D., & Calkins, A. (2000). *How to become a teacher*. Belmont, MA: Recruiting New Teachers, Inc.

Helmstetter, E., Curry, C. A., Brennan, M., & Sampson-Saul, M. (1998). Comparison of general and special education classrooms for students with severe disabilities. *Education and Training in Mental Retardation and Developmental Disabilities*, 33, 216–227.

Hilton, A., & Henderson, C. J. (1993). Parent involvement: A best practice or forgotten practice? *Education and Training in Mental Retardation*, 28, 199–211

Hilton, A., & Ringlaben, R. (Eds.). (1998). *Best and promising practices in developmental disabilities*. Austin, TX: Pro-Ed.

Horwath, A. (1998). Empowering family members to work as partners with professionals. In A. Hilton & R. Ringlaben (Eds.), *Best and promising practices in developmental disabilities* (pp. 287–293). Austin, TX: Pro-Ed.

Hourcade, J. J., Parette, H. P., & Huer, M. B. (1997). Family and cultural alert! Consideration in assistive technology assessment. *Teaching Exceptional Children*, 30, 40–44.

Kraft. S. G. (2001, February). Study of EHS shows modest but significant impact for kids and families. *Early Childhood Report*, 12, 1.

Lange, C. M., Ysseldyke, J. E., & Lehr, C. A. (1997). Parents' perspectives on school choice. *Teaching Exceptional Children*, 30, 14–19.

Linan-Thompson, S., & Jean, R. E. (1997). Completing the parent participation puzzle. Accepting diversity. *Teaching Exceptional Children*, 30, 46–50.

Newcomer, J. R., & Zirkel, P. A. (1999). An analysis of judicial outcomes of special education cases. *Exceptional Children*, 65, 469–480.

Palmer, D. S., Borthwick-Duffy, S. A., & Widaman, K. (1998). Parent perceptions of inclusive practices for their children with significant cognitive disabilities. *Exceptional Children*, 64, 271–282.

Silvestri, G. (1995). Occupational employment to 2005. *Monthly Labor Review*, 118, 60–84.

Smith, T. E. C., & Patton, J. R. (1998). *Section 504 and public schools: A practical guide*. Austin, TX: Pro-Ed.

Smith, T. E. C., Polloway, E. A., Patton, J. R., & Dowdy, C. A. (2004). *Teaching students with special needs in inclusive settings* (4th ed.). Boston: Allyn & Bacon.

Sparks, S. (1998). Multicultural practice in mental retardation and developmental disabilities. In A. Hilton & R. Ringlaben (Eds.), *Best and promising practices in developmental disabilities* (pp. 71–184). Austin, TX: Pro-Ed.

Thompson, L., Lobb, C., Elling, R., Herman, S., Jurkiewicz, T., & Hulleza, C. (1997). Pathways to family empowerment: Effects of family-centered delivery of early intervention services. *Exceptional Children*, 64, 99–113.

U.S. Department of Education. (2001). *Twenty-third annual report to Congress on the implementation of the Individuals with Disabilities Education Act*. Washington, DC: U.S. Government Printing Office.

U.S. Department of Education. (2002). *Twenty-fourth annual report to Congress on the implementation of the Individuals with Disabilities Education Act*. Washington, DC: U.S. Government Printing Office.

Williams, V. I., & Cartledge. G. (1997). Passing notes to parents. *Teaching Exceptional Children*, 30, 30–35.

CHAPTER 2
Working with Families of Students with Special Needs

Objectives

After reading this chapter, you will:

- Understand the family as it is in today's society
- Understand the need for family and school collaboration
- Understand some of the reactions families have when they determine that a member of the family has a disability
- Know the laws that protect family involvement
- Know strategies that enhance family involvement

Parents are the most important individuals in the lives of children with disabilities (Becker-Cottrill, McFarland, & Anderson, 2003; Lytle & Bordin, 2001). It is essential for school personnel to include the family in all key decisions affecting children with special needs (Grigal, Neubert, Moon, & Graham, 2003). Including parents in decision making is a legal requirement as well as an ethical and practical consideration (Smith, Polloway, Patton, & Dowdy, 2004). Advocates for expanding the role of families in educating their children adhere to the following assumptions:

CEC 1

Foundations

1. Parents are the first and most important teachers of their children.
2. The home is the child's first schoolhouse.
3. Children will learn more during the early years than at any other time in life.
4. All parents want to be good parents and care about their child's development. (Ehlers & Ruffin, 1990, p. 1)

School personnel should consider all of these assumptions when working with families of students with special needs and do all they can to encourage family involvement at all levels of a child's education. Even though the involvement of the family has long been recognized (Hilton & Henderson, 1993), professionals are just now beginning to realize the magnitude of the role that family members can play. As noted in Chapter 1, emphasis has shifted from providing recommendations to family members to professional collaboration with family members (Becker-Cottrill et al., 2003). Turnbull, Turnbull, Shank, and Smith (2004) define collaboration as "a dynamic process in which educators, students, and families share their resources and strengths to solve problems in a creative and responsive way" (p. 80). Cramer (1998) says that collaboration is joint problem solving and denotes an equality of status among the participants.

CEC 10

Collaboration

The involvement of family members is vitally important in the provision of services to individuals with special needs at all age levels (Stephenson & Dowrick, 2000). Unfortunately, simply recognizing that involving family members is good educational practice has not always resulted in actual involvement of families. Professionals must continue to put forth maximum effort to secure extensive involvement of families since the involvement of family members in intervention programs can greatly increase the effectiveness of services provided (Dabkowski, 2004).

INTASC 10

School and Community Involvement

Family members can be involved in many different educational activities, including assisting with IEP development (Dabkowski, 2004); social development (Elksnin & Elksnin, 2000); transition planning (Defur, Todd-Allen, & Getzel, 2001); decisions regarding inclusion (Palmer, Fuller, Arora, & Nelson, 2001; Salend & Duhaney, 2002); planning and implementing behavior support programs (Becker-Cottrill et al., 2003); and providing direct instruction (Smith et al., 2004). Families also have many talents and resources. Asking family members how they might wish to be involved in the school might provide opportunities for collaboration beyond traditional activities and lead to new venues never before considered.

THE FAMILY

In order for professionals to understand how to interact responsibly with families of children with special needs, they must have basic information about families and the dynamics found in families. Without this information, professionals will continue to underestimate the role that parents and family members play. Knowledge of family dynamics will assist school personnel in determining how to interact with various family members and how the family structure accomplishes the functions of family (Park, Turnbull, & Turnbull, 2002).

Definition of Family

Traditionally, families have been described as a group of individuals living together in a single dwelling. As Lambie (2000) says:

> Some people take a narrow view of mother, father, and children. Others broaden the view to include all those living in the home. Still others are very restrictive and, to the exclusion of adopted children, include only blood relation. (p. 5)

These traditional families generally included a mother, father, and one or more children. Fictional television families, such as those in *Roseanne*, *The Cosby Show*, *Still Standing*, *Everybody Loves Raymond*, and *Yes, Dear*, often portray this view of the family.

Today's family is defined in many different ways. Because school personnel need to work with the families of children in an effort to fully meet children's needs, a more inclusive interpretation of family is required. Taking a narrow view of family will leave out elements of a child's life that could have a major impact on educational programs.

Change in Family Structure

Changes have occurred in every component of our culture, including families and the dynamics of families. In fact, over the past several decades, significant social changes have occurred that affect families and family interactions with schools and other service agencies. Not only has the nature of family structure changed, but also the attitudes of our society toward work, school, teachers, authority figures, and even neighbors (Smith et al., 2004). These broader changes have resulted in major differences in the way service agencies, including schools, need to collaborate with families who have children with special needs. Table 2.1 summarizes some of the significant social changes that have

Table 2.1 Social changes in our society since the 1950s.

- Increased diversity in the United States
- Increased level of litigation related to educational issues
- Increased involvement of the federal government in education
- Legislation mandating services for children with disabilities
- Civil rights laws for racial minorities, women, and individuals with disabilities
- Increased number of divorces
- Increased levels of poverty
- Increased levels of single-parent homes
- Decline in the extended family community
- Changes in the family structure

BOX 2.1   *DESCRIPTION OF TYPICAL FAMILY IN THE 1950S AND TODAY*

Family in the 1950s

Mother and father in the home
Two or three siblings
Father works; mother stays home
Grandparents nearby
Children attend school in a culturally homogeneous environment

Family in the 21st Century

One-parent family
Both parents work
Grandparents not nearby
Children attend school in a culturally heterogeneous environment

---

occurred in our society since the middle of the 20th century. These changes have all affected the way persons with disabilities receive services. Box 2.1 describes a typical family found in the 1950s and a family with whom professionals might be working today.

Nearly every aspect of families has changed over the past 50 years. Whereas the majority of families used to be very similar in composition, families today represent diversity in all aspects. O'Shea and Riley (2001) state that "a typical family is a misnomer in American society" (p. 31). Today's families can be described using a wide variety of characteristics, including size, composition, member relationship, and role. Many of the family functions remain the same in today's family as in the families of the past, but the composition of the family has changed dramatically. Although family composition has changed, families continue to be the basic units that create neighborhoods, communities, states, and nations. Because families remain the basic unit in our culture and are so important in children's education, schools must learn to work with families of all types. Ignoring a particular family unit because it may not fit into a stereotypical view of what a family should be can only have a negative impact on children.

Families in the 21st century exhibit many different compositions. A large percentage of families today are single-parent families. Unfortunately, many of these families with a single head of household live in poverty. Allen (1992) noted that single mothers head 90% of families receiving welfare. The 2000 Census reported that single women headed 12.2% of all households and that 7.2% of all families with children were headed by single mothers.

In addition to single-mother families, single-parent families are headed by fathers, and, in some cases, grandparents, without either mother or father present. Extended family units with grandmother or grandfather living with the parents and child also exist. Many children also live in foster homes, where the foster parents or another individual may serve as a surrogate parent to fulfill the legal roles usually fulfilled by birth or adoptive parents. Table 2.2 describes family households, by type and relationships. As you can see, today's family represents a wide range of possible configurations.

Table 2.2 Family households by type and relationship.

Subject	Number	Percent
Household Population		
Population in occupied housing units	**273,643,273**	**100.0**
Owner-occupied housing units	187,965,615	68.7
Renter-occupied housing units	85,677,658	31.3
Per occupied housing unit	2.59	(X)
Per owner-occupied housing unit	2.69	(X)
Per renter-occupied housing unit	2.40	(X)
Household Type		
Owner-occupied housing units	**69,815,753**	**100.0**
Family households	53,071,538	76.0
Householder 15 to 64 years	42,502,253	60.9
Householder 65 years and over	10,569,285	15.1
Married-couple family	44,240,872	63.4
Male householder, no wife present	2,433,530	3.5
Female householder, no husband present	6,397,136	9.2
Nonfamily households	16,744,215	24.0
Householder 15 to 64 years	10,015,184	14.3
Householder 65 years and over	6,729,031	9.6
Male householder	7,004,848	10.0
Living alone	5,530,759	7.9
65 years and over	1,568,337	2.2
Not living alone	1,474,089	2.1
Female householder	9,739,367	14.0
Living alone	8,659,549	12.4
65 years and over	4,826,035	6.9
Not living alone	1,079,818	1.5
Renter-occupied housing units	**35,664,348**	**100.0**
Family households	18,715,809	52.5
Householder 15 to 64 years	17,317,563	48.6
Householder 65 years and over	1,398,246	3.9
Married-couple family	10,252,360	28.7
Male householder, no wife present	1,960,482	5.5
Female householder, no husband present	6,502,967	18.2

(continued)

Table 2.2 *Continued*

Subject	Number	Percent
Nonfamily households	16,948,539	47.5
Householder 15 to 64 years	13,504,347	37.9
Householder 65 years and over	3,444,192	9.7
Male householder	8,551,255	24.0
Living alone	6,248,347	17.5
65 years and over	827,296	2.3
Not living alone	2,302,908	6.5
Female householder	8,397,284	23.5
Living alone	6,791,420	19.0
65 years and over	2,501,189	7.0
Not living alone	1,605,864	4.5
Household Type		
Total households	**105,480,101**	**100.0**
Family households	71,787,347	68.1
Male householder	51,843,417	49.1
Female householder	19,943,930	18.9
Nonfamily households	33,692,754	31.9
Male householder	15,556,103	14.7
Living alone	11,779,106	11.2
Female householder	18,136,651	17.2
Living alone	15,450,969	14.6
Household Size		
Total households	**105,480,101**	**100.0**
1-person household	27,230,075	25.8
2-person household	34,418,046	32.6
3-person household	17,439,027	16.5
4-person household	14,973,089	14.2
5-person household	6,936,886	6.6
6-person household	2,636,134	2.5
7-or-more-person household	1,846,844	1.8
Average household size	2.59	(X)
Average family size	3.14	(X)

Subject	Number	Percent
Family Type and Presence of Own Children		
Families	**71,787,347**	**100.0**
With related children under 18 years	37,451,314	52.2
With own children under 18 years	34,588,368	48.2
Under 6 years only	8,020,067	11.2
Under 6 and 6 to 17 years	6,875,512	9.6
6 to 17 years only	19,692,789	27.4
Married-couple families	**54,493,232**	**100.0**
With related children under 18 years	26,117,104	47.9
With own children under 18 years	24,835,505	45.6
Under 6 years only	5,892,433	10.8
Under 6 and 6 to 17 years	5,316,384	9.8
6 to 17 years only	13,626,688	25.0
Female householder, no husband present	**12,900,103**	**100.0**
With related children under 18 years	8,794,940	68.2
With own children under 18 years	7,561,874	58.6
Under 6 years only	1,532,745	11.9
Under 6 and 6 to 17 years	1,274,233	9.9
6 to 17 years only	4,754,896	36.9

(X) Not applicable.

Source: U.S. Census Bureau, Census 2000.

In addition to these still somewhat traditional families, there are family units composed of nontraditional members, such as gay and lesbian couples. When working with these families, educators should remember that regardless of their opinions of what constitutes an ideal family, the rights of the family are to be respected. Without respect, collaboration with the family cannot occur. Regardless of whether or not the school personnel consider some structures as a family, they need to avoid actions based on personal biases and recognize the family unit as defined by the family. To do otherwise would be unethical and could have a negative impact on children. About the only thing that can be said accurately about today's families is that they are very diverse (Smith et al., 2004).

Professionals working with families should understand that family members generally want what is best for their child. Parents act to the best of their ability on behalf of their children, but act within the context of their culture, beliefs, and current situation. Therefore, professionals need to learn to value the culture and beliefs of

CEC 9

Professional and Ethical Practices

others and to act respectfully, honoring the differences encountered, or collaboration cannot occur.

TEACHER TIP 2.1

As a teacher, never assume that parents are not interested in their children. Remember, many children come from cultures that differ from your culture. Just because family members do not participate in school activities the way you might participate with your child does not mean those family members do not care about their child.

Critical Role of Families

The essential fact for school personnel to remember is that parents and grandparents or other family members acting in the role of parents should be involved in educational programs. Minimal family involvement is better than no family involvement. Thus, the actions of school personnel need to solicit family assistance and welcome family interactions when they occur. Family involvement is critical to the success of any teaming effort. To ensure that schools are supportive of family involvement, school personnel "need to engage in ongoing self-reflection and analysis to ensure a team structure that reduces stress and promotes active parent participation"

BOX 2.2

Letter to Parents

Dear Mr. & Mrs. Johnson:

I want to take this opportunity to tell you how pleased I am to have your son, Michael, in my first-grade classroom. He is a joy each and every day. Michael appears to really enjoy school, and I know I can always expect him to have a smile on his face. He gets along very well with all of his classmates, and is well liked by all of the students. He tries his best at all of his activities. One thing that I have noticed about Michael is that he seems to be a little behind in his reading. Because we are only halfway through the school year, this is not a reason for major concern. However, I did want to point out to you that he seems to be struggling and I do not want him to get frustrated. I would like to set up a time when it is convenient for you to come in so we can talk about some strategies that we can both use to help him catch up. I believe that he can do very well the remainder of this year and be ready for second grade. I just want us to be working with him together to make sure he is ready. Please let me know when a good time would be for you to come by; if I need to make a home visit I will be glad to.

Thank you,

Mrs. Smith

(Dabkowski, 2004, p. 37). Such self-reflection can assist school personnel in identifying the influence their actions have on family involvement. Reflection can also result in a better understanding of how various family factors impact family interactions with schools (Park et al., 2002). For example, routine communications with family members may either facilitate or impede involvement. Review the letter to parents in Box 2.2; reflect on the components of the letter that exhibit positive communications.

FAMILIES OF CHILDREN WITH SPECIAL NEEDS

When a new child enters a family, either through birth or adoption, the family structure and dynamics are altered. Obviously the first child changes the lives of the mother and father immensely as they turn part of their attention away from each other to providing for this new member of the family and begin their new life as parents.

CEC 1

Foundations

Subsequent births also affect the dynamics of the family unit, including the relationship between the parents and other children. If the child has a disability, the cultural view of disability may also be a factor. Additional areas of family life that often are impacted by the addition of a child with a disability include:

- Finances
- Amount and quality of time parents can devote to specific children
- Relationship between the husband and wife
- Relationship among other children and parents
- Future family goals

Reaction to a Child with a Disability

Reactions to learning that your child has a disability or a special need of any kind are usually mixed (Boushey, 2001; Linn, 2000). Some parents deny that there is a problem, others search for explanations, and some shop for cures (Boushey, 2001). Nevertheless, the hope for all family members is that the child with special needs will be accepted, and that family support systems will develop that will facilitate successful school and post-school experiences.

One factor that is often related to how families react to their child's problem is the severity of the disability and its impact on the family (Lian & Aloia, 1994). A second factor is the timing, that is, the age of the child when the disability is identified (Lian & Aloia, 1994). For example, families who realize that their child has special needs at birth may react differently than those who do not realize that a problem exists until the child is older. A final factor related to acceptance is the realization of some positive abilities of the child (Boushey, 2001). All of these factors are likely influenced by the family's cultural background (Harry, 1992).

PRAXIS 2

Legal and Societal Issues

Most families go through a series of stages in their acceptance of the fact that their child has special needs. Even though these stages have been labeled with various titles, they often include areas such as failing to believe that the child has a problem, looking for someone to "fix" the child, and accepting that the child has a disability.

Boushey (2001) describes the stages as (1) shock, (2) denial, (3) guilt, (4) isolation, (5) panic, (6) anger, (7) bargaining, and (8) acceptance and hope. For example, the family first experiences the "shock" of having a child with a disability. Next there is the "denial" or disbelief that there is actuality a disability. As the family slowly accepts the reality of the disability, then there is the fear that the disability is a result of actions, or inactions, of the parent(s) and the "guilt" that accompanies that fear or belief. The family often becomes "isolated" from others because of the differences of the child and of the child's needs. The voluntary and involuntary solitude slowly wraps the family and finally results in a "panic" that the family is now alone, lacking the support and resources of community. The panic turns to "anger" and the question becomes "Why me? Why my family?" Then the panic turns to the seeking for an answer and the "bargaining" begins, wherein parents say such things as "If only my child could . . . , then I would never complain again." Finally, the family will begin to see the reality of the situation, accept it as it is, and generate hope for the future. The family seems to have reached a stage of "acceptance and hope." The stages of grief are not linear and do not require that the sequence nor time spent in a stage be consistent for each family. However, most family members do go through these stages, although their journey may take different turns and different amounts of time. As each new stage in the child's life develops, family members may return to any of the previous stages. For example, as age peers begin a new phase in their life, the family may again grieve for the loss of the opportunity for their child to enter that phase with age friends.

TEACHER TIP 2.2

Family members experience a variety of reactions when they become aware that their child has a disability. Remember that family members move back and forth between different reactions. Even though you should always be aware that family members go through a variety of reactions, you should never try to rigidly apply these stages to families. Each person deals with the news that a family member has a disability in a different manner and in a personal way.

Regardless of the changes within the family when a child is born and specifically when the child has special needs, one of the first needs of the family is to develop an understanding of the disability that the child may have. Understanding the characteristics of mental retardation, learning disabilities, attention deficit disorder, hyperactivity, or another disability and the implications resulting from these characteristics are critical in a family's acceptance and support of the child. For example, parents with less knowledge may have unrealistic expectations for their child that could increase the possibility of childrearing difficulties and unsatisfactory relationships with school personnel. It is important for school personnel to provide access to information concerning specific conditions and to assist parents who are interested in meeting with support groups and other parents who have children with disabilities.

It is essential that school personnel, including teachers, counselors, and administrators, be aware of the many different reactions that family members may experience during discussions concerning their child and their child's needs. Additionally, school personnel should be sensitive to feelings that may surface during parent-school interactions. School personnel should react in a positive, supportive manner and work collaboratively with the parents to resolve issues and develop strategies. Ignoring the family's emotional status can lead school personnel to act inappropriately and in a manner devoid of support and be perceived by the families as lacking both understanding and collaborative intent. When working with family members of children who have special needs, school personnel should determine the readiness of a family to function in a collaborative school partnership and work to assist families in getting ready for such a partnership. Therefore, the school must first determine if the family understands the child's disability, strengths and weaknesses, their role in the child's education, and the capacity of the school to provide services. Determining these facts can help school personnel develop a plan to secure maximum family involvement.

FAMILY INVOLVEMENT AND SCHOOL PROGRAMS

Parents and other family members of students with special needs are in a unique position to become involved with the educational programs of their children. Family members have been involved in the child's life for several years before the school has even seen the student. The family has observed the child's first steps, listened to the child's first words, and provided opportunities for the child to grow and develop intellectually, emotionally, socially, and physically. The family has "important knowledge of the medical history of the child and his or her daily routines, habits, likes and dislikes, behaviors, and family needs" (Lytle & Bordin, 2001, p. 41). Family members are often the first to notice developmental delays, attention problems, sensory deficits, or other signs of problems. Therefore, when the child enters school, parents and other family members continue to be very involved in the child's education. Parents may find themselves as the child's most consistent advocate because they are the most knowledgeable concerning their child and may understand the disability their child is experiencing for a longer amount of time and in different contexts and settings than school personnel.

Family Advocacy Movement

Many family members of children with special needs have long advocated for special programs that will meet the needs of their child (Schloss, 1994). Indeed, parental advocacy is one of the primary reasons that schools began to provide programs that address the needs of these students (Smith et al., 2004). Educational systems are required to develop and implement programs that address the learning challenges of students with special needs as well as provide appropriate supports for other problems that may develop. In addition to families changing, the nature of services for students with special needs has also changed significantly over the past several years. As noted in Chapter 1, students with special needs have gone from total exclusion from school to the current trend of education in inclusive educational programs (Duhaney & Salend, 2000).

PRAXIS 2

Legal and Societal Issues

Public Law 94-142, the first federal mandate for a free appropriate public education for children with disabilities, was also the first law requiring parental involvement in the provision of educational services for students with special needs. As noted, prior to P.L. 94-142, schools frequently did not encourage family members to participate in educational programs of their children if such programs existed. Often, schools did not inform families of changes in children's grade placement or a change of classroom placement from general education to special education. In fact, parents often did not receive notification of assessment to determine disability, labeling of the child, and change of teachers or classroom environments. Sometimes the school even limited family involvement because of feelings that the school personnel were the "trained experts." The result was that many parents and other family members were often omitted from the decision-making process related to the education of their children. Some school personnel did make significant efforts to keep family members involved in the education of their children, but others did little, or nothing, to secure such involvement. Attitudes about family involvement and practices concerning family participation have changed dramatically in the last decade with the passage of law, the emergence of parent advocacy groups, and the development of a research base that supports the contribution that parents make to the education of their children.

Reasons for Increased Involvement

PRAXIS 2

Legal and Societal Issues

INTASC 10

School and Community Involvement

Several factors have resulted in the current level of family involvement in the education of students with special needs. First, the enactment of legislation mandating family involvement has had a major impact. IDEA and other legal mandates, which will be discussed extensively in other chapters, require that schools involve families in all stages of special education for students with disabilities, beginning with the referral of the child for special services (Dunlap, Newton, Fox, Benito, & Vaughn, 2001). The enactment of IDEA acknowledged that children with specific disabilities were eligible for a free appropriate public education, even though many had previously been excluded from public schools. The law requires schools to involve families in the education of their children and acknowledges the legal as well as ethical role that parents play with their children (Smith et al., 2004). The law and its subsequent amendments in IDEA, including the 2004 reauthorization, require schools to implement a number of procedural safeguards to ensure parental involvement. Subsequent chapters will address these issues. Lake and Billingsley (2000) state, "Collaboration between schools and parents rests on two Individual with Disabilities Act principles: parent participation and procedural due process" (p. 240).

In addition to IDEA requiring family involvement, Section 504 of the Rehabilitation Act of 1973 also requires schools to involve parents. Section 504, a civil rights act for persons with disabilities, applies to schools and the way schools interact with parents of students with disabilities (Smith, 2002). Both IDEA and Section 504 lay a firm legal foundation for parental involvement in the education of children with disabilities.

Second, the development of parent advocacy groups such as the Association for Retarded Children, now known as the Arc, has provided family members with knowledge and support. Family members have also learned that joining advocacy groups can be beneficial. The Arc became a strong advocacy group for children with mental retardation, whereas other groups focused on children with other special needs (Smith et al., 2004).

Finally, the research-based understanding by professionals that parent involvement is essential for student success has provided the basis for professionals to recognize the contribution that families can make in their child's educational program (Dunlap et al., 2001). This recognition has resulted in greater efforts by school personnel to include parents and other family members in all aspects of the educational process for students with special needs, including identification, referral for appropriate services, evaluation to determine specific needs, program planning, and finally, program implementation. Specific strategies to enhance the involvement of families in each of these steps will be discussed extensively in subsequent chapters.

Reasons for Lack of Involvement

Although families want what is best for their child, many different routes are taken to reach that goal. At some periods of time, parents and family members may not be as involved in their child's program as educators may think is necessary. It is important for professionals to recognize that there are many valid reasons why parents and other family members may not be involved. For example, in some instances, family members may not be able to get off of work; may not have transportation; may be intimidated by school personnel; or may not speak English very well. Others may choose nonparticipation because they have become accustomed to and accepting of schools making decisions for their children. Some may even feel that schools, at least partly, blame them for their child's problems or think that the school does not truly want or need their involvement. In addition, some family members actually avoid schools because of their personal history of school failure. Family members struggling with any of these reasons may have difficulties working with school personnel. As a result the school may inaccurately perceive the family's behaviors as parental apathy. Regardless of the reasons, school professionals should work hard to facilitate family involvement.

TEACHER TIP 2.3

When trying to increase the involvement of family members in their child's educational program, don't prejudge their level of involvement. Attempt to find out what issues may be limiting family involvement and see if you can assist. For example, if a family does not have transportation, assist in arranging for it or go to the home or another site easily accessible to the family. Most parents want to be involved; they may need some flexibility or support from the teacher.

Increasing Family Involvement

Just as parents of all children vary in their involvement with schools, so do families of children with special needs. Even though some families are extremely involved in the education of their children, others have very limited involvement (Dabkowski, 2004).

School and
Community
Involvement

Haring, Lovett, and Saren (1991) reported that 43% of families said they were some-what involved with the educational program of their child, but only 34% indicated they were actively involved. However, 23% of families said they had no involvement in the education of their children in public school special education programs. It is unlikely that these numbers have changed since this study was completed.

When family members are not involved in the education of their children, school personnel are not relieved of their responsibility to seek and encourage involvement. In fact, when families do not become involved, schools should take specific steps to assist and encourage involvement (Lytle & Bordin, 2001). Strategies for school personnel to utilize when seeking to increase family involvement include:

- Improving communication with family members through both frequency and quality of information provided
- Sharing positive and enjoyable school experiences of the child with family members
- Inviting family members to spend time in the child's classroom
- Offering to videotape the student in the classroom for family members, including examples of successful student learning
- Providing parents and other family members with information that may be helpful for meetings including the IEP, discipline, career counseling, and school meetings (adapted from Lytle & Bordin, 2001)

Read about the family described in Box 2.3 and develop some actions the school could take to increase family involvement.

The development of a sense of trust is critical in securing family involvement. Often family members do not trust the school's efforts to involve them; they may think that school personnel are simply getting forms signed for the child's records to protect the school. School personnel must be genuine in their interactions with family members and must desire family involvement, not simply a cursory involvement that can be gained from getting their signatures on forms.

Box 2.3

Linda and Walt are the parents of Melissa, a 14-year-old girl with learning disabilities. Melissa has been in the same school system since kindergarten. When Melissa was first diagnosed as having a learning disability and determined eligible for special education services in the third grade, Linda and Walt were very involved. They attended all of Melissa's IEP meetings, annual reviews, and any other meeting involved with their daughter's education. Since the fifth grade, however, Linda and Walt have become very uninvolved. It seemed to start in the fifth grade when Melissa's regular classroom teacher and resource room teacher acted as if they really didn't want Linda and Walt involved. As a result Linda and Walt sort of turned Melissa's educational program over to the school staff and have never really regained much involvement.

Melissa's teacher this year, in middle school, really wants Linda and Walt involved. With transition planning beginning, their involvement is very critical. However, even though Melissa's teacher has sent home numerous requests, the response from the parents has consistently been "we really don't have time; do what you think is best."

FAMILY AND SCHOOL COLLABORATION

There are many different levels of parent-school collaboration, beginning with the least intensive and least collaborative, written and telephone communication. More intensive than this are parent-school conferences, followed by group activities. Finally, the involvement of families in activities at the school and in the classroom is the most intense level of collaboration. Table 2.3 describes each of these levels. Although collaboration at any level is important, school personnel should attempt to work with parents at the more intensive end of the continuum.

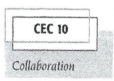

CEC 10

Collaboration

TEACHER TIP 2.4

Communication with parents should not just occur when you want something or when you need to deliver bad news. Remember to call parents regularly to tell them something good about their child or to report a class activity or project that involved their child. How often did one of your teachers call your parents just to say how great you were, or how often has one of your child's teachers called you to tell you the same thing? Frequent contact as the bearer of good news goes a long way in establishing good relationships.

Table 2.3 Description of levels of collaboration from least to most intensive.

Written Communication

School staff communicates with family members through written notes and letters. This provides a one-way mode of communication. Family members may or may not receive the note, understand the note, or respond to the note.

Telephone Communication

School staff communicates with family members through telephone call. This provides for two-way communication without any visual cues from either party. Opportunity for give and take; and opportunity to ensure that both parties understand communication.

Committee Meeting

School staff communicates with family members through face-to-face setting. This provides for two-way communication with visual cues. Opportunity for give and take; opportunity to ensure that both parties understand communication. May be an intimidating experience for family members.

Individual Meeting

School staff communicates with family members through face-to-face setting. This provides for two-way communication with visual cues. Opportunity for give and take; opportunity to ensure that both parties understand communication. May be less intimidating for family members. Better opportunity to establish a personal relationship and trust.

Need for Family and School Collaboration

Parents of children with special needs and school personnel are partners in providing appropriate educational services. However, parents are actually the "senior partners" because families "are the major influence affecting the growth and development of children" (Linn, 2000, p. 201). Most parents never stop feeling responsibility for the child, even when their child exits the home; many continue to feel some responsibility for their children's success well into adulthood. Often, school personnel do not acknowledge this "senior" role for parents, opting instead to consider themselves as the "key" members of the educational team. Although school personnel may know more about a particular topic than family members, the fact that family members have specific due-process rights regarding their child, as well as unique knowledge about their child, results in their involvement being both legally and professionally required. School personnel must recognize this unique role that family members can provide in educating children with special needs and make strong efforts to facilitate maximum involvement.

Hilton and Henderson (1993) surveyed 250 teachers concerning their attitudes toward parent involvement in the special education process. One key finding was that nearly 80% of those responding indicated that teachers already were overwhelmed with numerous tasks without having the extra task of working with parents. Even though many teachers see the value of including family members in the educational process, others view their involvement as burdensome. As long as school personnel exhibit negative attitudes toward family involvement, a major barrier to full involvement will remain in place.

FAMILY INVOLVEMENT AND POST-SCHOOL COLLABORATION

Once students exit school, the impact of family involvement should not cease. In some ways, parents may need to play a more extensive role after their children exit the school system than when their children are in school. Vocational rehabilitation and other adult service agencies provide services and supports based on requests and funds available and may not be as efficient as schools in meeting the needs of individuals with special needs.

PRAXIS 2

Legal and Societal Issues

TEACHER TIP 2.5

Many parents are lost when their son or daughter with a disability is getting ready to exit school. Prepare a pamphlet of resources for adults with disabilities and explain these services to parents. Help them connect with rehabilitation agencies and other adult-service providers. Even though some of these actions may be part of the student's transition plan, it is helpful to provide parents with written information concerning adult services available to their child.

Adults with special needs require support in many different essential life areas, including employment, housing, social situations, and post-secondary training, and thus may require a wider array of supports than children with special needs. School personnel can help prepare family members for this extended support role during transition planning (Defur et al., 2001). This new role may include a variety of tasks, such as assisting their adult child with disabilities with self-determination and self-advocacy, providing supports for employment and living arrangements, and in some instances serving as a partial or full guardian. Family members can be extremely helpful in supporting young adults with disabilities by fostering self-determination and self-advocacy skills during this time of their life (Zhang, Katsiyannis, & Zhang, 2002).

SPECIFIC COLLABORATION ACTIVITIES

Parents and family members can become involved in a wide variety of collaborative activities with school personnel. These include involvement in planning programs, implementing programs, and evaluating programs. The specific activities will vary depending on the nature of the child, age of the child, and capabilities and resources of family members. Some specific activities in which parents and other family members can become involved include:

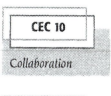

CEC 10

Collaboration

INTASC 10

School and Community Involvement

- Referral and the referral process
- Assessment and the assessment process
- IEP, IFSP, and transition plan development and implementation
- Support in homework and other school-related activities
- Support in behavior intervention plans
- Support during transition to post-school environments
- Support for young adults after their transition from school

Many of these activities will be described more fully in later chapters.

Although there are many different collaborative activities that can occur between schools and parents, effective collaborative relationships may not occur. Blue-Banning, Summers, Frankland, Nelson, and Beegle (2004) found six major themes that affected parent-school collaboration. These include: (1) communication, (2) commitment, (3) equality, (4) skills, (5) trust, and (6) respect. Recognizing that the methods and levels of involvement of family members and school staff will vary with each child, the most important thing to remember is that any involvement is generally better than no involvement. It is the responsibility of school staff to facilitate collaborative activities with family members. Family involvement can make an incredible difference in the success of the child, both in school and after the child becomes an adult.

SUMMARY

This chapter is a brief introduction to the role of families of children and adults with special needs. The fact that the nature of families has changed dramatically over the past few decades was discussed. It was noted that the fictional view of families, depicted in *Everybody Loves Raymond* and *Still Standing*, does not currently exist in many situations. Rather, families of today often differ extensively and may include only one parent, be composed of blended families, include homeless families, include extended families, include families with grandparents raising the children, and may include families with parents of the same sex. Professionals working with children and adults with special needs must be sensitive to the varying family styles they will encounter and be prepared to work with each different family.

The critical role of families within the educational system and the importance of families in all areas related to their child with special needs was presented. Family members must be involved with the education of their child with special needs. Although IDEA requires a certain level of family involvement, school personnel often need to take specific steps to support and encourage involvement. Without support and encouragement by school personnel, many parents may choose not to participate at a level that truly enhances the educational opportunities of their child. This is of great concern because the involvement of parents and family members in the school and with school personnel can be critical in the successful implementation of educational programs for all students. For children with special needs, parental involvement and family-school collaboration are even more critical.

QUESTIONS FOR DISCUSSION

1. Assumptions about families were reported to include that parents are a child's first and most important teacher, home is the first school house, children learn more during early years than later, and all parents want to be good parents. Do you agree or disagree with these assumptions? What happens when children are in homes that do not reflect these assumptions?

2. Define "family" in your terms. How does this definition of family differ from traditional definitions? Do families, per your definition, present more or fewer problems for school personnel than a more traditional view of families? Why or why not?

3. Aside from the legal reasons for involving families in the education of children with disabilities, what are some other reasons why families should be involved? Who is responsible for facilitating this involvement, and how can this be accomplished?

REFERENCES

Allen, K. E. (1992). *The exceptional child: Mainstreaming in early childhood education* (2nd ed.) Albany, NY: Delmar.

Becker-Cottrill, B., McFarland, J., & Anderson, V. (2003). A model of positive behavioral support for individuals with autism and their families: The family focus process. *Focus on Autism and Other Developmental Disabilities, 18,* 113–123.

Blue-Banning, M., Summers, J. A., Frankland, H. C., Nelson, L. L., & Beegle, G. (2004). Dimensions of family and professional partnerships: Constructive guidelines for collaboration. *Exceptional Children, 70,* 167–184.

Boushey, A. (2001). The grief cycle—One parent's trip around. *Focus on Autism and Other Developmental Disabilities, 16,* 27–30.

Cramer, S. (1998). *Collaboration: A success strategy for special educators.* Boston: Allyn & Bacon.

Dabkowski, D. M. (2004). Encouraging active parent participation in IEP team meetings. *Teaching Exceptional Children, 36,* 34–39.

Defur, S. H., Todd-Allen, M., & Getzel, E. E. (2001). Parent participation in the transition planning process. *Career Development for Exceptional Individuals, 24,* 19–36.

Duhaney, L. M. G., & Salend, J. S. (2000). Parental perceptions of inclusive educational placements. *Remedial and Special Education, 21,* 121–128.

Dunlap, G., Newton, J. S., Fox, L., Benito, N., & Vaughn, B. (2001). Family involvement in functional assessment and positive behavior support. *Focus on Autism and Other Developmental Disabilities, 16,* 215–221.

Ehlers, V. L., & Ruffin, M. (1990). The Missouri project—Parents as teachers. *Focus on Exceptional Children, 23,* 1–14.

Elksnin, L. K., & Elksnin, N. (2000). Teaching parents to teach their children to be prosocial. *Intervention in School and Clinic, 36,* 27–35.

Grigal, M., Neubert, D. A., Moon, M. S., & Graham, S. (2003). Parents' and teachers' views of self-determination for secondary students with disabilities. *Exceptional Children, 70,* 97–112.

Haring, K. A., Lovett, D. L., & Saren, D. (1991). Parent perceptions of their adult offspring with disabilities. *Teaching Exceptional Children, 23,* 6–10.

Harry, B. (1992). *Cultural diversity, families, and the special education system: Communication and empowerment.* New York: Teachers College Press.

Hilton, A., & Henderson, C. J. (1993). Parent involvement: A best practice or forgotten practice? *Education and Training in Mental Retardation, 28,* 199–210.

Lake, J., & Billingsley, B. (2000). An analysis of factors that contribute to parent-school conflict in special education. *Remedial and Special Education, 21,* 240–251.

Lambie, R. (2000). *Family systems within educational contexts.* Denver: Love.

Lian, M. J., & Aloia, G. F. (1994). Parental responses, roles, and responsibilities. In S. K. Alper, P. J. Schloss, & C. N. Schloss (Eds.), *Families of students with disabilities: Consultation and advocacy* (pp. 51–93). Boston: Allyn & Bacon.

Linn, S. (2000). Coping and adaptation in families of children with cerebral palsy. *Exceptional Children, 66,* 201–218.

Lytle, R. K., & Bordin, J. (2001). Enhancing the IEP team: Strategies for parents and professionals. *Teaching Exceptional Children, 33,* 40–44.

O'Shea, D. J., & Riley, J. E. (2001). *Families and teachers of individuals with disabilities: Collaboration orientations and responsive practices.* Needham, MA: Allyn and Bacon.

Palmer, D. S., Fuller, K., Arora, T., & Nelson, M. (2001). Taking sides: Parents views on inclusion for their children with severe disabilities. *Exceptional Children, 67,* 467–475.

Park, J., Turnbull, A. P. & Turnbull, H. R. (2002). Impacts of poverty on quality of life in families of children with disabilities. *Exceptional Children, 68,* 151–170.

Salend, J. S., & Duhaney, L. M. G. (2002). What do families have to say about inclusion? *Teaching Exceptional Children, 35,* 62–66.

Schloss, P. J. (1994). Historical and legal foundations for parent advocacy. In S. K. Alper, P. J. Schloss, & C. N. Schloss (Eds.), *Families of students with disabilities: Consultation and advocacy* (pp. 17–49). Boston: Allyn & Bacon.

Smith, T. E. C. (2002). Section 504: Basic requirement for schools. *Intervention in School and Clinic, 37,* 2–6.

Smith, T. E. C., Polloway, E. A., Patton, J. R., & Dowdy, C. A. (2004). *Teaching students with special needs in inclusive settings* (4th ed.) Boston: Allyn & Bacon.

Stephenson, J. R., & Dowrick, M. (2000). Parent priorities in communication intervention for young students with severe disabilities. *Education and Training in Mental Retardation and Developmental Disabilities, 35,* 25–35.

Turnbull, R., Turnbull, A., Shank, M., & Smith, S. J (2004). *Exceptional lives: Special education in today's school* (4th ed.). Upper Saddle River, NJ: Pearson/Merrill Prentice Hall.

Zhang, D., Katsiyannis, A., & Zhang, J. (2002). Teacher and parent practice on fostering self-determination of high school students with mild disabilities. *Career Development for Exceptional Individuals, 25,* 157–169.

CHAPTER 3
Working with Families: Guiding Principles

Objectives

After reading this chapter, you will:

- Understand why partnerships between schools and families are in the best interest of all parties
- Understand how family involvement impacts student success, family empowerment, co-advocacy, and school environments
- Know the responsibility of the families and schools in securing family involvement

- Develop a better understanding of the uniqueness of families
- Recognize the role that professionals play in family involvement

"Educators and parents of children with disabilities must be partners in ensuring that appropriate education is available to children" (Smith, Polloway, Patton, & Dowdy, 2004, p. 76). Although guiding principles have been developed for many aspects of life and activities that occur within the school, educators have still not agreed upon a set of principles for family involvement and family-school partnerships. There are, however, several principles that should be considered when working with families. These include:

- Enhancing a sense of community among families (Dunst, Johansen, Trivette, & Hamby, 1991)
- Considering family members as "equals" or even "senior partners" in the educational process (Smith et al., 2004)
- Sharing responsibility (Dunst et al., 1991)
- Considering family cultural factors (Parette & Petch-Hogan, 2000)
- Focusing on collaboration between schools and family members (Ruble & Dalrymple, 2002)
- Protecting family integrity (Dunst et al., 1991)
- Enhancing self-advocacy skills (Bassett & Lehman, 2002)

Each of these principles is interrelated, and many of the strategies associated with one principle may be useful for other principles. These principles provide a foundation for effective family involvement and partnerships. The following statements summarize the principles (Dunst et al., 1991):

- Partnerships are in everyone's best interest.
- Family involvement is a right as well as a responsibility.
- Every family is unique, but commonalities do exist.
- The objective of family-school partnerships is to work for the empowerment of families.

PARTNERSHIPS ARE BENEFICIAL TO EVERYONE

A strong interactive partnership between school and families has been shown to be essential in achieving the best outcomes for children with disabilities (Grigal, Neubert, Moon, & Graham, 2003). According to some, families should even be treated as "senior partners" in this partnership because of their overall responsibility for their children (Smith et al., 2004). They are experts with regard to their children (Dunlap, Newton, Fox, Benito, & Vaughn, 2001). Families are essential in the educational process for several reasons, including:

- Family members are the child's first teachers.
- Family members know the child better than school personnel.
- The home setting is where children learn to generalize their learning to functional environments.

- Family members are associated with the child before and long after the school years.
- Family members can provide support for educational programs beyond the school day.
- Family members can provide support for homework.
- Family members can reinforce and support behavior intervention programs.
- Family members can add invaluable information to the assessment process.

The value of family involvement cannot be overemphasized, and school personnel must take actions to ensure such involvement. In order to do so, an understanding of some of the basic elements affecting parent-school partnerships must be understood. Table 3.1 lists the six themes identified by Blue-Banning, Summers, Frankland, Nelson, and Beegle (2004) and describes indicators for each theme.

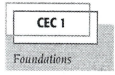

CEC 1

Foundations

Table 3.1   Themes affecting parent-school partnerships.

Collaborative Partnership Theme	Indicators
Communication: The quality of communication is positive, understandable, and respectful among all members at all levels of the partnership. The quantity of communication is also at a level to enable efficient and effective coordination and understanding among all members.	Sharing resources Being clear Being honest Communicating positively Being tactful Being open Listening Communicating frequently Coordinating information
Commitment: The members of the partnership share a sense of assurance about (a) each other's devotion and loyalty to the child and family, and (b) each other's belief in the importance of the goals being pursued on behalf of the child and family.	Demonstrating commitment Being flexible Regarding work as "more than a job" Regarding child and family as "more than a case" Encouraging the child and family Being accessible to the child and family Being consistent Being sensitive to emotions
Equality: The members of the partnership feel a sense of equity in decision making and service implementation, and actively work to ensure that all other members of the partnership feel equally powerful in their ability to influence outcomes for children and families.	Avoiding use of "clout" Empowering partners Validating others Advocating for child or family with other professionals Allowing reciprocity among members Being willing to explore all options Fostering harmony among all partners Coming to the table/avoiding "turfism" Acting "equal"

(continued)

Table 3.1 *Continued*

Collaborative Partnership Theme	Indicators
Skills: Members of the partnership perceive that others on the team demonstrate competence, including service providers' ability to fulfill their roles and to demonstrate "recommended practice" approaches to working with children and families.	Taking action Having expectations for child's progress Meeting individual special needs Considering the whole child or family Being willing to learn
Trust: The members of the partnership share a sense of assurance about the reliability or dependability of the character, ability, strength, or truth of the other members of the partnership.	Being reliable Keeping the child safe Being discreet
Respect: The members of the partnership regard each other with esteem and demonstrate that esteem through actions and communications.	Valuing the child Being nonjudgmental Being courteous Exercising nondiscrimination Avoiding intrusion

Source: From "Dimensions of Family and Professional Partnerships: Constructive Guidelines for Collaboration," by M. Blue-Banning, J. A. Summers, H. C. Frankland, L. L. Nelson, and G. Beegle, 2004: *Exceptional Children, 70,* p. 174. Copyright 2004 by the Council for Exceptional Children. Used with permission.

Family Empowerment

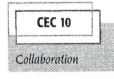

CEC 10

Collaboration

INTASC 10

School and Community Involvement

As noted, family members are involved as partners in the education of their children; they become empowered. In some instances, family members do not have the skills necessary to participate successfully. In these situations, educators may play a major role in supporting families as they learn the skills necessary to participate (Sparks, 1998). As the basic skills are learned (for example, self-advocacy, listening, group participation), family members can begin to initiate activities that will continue this growth. The empowered family is not only able to work with educators in achieving what is best for the child in school but also to advocate for the child in the community. Educators who collaborate as partners with families rather than interacting with families in a traditional helper-helpee relationship are most effective (Turnbull & Turnbull, 2001). Read the scenario in Box 3.1. What actions does the teacher take that impede family empowerment?

Box 3.1

Betty is the special education resource room teacher at Alm Elementary School. One of her students, Michael, is 11 years old and has a diagnosis of mild mental retardation. Betty is having a meeting with Michael's parents, Mike and Molly, at the beginning of the school year to discuss their role in Michael's education. Betty begins the discussion by stating the following: *I just want to make sure that I help*

Michael as much as I can this year. And, of course, I am here to help you deal with Mike's needs any way that I can. I want to start out by asking that we work together on making sure that Michael does his homework. I am a firm believer that all students, including those in special education, learn to take responsibility for themselves. Therefore, I would like you to monitor his homework assignment note-book every night, and make sure that he at least attempts to do all of the work. Completing work is a "big deal" for me. Next, I want to help you cope with some of Michael's growing behavior problems. I have a little behavior management system that I use in the classroom that I think you can use at home very easily, and it should work well. I'll leave you copies of the forms that I use and a general de-scription of what I think you should be doing. If you implement the plan, I think this will help you deal with Michael's behavior at home, and it will definitely reinforce the things I am trying to get Michael to do in the classroom.

Michael's parents then say: *We really want to get more involved in Michael's educational pro-gram this year, and really want to be members of the team that decides what Michael needs and how to deliver it to him. We want to be part of that team that actually provides some instruction and support.*

Betty then says: *I think it is so wonderful when parents want to help. I just want you to remember that teaching these children is not an easy task. We always want parents to be involved, but we want you to be able to assist us in carrying out our plan for these children. If parents do too much, it some-times interferes with our efforts in the school to carry out the IEP.*

Teacher Tip 3.1

At the beginning of the school year, provide families with a notebook for their child. Include important information with labeled dividers:

- Names and contact information for persons involved with their child
- Daily schedule
- Copy of IEP
- Copy of "Parental Rights and Responsibilities"
- Notes from school
- Copies of permission forms and letters
- Testing and evaluation reports
- Samples of student work

Suggest that families bring this notebook with them each time they meet with the school concerning their child.

Co-Advocacy

One goal of family involvement is the development of parent-school partnerships in which all can act as co-advocates for students. In the interest of student growth, family empowerment, and healthy schools, it is essential that some of the traditional authority and decision-making power of the school be shared with families. This means the school will need to exceed the legally required minimums of family involvement by developing school-home relationships in which family members are supported in more substantive

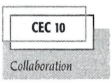

CEC 10

Collaboration

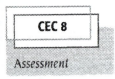

CEC 8

Assessment

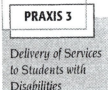

PRAXIS 3

*Delivery of Services
to Students with
Disabilities*

program participation. This type of involvement also means giving up some of the historical ownership that both parents and school staff have maintained over certain issues and sharing responsibility for activities. Hammitte and Nelson (2001) identify three major areas in which such co-advocacy can occur: (1) assessment, (2) goal setting, and (3) program implementation. Traditionally, the school has assumed that it should make decisions in these three areas either alone or with minimal input from family members. But true co-advocacy requires equal participation from family members and school staff.

One of the outcomes of high levels of family involvement is increased cooperation between professionals and families. This increased level of cooperation leads to increasing the likelihood of the ability of professionals and families to co-advocate for students with disabilities. When a high level of cooperation is gained, time becomes available for developing effective programs for students rather than being spent in adversarial activities.

Healthy School Environments

PRAXIS 2

*Legal and Societal
Issues*

Violence in schools has been identified as one of the major factors in reducing the effectiveness of public schools. Schools have been searching for successful methods to reduce the violence and have found that bringing family members into the school buildings has been successful in reducing violence. Thus, the mere presence of family members in the school is beneficial.

As Winebrenner (1996) reported, when family members are present within schools and at school activities, they send a message to their children that school is worthwhile. Parents show their interest in many ways. Some of these include but are not limited to:

- Classroom volunteers
- Aide
- Guest speaker
- Guest teacher
- Member of school site council
- Mentor for other parents
- Tutor
- Chaperone
- Campus security
- Leader of parent groups

CEC 10

Collaboration

School professionals must remember that not all parents are able to be present in the school. Inflexible work schedules, transportation needs, or health problems are examples of issues that may keep some family members from being present in the school. For these family members, teachers might secure their involvement with activities they could complete at home, such as helping their child's teacher prepare materials. The involvement of families in the educational environments of their children is essential in developing healthy school environments for students with disabilities.

TEACHER TIP 3.2

Teachers should use language that indicates respect for the school volunteers. Provide a nametag. Use a respectful form of address consistent with one used with other teachers (for example, Miss Kim or Mrs. Jones, Mr. Sam or Mr. Garcia). Provide adult seating in an "honored space" for volunteers.

FAMILY INVOLVEMENT IS A RIGHT AND A RESPONSIBILITY

Today, as we have discussed, families are considered to be an important and essential component of the educational community. Family involvement and family-school partnerships are important to all educators. Through IDEA, families with children who have disabilities must be offered a great level of involvement in educational decision making concerning their children. IDEA (2004) guarantees families the right to:

CEC 1

Foundations

PRAXIS 2

Legal and Societal Issues

- Unbiased education assessment
- Inclusion in the decisions concerning placement of their child
- Inclusion in the planning and development of an individual educational plan
- Confidential treatment of materials concerning their child
- Not participate if they decide
- Engage in mediation or a resolution session in an attempt to resolve disputes with the school
- Take schools and districts to a hearing for issues relating to the special education of their child

Section 504 of the Rehabilitation Act of 1973 also requires that schools afford parents certain rights. In fact, Section 504 and the IDEA guarantee that parents have specific legal rights related to educational services for their children. These rights are viewed not as the maximum level but as the beginning point for schools to assure family participation at the level the family chooses. School personnel should go beyond the minimum legal rights to develop true collaborative relationships with family members.

Another major federal legislation requiring the involvement of family members is the No Child Left Behind Act of 2001. This law "is a landmark in education reform designed to improve student achievement and change the culture of America's schools." (U. S. Department of Education, 2002) The act requires schools to provide extensive information on students' progress so that parents know where their child stands academically. It also provides information to parents related to the performance of their child's school and provides opportunities for parents to receive tutoring for their child or even transfer their child to an adequately performing school in some circumstances (U.S. Department of Education, 2004).

Responsibility of Schools

Professionals have a responsibility to provide an appropriate education for the students they serve. Research and effective practice make it clear that this requires moving

Table 3.2   CEC Standards: parent relationships.

Professionals seek to develop relationships with parents based on mutual respect for their roles in achieving benefits for the exceptional person. Special education professionals:

1. Develop effective communication with parents, avoiding technical terminology, using the primary language of the home, and other modes of communication when appropriate.
2. Seek and use parents' knowledge and expertise in planning, conducting, and evaluating special education and related services for persons with exceptionalities.
3. Maintain communications between parents and professionals with appropriate respect for privacy and confidentiality.
4. Extend opportunities for parent education utilizing accurate information and professional methods.
5. Inform parents of the educational rights of their children and of any proposed or actual practices which violate those rights.
6. Recognize and respect cultural diversities which exist in some families with persons with exceptionalities.
7. Recognize that the relationship of home and community environmental conditions affects the behavior and outlook of the exceptional person.

Source: Retrieved December 8, 2003, from **www.cec.sped.org/ps/code.html**.

PRAXIS 3

Delivery of Services to Students with Disabilities

beyond the legal minimums regarding family involvement. The Council for Exceptional Children's *Code of Ethics and Professional Standards* devotes a section specifically to "Parent Relationships," stating that professionals are to "seek to develop relationships with parents based on mutual respect for their roles in achieving benefits for the exceptional person" (CEC, 2003, p. 3). See Table 3.2.

When parents and families first begin working with schools on the education of their child, they may not be knowledgeable concerning their role and its requirements in the planning, conducting, and evaluating of programs for their child. Therefore, CEC states that professionals should "extend opportunities for parent education utilizing accurate information and professional methods" (2003, p. 3). When needed, professionals should attempt to offer educational opportunities that meet the needs of the families of students with disabilities. Sileo, Sileo, and Prater (1996) identified four areas in which parents might request information in order to facilitate their involvement as members of family-school partnerships. These areas might include:

1. Parent education programs that focus on skills
2. Parent education programs that help parents influence their children's education
3. Awareness programs to help family members' understanding of how to interact as partners
4. Informational programs and employment opportunities in areas that benefit both the school and the family

Educators who seek to encourage and support partnerships with families should adopt and implement practices that include developing and providing programs requested by the families that are relevant to their needs.

TEACHER TIP 3.3

Develop a pamphlet on parent advocacy skills. Include contact information on local advocacy groups. Also include related websites, such as **www.wrightslaw.com** or **www.cec.sped.org**.

The President's Commission on Excellence in Special Education issued a report in 2002 entitled *A New Era: Revitalizing Special Education for Children and Their Families*. One of the major recommendations in the report is to increase parental empowerment and school choice. Under this recommendation, the report states "Parents should be provided with meaningful information about their children's progress, based on objective assessment results, and with educational options" (p. 35). In addition to this recommendation, the report states "IDEA should empower parents as key players and decision-makers in their children's education" (p. 35).

Responsibilities for Families

There is little argument that family involvement is not only a right but also a responsibility for family members. To fulfill their parental responsibility, parents will need support from their educational partners to:

1. Learn about the services being provided to their child with disabilities.
2. Learn about the curriculum that is being followed by the school.
3. Become knowledgeable of the school and district policies that affect their child.
4. Influence administrative decisions concerning their child.
5. Influence policymaking of the organization providing services.

Educators must realize that parent responsibilities will not be fulfilled unless they cooperate and work with families assisting them in the process of learning about and working within the educational system. However, as significant changes continue to occur in our social structures, family involvement has become more difficult. School personnel need to recognize that soliciting family involvement is their responsibility; but simply inviting parents to attend meetings is not sufficient. Educators must take specific steps to encourage and reinforce family involvement. Read the scenario in Box 3.2. What actions could you take, as the child's teacher, to obtain more parental responsibility?

> **CEC 9**
>
> *Professional and Ethical Practices*

Box 3.2

Charles and Sarah Taylor have a daughter, Helen, who is in the seventh grade at Marrison Middle School. Helen has been referred for special education because she is more than 2 years below her grade level in reading, math, and written expression. Although she has had difficulties since the middle of the third grade, Mr. and Mrs. Taylor have resolutely refused special services, fearing that such services would stigmatize Helen. They have finally come to realize that Helen needs, and would benefit from, special education. They are at the assessment/IEP conference, but they are very reluctant to say anything. They feel like they have done all they could do during Helen's first 7 years of school and it has not been beneficial. Therefore, they are ready to turn over everything to Helen's teachers. When asked if they have any questions, comments, or suggestions, they say "no, we just are not knowledgeable enough to know what to do." Helen's teachers who are at the conference feel like Mr. and Mrs. Taylor could provide some very useful information and suggestions, but they are at a loss about how to get the parents more involved.

COMMONALITIES AND UNIQUENESS OF FAMILIES

When working with families, it is essential to focus on the family as a unique entity (Bennett, Lee, & Lueke, 1998). Although no two families are exactly alike, there are characteristics common to most families. These characteristics include:

- Experiencing the various stages of the family life cycle
- Family needs
- Family strengths and support systems
- Family structure
- Cultural heritage

The uniqueness of each family is a result of the manner in which the common characteristics unite. O'Shea and Riley (2001) define family as "two or more individuals who live together and are related to one another by blood or marriage" (p. 30). But families vary in many ways, and defining "family" can be a challenge. Obviously, the traditional definition of family has changed from a mother and father and one or more children, to a much broader view of what constitutes a family.

Families can be viewed as not just individuals but as "a social system in which each member is affecting and being affected by the other members" (Shea & Bauer, 1991, p. 4). Those who espouse this view of family use an approach known as the family systems approach, in which one considers the impact of characteristics of the family on the family members and views the family as an interactive, dynamic system where one change can result in major changes to subtle affects. The approach notes that families are integrated systems with unique characteristics, and that family members are interdependent within the family (O'Shea, O'Shea, & Algozzine, 1998). Thus, when an individual family member encounters change, the family experiences a shifting of relationships among the family members.

Family relationships also are influenced by a set of understood family norms or rules that organize and govern the interactions among the family members. These family norms result from religious, cultural, and ethnic beliefs to which family members ascribe (McCubbin, Thompson, Thompson, McCubbin, & Kaston, 1993). These beliefs provide the framework and underpinning for family behaviors and the family's unique pattern of functioning.

Therefore, individual family member behavior can be understood as a product of a balance of forces within the family (Davis & Malone, 2001). The first force is that of the need to maintain closeness, preserve harmony, and assume responsibility for the members of the group. The second force is the drive toward individualization and seeking of personal goals. The family works toward the achievement of these two goals by supporting each member of the group. When balance occurs, the family supports both individualization and togetherness. When the forces are in conflict or out of balance, then anxiety occurs, which may impact each family member. Changes and choices may result in the family needing assistance in maintaining that essential balance necessary for family health (Falik, 1995).

Professionals need to recognize that the family is a dynamic social system whose uniqueness must not only be recognized but honored, while also remembering that actions toward one family member may result in often unanticipated reactions from other members of the group. Read the scenario in Box 3.3. As a teacher, what concerns would you have when working with family members?

TEACHER TIP 3.4

Ask families to complete an information form concerning possible instructional objectives and to bring the form to the meeting. Possible questions include:

- What do you see your child doing after leaving school?
- What do you want to see your child doing 5 years from now?
- What do you want your child to learn in school this year?
- It would help me and my family if my child could: _____

Box 3.3

Frankie comes from a home in which his father is a very dominant factor. Frankie's mother, Darlene, wants to go to meetings at the school and help Frankie with his work, but her husband, Frankie's father, won't allow it. He says that the school is just a place where kids go and get into trouble and he does not want to help the school make a failure out of his son. Frankie's father had major difficulties in school when he was young; he actually dropped out of school when he was 16. At 10, Frankie has a few more years before he too can drop out. Frankie has been diagnosed as having emotional problems. Darlene finally convinced Frankie's father to allow the testing; however, once the diagnosis was developed, the father said he would not allow Frankie to be put in special education "with all the retarded kids." As a result, Frankie has been having more and more problems. Not only is he having difficulties in his academic work, but his behavior seems to be getting much worse. He is becoming very defiant and is disruptive in the classroom. Frankie's teacher, Ms. Braken, has communicated with Darlene on numerous occasions and has asked if she and Frankie's father would come in for a conference. Darlene wants to, but Frankie's father, Harry, says definitely "no." Until school staff can discuss Frankie's situation with his parents and develop a plan of action, and even permission for special education, his situation will continue to deteriorate.

Professional and
Ethical Practices

Collaboration

IMPORTANT CONCEPTS RELATED TO FAMILY INVOLVEMENT

Parent-professional partnerships generally revolve around the team approach to serving students with disabilities. If such a team is to be successful, team members must be willing to relinquish some of their traditional roles so that all team members have an equal status in the team. Hammitte and Nelson (2001) list the following as areas in which parents and schools can collaborate to facilitate successful programs for students: assessment, goal setting, and program implementation.

Having explored the general principles of working with families, it is now important to examine four additional concepts related to families. The first concept is that of family satisfaction. Then the concepts of the importance of proactive services and the role of the professional will be examined. Finally, the idea that there is never too much family involvement will be considered.

Family Satisfaction—If Not a Principle, a Concern

Family satisfaction is an essential element for parent-school partnerships to be successful. Thus, professionals need to work with family members to achieve ongoing satisfaction and effective family involvement. Although this is an important concept, it is a difficult one to measure. In virtually all research asking family members about their satisfaction with the special education process, the results have been the same. Most parents are satisfied with the services that are being provided (Hodapp, Freeman, & Kasari, 1998; McDonnell, 1997). This satisfaction with current practices may lead families to a feeling of complacency and result in reduced parent-family advocacy. Therefore, professionals must realize that even if most families report satisfaction with the services that are being provided, more needs to be done to increase the families' involvement.

Having family members report satisfaction, without any involvement, is not a desired outcome. Schools should seek not only satisfied, but involved families. To be able to report that the majority of parents are satisfied with their child's educational program may or may not be significant. In order to ensure true family satisfaction, the degree of satisfaction from involved parents presents a more valid picture of satisfaction level.

The Importance of Proactive Services

Family members frequently report that the only contact they have with educational professionals is when their child is in trouble or has had problems in the educational setting. This crisis-oriented, reactive approach does not encourage family involvement nor develop collaboration.

Educators must be proactive in their interactions with families. Suggested approaches and specific strategies for becoming more proactive are discussed in the chapter on communication. The overall principle, though, is one of relationship building. Strong positive relationships are essential if a professional is going to collaborate effectively with families. Without these strong positive relationships being in place, close collaboration cannot occur.

Recognition of the Role of the Professional

School personnel play many roles in the education of children with special needs. The two most critical roles include facilitating access to needed services for the child and family, and supporting the family in increasing its involvement and empowerment. Facilitation is ensuring that the family's needs are met; empowerment is when families become independent advocates for the needs of their children. School personnel should serve both as facilitators for services and supports for family empowerment. If the family is successful in becoming empowered, then they will assume many of the roles of professionals.

CEC 9

Professional and Ethical Practices

Although the educator is a facilitator of family involvement, he/she must realize that there are and will continue to be other service providers in the life cycle of the family. For many families of a child with disabilities, there have already been a number of professionals assisting the family. Families enter the school system with a history of both positive and negative experiences with professionals, and this history often impacts and influences their relationship with educators. Further, it is important to recognize that there may be additional professionals currently involved in providing services to the family. It is essential that the educator understand that education is only one aspect of the services being used by a family. In fact, education may not be the most important service for the family at this time. Families who are unable to be involved with schools beyond being a receiver of information should not be viewed as uncaring or uninvolved in the lives of their children, but rather as a family with a personal prioritization of needs.

Family-to-family and family-to-professionals are important modes of the information-gathering role of parents. Professionals often view these sources of information in a negative light. Educators may believe that this information confounds the task of providing direct services or confuses families concerning the realities of the educational system. But to be proactive and collaborative educators should encourage families in their information seeking, as it is a step toward independence, self-advocacy, and family empowerment. However, when doing this, the educator may find it helpful to provide families with information concerning:

- Sources of information about educational services
- Appropriate hierarchical order in seeking school-related information (i.e., not going to the superintendent prior to the classroom teacher and the principal)
- Differences in services of education and other human service agencies
- Role and knowledge of medical professionals in the community
- Individual nature of individualized educational planning

Family Empowerment and Family Involvement

INTASC 10

School and Community Involvement

As noted numerous times, family involvement and empowerment is a goal that every school district and professional should seek. Emerging from the principle that family involvement is beneficial to everyone is the view that more is better. "More is better" means that more family involvement efforts not only improve the educational process, but that family involvement benefits everyone. Although reaching this goal may never be achieved with some families, professionals should strive to help families move as far toward full empowerment as possible. Any level of family empowerment is better than no level of empowerment.

QUESTIONS FOR DISCUSSION

1. Family empowerment appears to be a goal for families who have children with disabilities. What is family empowerment and why should schools help families achieve this level of involment? Aren't "empowered families" more likely to cause problems for the school? Why or why not?

2. Parent involvement is both a legal right and a responsibility. Discuss these two factors related to family involvement. Can you have one without the other? Which is the more important reason for families to be involved with their child's education, legal right or responsibility? Discuss why you choose your response.

3. Is there really never too much family involvement? Give some examples where family involvement might be overboard. Now, discuss whether it is better to have "overly involved" families or families that are very uninvolved.

SUMMARY

There has been no professional codification of principles for family involvement and family-school partnerships. It is recognized in the field that family-school partnerships are in everyone's best interest because such partnerships lead to family empowerment, acts of co-advocacy, and healthy schools. Unique to special education, family involvement is a right and a responsibility of both the school and the family. Of great importance is the recognition that each family is unique. Family occupies a unique place in the life cycle of each member; families have unique strengths and needs; each family has a unique structure influenced by culture, family attributes, and composition; and, lastly, the family is a dynamic organism that has changing attributes including strengths, needs, and composition. By understanding the general principles and supporting concepts presented, the goal of successful family-school partnerships is more likely to be achieved.

REFERENCES

Bassett, D. S., & Lehmann, J. (2002). *Student-focused conferencing and planning*. (Transition Series). Austin, TX: Pro-Ed.

Bennett, T., Lee, H., & Lueke, B. (1998) Expectations and concerns: What mothers and fathers say about inclusion. *Education and Training in Mental Retardation and Developmental Disabilities, 33*, 108–122.

Blue-Banning, M., Summers, J. A., Frankland, H. C., Nelson, L. L., & Beegle, G. (2004). Dimensions of family and professional partnerships: Constructive guidelines for collaboration. *Exceptional Children, 70*, 167–184.

Council for Exceptional Children (CEC). (2003). *CEC Code of Ethics and Professional Standards*. Retrieved from December 7, 2003, from www.cec.sped.org/ps/code.html.

Davis, P. S., & Malone, D. M. (2001). Family assessment. In D. J. Oshea, L. J. O'shea, R. Algozzine, & D. J. Hammitte (Eds.) *Families and teachers of individuals with disabilities.* Boston: Allyn & Bacon.

Dunlap, G., Newton, J. S., Fox, L., Benito, N., & Vaughn, B. (2001). Family involvement in functional assessment and positive behavior support. *Focus on Autism and Other Developmental Disabilities,* 16, 215–221.

Dunst, C. J., Johansen, C., Trivette, C. M., & Hamby, D. (1991). Family-oriented early intervention policies: Family centered or not? *Exceptional Children,* 58, 115–126.

Falik, L. H. (1995). Family patterns of reaction to a child with learning disabilities: A mediational perspective. *Journal of Learning Disabilities,* 28, 335–341

Grigal, M., Neubert, D. A., Moon, M. S., & Graham, S. (2003). Parents' and teachers' views of self-determination for secondary students with disabilities. *Exceptional Children,* 70, 92–112.

Hammitte, D. J., & Nelson, B. M. (2001). Families of children in early childhood special education. In D. J. O'Shea, L. J. O'Shea, R. Algozine, & D. J. Hammitte (Eds.), *Families and teachers of individuals with disabilities* (pp. 129–154). Boston: Allyn & Bacon.

Hodapp, R. M., Freeman, S. F. N., & Kasari, C. L. (1998). Parental educational preferences for students with mental retardation: Effects of etiology and current placement. *Education and Training in Mental Retardation and Developmental Disabilities,* 33, 342–349.

H. R. 1350, Individuals with Disabilities Education Improvement act of 2004.

McCubbin, H. I., Thompson, E. A., Thompson, A. I., McCubbin, M. A., & Kaston, A. J. (1993). Culture, ethnicity, and the family: Critical factors in childhood chronic illness and disability. *Pediatrics,* 91, 1063–1070.

McDonnell, J. (1997). The integration of students with severe handicaps into regular public schools: An analysis of parents' perceptions of potential outcomes. *Education and Training in Mental Retardation,* 22, 98–111.

O'Shea, D. J., O'Shea, L. J. & Algozzine, R. (1998). *Learning Disabilities: From theory to practice.* Upper Saddle River, NJ: Merrill/Prentice Hall.

O'Shea, D. J., & Riley, J. E. (2001). *Families and teachers of individuals with disabilities: Collaboration orientations and responsive practices.* Needham, MA: Allyn & Bacon.

Parette, H. P., & Petch-Hogan, B. (2000). Facilitating culturally/linguistically diverse family involvement. *Teaching Exceptional Children,* 33, 4–10.

President's Commission on Excellence in Special Education. (2002). *A new era: Revitalizing special education for children and their families.* Retrieved January 24, 2004 from www.ed.uiuc.edu/news/2002/specialed report.htm.

Ruble, L. A., & Dalrymple, N. J. (2002). COMPASS: A parent-teacher collaborative model for students with autism. *Focus on Autism and Other Developmental Disabilities,* 17, 76–83.

Shea, T. M., & Bauer, A. (1991). *Parents and teachers of children with exceptionalities: A handbook for collaboration* (2nd ed.). Boston: Allyn & Bacon.

Sileo, T. W., Sileo, A. P., & Prater, M. A. (1996). Parent and professional partnerships in special education: Multicultural considerations. *Intervention in School and Clinic,* 31, 152.

Smith, T. E. C., Polloway, E. A., Patton, J. R., & Dowdy, C. A. (2004). *Teaching students with special needs in inclusive settings* (4th ed.). Boston: Allyn & Bacon.

Sparks, S. (1998). Multicultural practice in mental retardation and developmental disabilities. In A. Hilton & R. Ringlaben (Eds.), *Best and promising practices in developmental disabilities* (pp. 71–184). Austin, TX: Pro-Ed.

Turnbull, A. P., & Turnbull, H. R. (2001). *Families, professionals, and exceptionality: Collaborating for empowerment* (4th ed.). Upper Saddle River, NJ: Merrill/Prentice Hall.

U. S. Department of Education (2002). "No Child Left Behind" Washington, D. C.: author.

U. S. Department of Education (2004). *Guide to No Child Left Behind.* Washington, DC: Author.

Winebrenner, S. (1996). *Teaching kids with learning difficulties in the regular classroom.* Minneapolis, MN: Free Spirit.

CHAPTER 4
Working with Families:
Understanding Family Factors

● ● ● ● ● ● ● ● ● ● ● ● ● ● ● ● ● ● ● ○ ○ ◇

Objectives

After reading this chapter, you will:

- Describe stress and understand how it impacts families with children with disabilities
- Understand the life cycle of the family
- Describe how family members experience grief and loss as a result of a child with a disability

- Describe potential school-related problems resulting from disabilities and other learning needs
- Describe important transitions that families with children with disabilities must make as a result of disabilities
- Understand how professionals can avoid adding to the stress experienced by families with children with disabilities
- Describe various models to assist family members in dealing with their stress

Stress is a normal part of the parenting process. Even so, having a child with a disability often increases the stress on the family members and the family unit. It is therefore critical when working with families that one understands the stressors involved in raising a child with disabilities. To understand, one must be aware of the life cycle of the family, the information on grief and loss, and the research on stress and coping. After developing a theoretical basis, two models to use in working with families will be discussed. The first is the Family Systems Approach (Turnbull & Turnbull, 2001; Whitechurch & Constantine, 1993) and the second is the Hilton Coping Model (Hilton, 1998). The Family Systems Approach sees the family as a dynamic unit that provides the environment for all children to learn and grow. The Hilton Coping Model provides a method of understanding the coping strategies of individual family members. By examining both facets of family interactions, the whole and the individual, the professional can become a more effective family partner.

LIFE CYCLE OF THE FAMILY

As noted in previous chapters, the family of a child with disabilities experiences predictable changes that have been referred to as a family life cycle. Turnbull and Turnbull (2001) have identified four critical stages of the family life cycle. The four stages of this model are based on the child's age and include early childhood, school age, adolescence, and adulthood. Hanline (1991) provided a list of some of the issues that occur at different stages. At the early childhood stage (birth to 5 years), the issues listed were:

- Obtaining an accurate diagnosis
- Informing family and friends
- Locating services
- Developing relationships with professionals

During the school-age stage (6 through 12 years), the issues often encountered include:

- Becoming aware of a new service system
- Learning legal rights and responsibilities
- Clarifying issues of pull-out service versus inclusion
- Arranging extracurricular activities

During the adolescence stage (13 through 21 years), a number of different concerns may surface. These include:

- Addressing the long-term nature of the disability
- Realizing the impact of long-term dependence issues

- Confronting the child's sexuality
- Addressing isolation from and rejection by the adolescent's peers
- Finding age-appropriate activities
- Planning for career/vocational outcomes
- Addressing postsecondary educational concerns

During the adult stage (21 years and older), the family is faced not only with the continuation of many of the issues of adolescence but with the additional ones of adulthood. These include:

- Identifying adult living arrangements
- Providing socialization activities away from the family
- Addressing issues of guardianship and parental death

The number of issues and the level of stress introduced to the family are unique to each family. Although most families need support throughout the family's life cycle, the amount of support needed depends on the individual family's strengths and self-sufficiency. But whatever the issues and level of stress, all families have the same goal that they will "remain intact as a family over time, meet the developmental needs of the child over time, and develop the kinds of relationships that remain resilient and vital over time" (Hanline, 1991, p. 263).

TEACHER TIP 4.1

Before developing opinions related to family involvement in the educational process of their child, make an effort to determine the stage of the life cycle of the family. This can have a significant impact on actions of family members.

GRIEF AND LOSS

At an early point in the family life cycle, families learn that their child has a disability. The family then must address the twin issues of grief and loss. These reactions and feelings relate to grieving for the loss of the "perfect child" (Ellis, 1989) and/or to the feelings that their dreams for their child have been lost (Gargiulo & Graves, 1991). Olshansky (1962) characterized this process as the "chronic sorrow syndrome" and Jaffe (1991) points out that parents experience feelings of guilt, anger, disappointment, withdrawal, sadness, and denial early in the process and later experience feelings of depression, helplessness, ambivalence, and being burdened. These feelings do not occur only at the time of identification but occur throughout the life of the child and his/her family (Hanline, 1991; Spidel, 1995). The feelings of loss occur regardless of the age of the child at identification or recognition of the disability and regardless of the level of severity of the disability identified (Gargiulo & Kilgo, 2000). However, the intensity of these reactions may vary depending on the two specific factors: first, the age of the child when identification occurs, and second, the severity of the child's condition. Either factor may increase the level of stress experienced by parents.

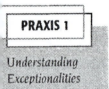

Other factors influencing reactions of the parents to the information that their child has a disability include the parents' socioeconomic status, their physician's attitude, the presence of other children and a spouse in the home, their prior information about the disability, their cultural/ethnic values, the availability of support systems, their religion, the presence of other children with disabilities in the family, and the level of family functioning (Lambie & Daniels-Mohring, 1993; Mary, 1990).

Early work by Kubler-Ross (1969) with parents of children with disabilities focused on the grieving process. This work has become the basis for the currently accepted model used to explain parental reaction and overt behavior toward professionals. Kubler-Ross and others identified the following five stages of grieving:

- **Denial:** The unconscious avoidance of the anxiety related to the event. For example, when in denial a person may often have a feeling of numbness or confusion, and sometimes a disorganization of thought. They may not hear what is being communicated and may require follow-up after the emotional numbness passes.
- **Bargaining:** The time of fantasy thinking. For example, the person may exhibit the belief that "if I work really hard, I can fix this or at least make it better."
- **Anger:** The time when the bargaining phase wears off and there is realization that it will not be "fixed." For example, the person may respond with statements such as "Why me?" or respond in anger at a spouse, doctor, or professionals who may be seen as insensitive.
- **Depression:** Anger turned inward. For example, although the acceptance of the event can result in a realistic assessment of the situation and its implications, in some instances the resultant anger can turn inward and result in depression. Sometimes the person may have feelings of emptiness following the anger and depression that may interact, producing a feeling of "life without meaning."
- **Acceptance:** A feeling of balance may return. For example, at this stage the event and its impact can be discussed. Guilt is lessened and realistic plans can be made.

The basic concepts of the Kubler-Ross model are used extensively in the training of special educators, counselors, and health care professionals (e.g., Spidel, 1995). These individuals in turn use the model to help parents understand their experiences. Several assumptions accompany the Kubler-Ross model. These include:

- Parents go through all stages.
- Parents move from one stage to another in a sequential pattern.
- Movement is a sequential and orderly process.
- Parents have the goal of acceptance and resumption of their lives.
- Failure to progress at a reasonable rate or remaining at one stage indicates a problem in the parent's life or lack of acceptance or resolution of an issue or feeling.
- Unresolved feelings are abnormal, are destructive to the family, and need resolution.

Marsh (1993) points out weaknesses with the stage model, including its inability to handle the variety, intensity, and direction of change that parents report. Furthermore, when comparing parental reports and interviews of their reactions, many of the assumptions of the stage models are unsupported (Marsh, 1993). It is clear that parents experience the grieving process at different rates, that parents return to previous specific feelings during times of stress, that feelings of loss continue for the life of the parents, and that parental acceptance may never be completely reached. In fact, some parents say that acceptance may be an inappropriate goal (Marsh, 1993). Current models of parental reactions and grieving are not useful in explaining such differences (Mary, 1990).

TEACHING TIP 4.2

When interacting with family members who do not accept their child's disability, provide positive characteristics of individuals with similar disabilities. Often, parents just need to realize that their child with a specific disability is still capable of achieving a great deal as a adult, even if it is simply supported living.

STRESS

Although all parents experience stress during the parenting process, increased stress within a family has been associated with having a child with a disability (Beckman, 1991; Jaffe, 1991; Meyer & Bailey, 1993; Raghavan, Weisner, & Patel, 1999). Additionally, grief and loss are two factors that may increase the stress in families of children with disabilities. Stress can also come from the structure of the family unit, from individual family members, and, ironically, from the professionals who are working to help the family. But no matter the source of the stress, it may result in changes in relationships within the family (Lyon & Lyon, 1991); increase emotional problems for the parent (Nadler, Lewinstein, & Rahav, 1991); result in poor communication and possible conflicts with professionals (Gargiulo & Graves, 1991; Hancock, Wilgosh, & McDonald, 1990); result in changes in belief systems (Erin, Rudin, & Njoronge, 1991); and in the end may result in a loss of sense of competence and/or self-esteem (Hanline, 1991).

Stress from the Family Structure

Family structure strongly influences the needs of the family and the presence of stress in the family. As discussed, the majority of families no longer only consist of two parents and several children. The impact of different cultures, divorce, remarriage, re-combination of families, other children with disabilities, and sexual preference of family members all may create stress and influence needs of families of children with disabilities (Parette & Petch-Hogan, 2000). Differing family structures provide additional challenges for the professional who is attempting to build partnerships and encourage family involvement. Examples of potential school-related problems encountered when children live in two separate households during the school year include:

- Variable amounts of time available for homework and school problems
- Pressures competing for family resources
- Additional parent conferences
- Households made up of only one adult

- Children with four or more parents
- Differing values in the two households concerning school behavior and performance

Stress, though, does not affect all members of the family in the same way (e.g., Beckman, 1991; Jaffe, 1991) and each family member's need for support during times of stress may be different. It is important, therefore, to recognize especially that mothers and fathers within the same family often have different needs for support (Beckman, 1991). For example, mothers tend to report higher need for support than fathers do. In addition, the personal strengths (coping resources and styles) of each family member and the availability of support systems for the family often mediate the effects of stress (Seligman, 2000).

According to Hanline (1991), transitions and transitional events may magnify stress within a family, result in an increased focus on the special needs of the child, and may renew the feelings of sorrow previously addressed by the family. Further, these transitions may be more difficult because they may occur at different times than for children in other families. Following is a list of transitions and transitional events that may increase stress within the family.

- Diagnosis of the disability is made.
- Developmental milestones are missed.
- Younger siblings developmentally pass the child with the disability.
- Puberty begins.
- Significant birthdays are reached (for example, 16th, 21st).
- A medical crisis occurs.
- A behavioral crisis occurs.
- An out-of-home placement is considered.

The ability of parents or family members to handle the stress of these and other transitions and events is also affected by the number of stressful events or challenges that occur simultaneously. When multiple events occur, resources for coping may become depleted, and, thus, limit the ability to handle the additional event. Families and educators can work together to reduce the stress of transitions and critical events through discussion and planning for these critical times (Sandler, 1998).

TEACHER TIP 4.3

Before making suggestions to families, make sure you are cognizant of the family's identification of their needs. Listen to what the family is saying before you offer advice. Effective helpers listen for both the information and feelings.

Stress from the Family Members

Families may also experience stress from the family itself. For example, Sandler (1998) points out that grandparents are often an important part of the family's support system. As such, grandparents can directly influence the child's development through childcare and teaching or indirectly through the provision of support to the parents. On the other hand, grandparents may provide high levels of stress because they lack an understanding of the disability and/or have inappropriate expectations for the child, parents, and family unit.

The reaction of siblings to the brother or sister with a disability also can be a stressor. Siblings have reported the same feelings of loss and grief as did their adult family members. Additionally siblings reported feelings of guilt and confusion. Siblings, unlike adult members of the family, lack the maturity and experience to cope with these feelings. Siblings of children with disabilities need parents and other adults to:

- Express love for the sibling
- Provide siblings with information concerning the disability
- Keep the sibling informed concerning changes and stress on the family
- Include the sibling in family and school meetings
- Work for equity within the family duties and responsibilities
- Prevent siblings from becoming second parents in the areas of care and discipline
- Be aware that the needs of all the children will change through the family life cycle

Sibling needs will influence the functioning of the family and impact the child with disabilities. Educators and families should remember the needs of the siblings, include them in activities and meetings, and develop support groups specifically for them. It is also important that the educator recognize that the family's ability to work with the school may be impacted by the presence of other children in the family.

Stress from Professionals

Interactions between parents and professionals may become a source of parental stress (Bennett, Lee, & Lueke, 1998; Parette & Petch-Hogan, 2000). For instance, professionals who do not view the involvement of parents in the school environment as important and do not provide information and support to the family may increase parental stress (Bennett et al., 1998; Hilton & Henderson, 1993; Horwath, 1998; Smith, 1993). On the other hand, if the professional attempts to provide support to parents who do not perceive that they need help, that also may increase parental levels of stress (Meyer & Bailey, 1993). Paul, Porter, and Falk (1993) point out the importance of professionals being aware of, and sensitive to, the feelings of the family members concerning "outside" assistance.

> **INTASC 10**
>
> School and Community Involvement

TEACHER TIP 4.4

Never force supports on a family. Engage family members in discussions that will allow them to help determine their needs and seek supports rather than trying to impose supports if the family does not want help.

Table 4.1   Areas of potential stress for families.

- Shattered dream of the perfect child
- Difference in the child's looks
- Increased attention requirements
- Increased routine-caregiving difficulty
- Parent, family, and societal attitudes towards disabilities
- Frustration
- Humiliation
- Lowered self-esteem
- Time reduction with other family members
- Loss of friends and other relationships
- Avoidance of social situations/events
- Loss of rewards for parents
- Lack of specific information
- Increased childrearing costs
- Medical concerns
- Conflict of opinions
- Confused expectations
- Problems in communication with family members
- Questions concerning the future
- Vulnerability of the child

Source: Adapted from *Counseling Parents of Exceptional children* (p. 113), by J. C. Stewart, 1986, Columbus, OH: Merrill.

Box 4.1   *STRESS FOR A MOTHER*

Mary Sloan found out last year that her 8-year-old son, Thomas, had mild mental retardation. She dealt with the diagnosis fairly well, and actually acknowledged that she had long thought he was not "right." Last month her husband, Phillip, left the family. He told Mary he was not coming back. Mary has found a second job to help her deal with family finances, but this takes her out of the house three evenings each week and makes her tired because of lack of rest. When she is working her night job, her daughter, 13-year-old Monica, is in charge. Monica resents having to keep her younger brother three nights each week; it is beginning to hamper her teenage social life. Mary recently found out that the school district wants to move Thomas to another school where they can place him in a more restricted setting. Even though the district has agreed to provide transportation, Thomas must be ready for the bus at 7:05, meaning getting him up at least 30 minutes earlier than now. Mary's boss at her day job has recently complained that Mary is getting to work late and seems to be tired. Mary is trying to cope with mounting stress.

Additional factors that may compound parental stress include a professional's lack of knowledge, respect, and/or appreciation of family values and cultural differences (Smith, 1993). In addition, school expectations may contradict parental expectations, thus resulting in friction instead of collaboration. Therefore, in order for professionals not to increase family stress, it is essential that they can recognize potential sources of family stress (Lustig & Akey, 1999). Stewart (1986), after an extensive literature review on the factors associated with parenting a child with disabilities, developed a list of potential areas or times of stress for families (see Table 4.1). Read the scenario in Box 4.1 and then identify areas of stress experienced by this family.

MANAGING STRESS

Professionals must recognize that stress originates from many sources (see Table 4.2). Nevertheless, Sandler (1998) points out that many of the stresses may be anticipated and dealt with on a proactive basis. Despite the seemingly limitless number of potential stressors, stress should be considered a normal factor, and, by itself, does not cause families to become dysfunctional (Garber, 1992; Hughes, 1999; Lambie & Daniels-Mohring, 1993).

Although identification of stressors is critical in determining service needs, equally important is the identification of the family's ability to handle stress. The family's ability to handle the stress is determined by family strengths and support systems.

Table 4.2   Sources for family stress.

- Extensive amounts of time spent on daily care and/or long or intense medical care needs (Spidel, 1995)
- Increased parental responsibilities (Waggoner & Wilgosh, 1990)
- Increased financial responsibilities (Birenbaum & Cohen, 1993)
- Dealing with health care and education professionals (Birenbaum & Cohen, 1993; Meyer & Bailey, 1993; Waggoner & Wilgosh, 1990)
- Loss of control of decision making (Meyer & Bailey, 1993)
- Social network contradictions (Lambie & Daniels-Mohring, 1993)
- Cultural demands and confusion (Lambie & Daniels-Mohring, 1993)
- Unmet needs or lack of services (Bennett et al., 1998; Garber, 1992; Mayer, 1994)
- Transitions and critical events (Hanline, 1991; Lambie & Daniels-Mohring, 1993; Lustig & Akey, 1999; Sandler, 1998)
- Deficits of the individual child (Lambie & Daniels-Mohring, 1993)
- Demands of other family members (Lambie & Daniels-Mohring, 1993)

Personal Strengths of Family Members

As pointed out by Meyer and Bailey (1993), coping is a multifaceted concept and varies from family member to family member. Personal strengths of family members play a major role in the development of family strengths. Both psychological well-being (Lambie & Daniels-Mohring, 1993) and capacity to interact with the outside world (Seligman, 2000) have been identified as essential for parents to develop and maintain contact with needed support systems.

Personal strengths may be viewed as the inner knowledge, skills, experiences, attitudes, and beliefs with which an individual enters the process. Each of these areas can play a positive or negative role in coping. For example, depending on the parents' belief system, religion and cultural values can cause the family to view the child with disabilities as either a gift or a punishment (Mary, 1990).

An important aspect of personal strength is the self-perceived competence of family members. For instance, there is evidence that mothers who have increased perceived competence in their ability to parent a child with disabilities experience less stress and fewer episodes of self-doubt and guilt. It is important to note that these perceptions of personal competence may change as the child develops (Hadley & Hanzlik, 1990). Thompson and Gustafson (1996) compared mothers of children with disabilities to mothers of children without disabilities and found that both sets were essentially the same on measures of depression, stress, social isolation, and alcohol problems. In comparison to mothers, studies indicate that fathers of children with disabilities who ascribe to a traditional role experienced more stress than the mothers (Seligman & Darling, 1997). Later research indicates no difference in stress levels (Ainge, Covin, & Baker, 1998; Dyson, 1997), but that the stress may come from different sources (Beckman, 1991; Roach, Orsmond, & Barratt, 1999). It appears that both fathers and mothers are able to adjust to the presence of a child with a disability and to parent a child with a disability with feelings of personal strength and competency. Garber (1992) described personal strengths that help parents cope as good physical health, problem-solving skills, and positive perception. Karpel (1986) identified a slightly different list of essential personal strengths, including self-respect, protectiveness, tolerance, affection, flexibility, hope, and family pride. For parents of children with disabilities it appears that each of these factors can be influenced either positively or negatively. For example, good physical health requires proper food intake, limited or no intake of alcohol and drugs, exercise, and so forth (see Table 4.3).

Cultural and religious values of the parent and the family are also related to self-perception of competence. Research (Hughes, 1999; Smith, 1993) suggests that some cultures view disabilities as ordained by fate, thus providing the parent with the goal of attaining harmony with nature. Family members possessing cultural beliefs such as these may not experience the same emotional and stress-related reaction as family members who view disabilities differently. Therefore, they may be able to cope better with the challenges.

Using the personal strengths approach enables a parent to access supports available within the family and the community. Such strengths are then critical in the

Table 4.3 Factors influencing a family member's coping.

Factor	Positive Indicator	Negative Indicator
Physical Health	Good health	Poor health
Exercise	Regular program	Little or irregular
Sleep Patterns	Full night's sleep	Sleeplessness
Use of Drugs and Alcohol	Little or no usage	Moderate to high usage
Food and Vitamins	Balanced diet	Below minimums
Attitudes	Open; optimistic; humor	Pessimistic; closed
Self-Esteem	High	Low
Flexibility	Very flexible; good problem solving	Inflexible; rigid
Hope	Optimistic	Pessimistic
Religion	Positive view of child; gift	Negative view of child; burden; punishment
Cultural View	Positive view of child; community support	Negative view of child; independent struggle
Perceived Competence	High self-perception; "can do" attitude	Low self-perception; helplessness; high self-doubt

reduction of stress and in effective parenting. A parent's personal strengths can be improved through training and personal growth activities such as:

- Reading books relating to personal weaknesses
- Taking part in physical activities regularly
- Attending counseling/therapy sessions
- Interacting with experts/others who have had similar experiences
- Taking courses on parenting and/or weakness areas
- Meeting parents with strong coping skills
- Volunteering or observing in the classroom
- Learning relaxation techniques

TEACHER TIP 4.5

Remember that all families are different, not only in their reactions to having children with disabilities but also in their personal strengths and weaknesses that allow them to deal with the presence of a child with a disability. Individualize your interactions with each family and family members.

Siblings in a Support Role

It has been shown that family members can provide support at times and stress at other times (Lustig & Akey, 1999). That is particularly true in the case of siblings. It has been found that siblings vary greatly from child to child and family to family in their reactions to having a child with a disability and the support they can offer (Bailey, Skinner, Rodriquez, Gut, & Correa, 1999). For example, siblings often provide support in child-rearing, or at least supervision of children with disabilities (Stoneman, Brody, Davis, Crapps, & Malone, 1991). However, the same siblings during adolescence may not be as willing to help and may experience feelings of loss that can add stress to the family.

TEACHER TIP 4.6

Start a sibling support group for siblings of children with disabilities in your school. Use this group to provide information and peer supports.

Family Unit in Support Roles

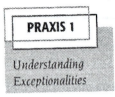

PRAXIS 1

Understanding Exceptionalities

Ronnau and Poertner (1993) stated that professionals should recognize the importance of identifying strengths of the family unit when working together with families. Family unit strengths include the strengths related to the interworkings of the family itself. Some family units are extremely powerful in working and maintaining the well-being of their members. Other families do not function as units at all, but function as individuals pulling at each other in an attempt to meet personal needs. For example, a family strength is the ability to maintain the family's economic health (Paul et al., 1993). Families with higher incomes may be better able to obtain respite care, other external supports, and out-of-home activities for their children (Stoneman et al., 1991) than families with lower incomes.

PRAXIS 1

Understanding Exceptionalities

The cultural and functional definition of extended family provides many differing structures in today's world, but the value of the extended family in providing support as a family unit is unquestionable (Sandler, 1998). According to Smith (1993), some families come from cultures in which extended and multiple families often live in one household and collaborate in caregiving and parenting functions. For instance, in the Chinese culture the traditional family often has tight kinship relationships (Wang, 1993). Similar kinship has a historical background within the African American culture, although extended families tend to go beyond the traditional family to include non-blood extended families (Thomas, 1993). In general, families with children with disabilities tend to look inward to the family unit for support rather than outward for community resources (Serafica, 1990; Wang, 1993).

Community Support

A family member's ability to cope with the increased challenges resulting from raising a child with disabilities is related to the availability of support systems (Lustig &

Akey, 1999). Support systems can be formal (individuals or groups designed to help people who need support) or informal (friends or acquaintances). Family adjustment often reflects the amount of support received from relatives as well as the availability of services in the community (Jaffe, 1991).

INTASC 10

School and Community Involvement

Potential resources can be found in the community. Seligman (1991) found that friends, day care providers, babysitters, and professionals provided essential assistance and support to families of children with disabilities. Religion and the religious community can also play an important role in supporting the family with disabilities (Hughes, 1999; Linn, 2000; Webb-Mitchell, 1993). In some cultures, for example, the African American culture, the church is a major source of social support (Thomas, 1993). Furthermore, the church can provide crisis support, act as a surrogate family when needed, provide role models for siblings, and convey feelings of hope.

Members of families of children with disabilities often find support and direction from other parents of children with disabilities (Hintermann, 2000; Horwath, 1998; Mayer, 1994). However, it appears that American Indian and Hispanic parents are less likely to seek the support of other parents than Anglo parents (Sontag & Schacht, 1994). Nonetheless, all families may be able to find some level of support from other parents. According to Lustig and Akey (1999), parent-to-parent groups may provide critical assistance to families in gaining social support and access to informal support services. These groups may be formal or informal but consist of parents who have children with disabilities. Examples of these groups include local chapters of the Arc and the National Society for Children with Autism.

According to Simeonsson and Simeonsson (1993), parents' needs for support vary at different times in the families' development. Professionals can ensure that the family has access to information concerning formal support services. Family resource programs can assist in providing parent information and education (Paul et al., 1993). Each state has a Parent Information Center as well as a Protection and Advocacy Center. These centers can provide information and educational materials upon request.

Seeking assistance from professionals and others has been reported as a critical coping skill (Nadler et al., 1991), but its usefulness can differ according to one's culture. For example, Sontag and Schacht (1994) found that Anglo parents more often than both Hispanic and American Indian parents felt professionals didn't listen to them. On the other hand, they found that Hispanic and American Indian parents reported greater need to receive information about how to obtain services than Anglo parents did. There is also evidence that the category of disability may also be a factor in a family member's perceptions of the value of professionals (Hodapp, Freeman, & Kasari, 1998).

TEACHER TIP 4.7

A key role for school personnel may be to help families identify community supports. Have a list of supports and contacts available for families and be willing to discuss these supports if family members are interested.

Table 4.4   Potential informal and formal sources of support.

Informal
    Family members
    Friends
    Social groups
    Other parents
Formal
    Social service providers
    Alternative medical providers
    Church
    Psychologists
    Educators
    Social workers
    Professional groups

INTASC 10

School and Community Involvement

To successfully meet the challenges presented by children with disabilities, most families benefit from the use of support systems. The family may act as a support system for its members; however, families may need outside sources of support in times of high stress or crises. For example, Turnbull and Turnbull (2001) suggest that a parent's use of interpersonal and intrapersonal resources acts to buffer stress. It has long been recognized that parents of children with disabilities who are able to increase their access and use of social supports reduce their levels of stress. For example, Simpson (1996) found that single mothers experienced increased stress when support was reduced. Mothers of preterm babies who experienced elevated levels of stress were found to have less support than mothers who experienced a lower level of stress (Beckman, 1991). See Table 4.4 for a list of potential sources of support that educators and families may wish to identify.

THEORETICAL MODELS FOR COPING WITH STRESS

It is important that families and educators view stress as normal and predictable. It is also important that they believe stress can be altered through personal actions. Therefore, it is important that families and professionals learn how to identify stressors and work toward the reduction of stress as a goal of their partnership. The Family Systems Approach and the Hilton Coping Model provide theoretical models for working with families to identify and reduce stress.

Family Systems Approach

It is essential for professionals to view the family or family members as a dynamic system. One of the more significant changes within special education is the shift from focusing on the individual with a disability to that of focusing on the family (Allen & Petr, 1996; Turnbull, Turbiville, & Turnbull, 2000; Turnbull & Turnbull, 2001). The result of this shift has been the adoption of the Family Systems Approach for establishing family and professionals partnerships.

The Family Systems Approach is based on three principles: (1) input/output, (2) concepts of wholeness and subsystems, and (3) the boundaries (Turnbull & Turnbull, 2001, Whitechurch & Constantine, 1993). Inputs are the family's characteristics, the family members' individual characteristics, and the special challenges faced within the family (Turnbull & Turnbull, 2001). Outputs are the result of the family interactions as they interact with each other to perform their roles related to family functions (Turnbull & Turnbull, 2001). The second principle is that of the concept that the family must be understood as an entity and the family perspective must be discovered, not that of the individual child, mother, or father. The family is greater than its members, just as the sum is greater than its parts (Turnbull & Turnbull, 2001). The last principle is that of boundaries. Boundaries are created by interactions of family members and by the interaction of the family as a whole with those persons who are not members of the family. The openness and closedness of the boundaries affects the degree of collaboration in which the family will engage (Turnbull & Turnbull, 2001).

The family as a dynamic system provides the environment for all children to learn and grow. Bronfenbrenner (1990) expanded this concept to include the "family as teacher." However, research later demonstrated that many parents felt conflicted by this role. Some found the role of teacher as stress producing and expressed the anxiety that unless every interaction became an educational opportunity, the parent felt guilty (Robbins, Dunlap, & Plienis, 1991). The current role of parent-teacher collaboration with families is that of being involved in planning for the child's future, assisting in homework, and providing practice and instruction for domestic and community skills training (Turnbull & Turnbull, 2001). Professionals must be aware of the preferences of each unique family. Any plans must reflect the roles that the family chooses.

Recognizing that families are diverse and unique and that families are dynamic social systems requires the professional to gather information before, during, and often after any interaction with a family member. Such information is critical to meeting the needs of the student in the educational setting and to the empowerment of the student's family when family members and educators interact. When gathering information, the educator must recognize that not only is there great diversity in patterns of family behavior, but that individual family members show wide variance in reactions to the identification of a child as having a disability (Hughes, 1999; Mary, 1990); how they handle the stress of child raising (Hanline, 1991); their personal needs (Turnbull & Turnbull, 2001) and their philosophies (Erin et al., 1991); how they react to and interact with professionals (Bailey et al., 1998; Turnbull & Turnbull, 2001); their methods of coping and use of other personal strengths (Meyer & Bailey, 1993); and their use of support systems (Hughes, 1999). These differences make each family member unique in their view of their experiences (Mary, 1990; Turnbull & Turnbull, 2001) and in how they interact with the educational community (Seligman, 2000). These differences often increase the difficulty for professionals to decipher the needs

CEC 1

Foundations

INTASC 10

School and Community Involvement

of family members, thereby limiting the effectiveness of their work with families (Palmer, Borthwick-Duffy, & Widaman, 1998a, 1998b; Spidel, 1995).

TEACHER TIP 4.8

Develop an informational folder for each different cultural group found in your community. Review this information before meeting with the family to ensure that you are aware of cultural issues that you should consider. Such information might also include volunteer interpreters to assist when there are families with different language needs.

The Hilton Coping Model

Understanding the strategies used by family members when coping with stress is critical to understanding family members of children who have disabilities. The goal of parents and families of children with disabilities to function successfully is essential to the progress and ultimate success of the child in school and ultimately in life. This goal is often referred to as coping or adjustment.

Seligman (2000) states that personal resources impact coping with stress. These personal resources include five categories of coping strategies: social networks, problem-solving skills, general and specific beliefs, utilitarian resources, and health/energy/moral. Later research suggested that these categories are interrelated and that the impact of stress must be included in any multidimensional model for understanding parents with disabilities (Seligman, 2000).

An effective method for understanding the coping strategies of parents and families is to examine the personal strengths of the family members as well as the support systems the family has in place. Hilton (1998) proposed a model for understanding individual family members. The model uses concentric circles to provide a graphic view of how families cope. In this model the center circle represents the personal strengths possessed by individual family members, including the individual family member's understandings, skills, and strengths. Understanding, skills, and strengths include personal philosophy about disabilities, internal ability to handle stress and feelings concerning personal control, previous experiences such as exposure to persons with disabilities, and cultural dimensions including their religion, their upbringing, and the amount and type of education. The level of these factors within the individual determines the size of this center circle.

The next circle is the support systems available to the person. Examples of such supports might include neighbors providing babysitting, parent support groups, social service agencies, respite care, family members, or schools. In terms of Hilton's model (1998), as supports are identified and accessed the outside circle grows and acts as a buffer to the inner circle.

Outside the outer circle are the feelings associated with loss. These feelings are readily accessible to the individual. The variety of feelings experienced, that is, available, is limited only by the individual. At the time of initial identification of the child

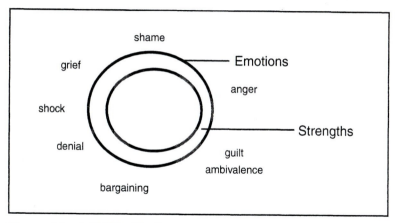

Figure 4.1   *Initial identification.*
Source: From "A Multidimensional Model for Understanding and Working with Families of Children Who Have Disabilities," by A. Hilton, 1998, in A. Hilton & R. Ringlaben (Eds.), Best and promising practices in developmental disabilities (*pp. 275–286*), Austin, TX: Pro-Ed.

as having a disability, the support-system circle is relatively small. The feelings, determined by a family member's personal emotional makeup, are close to the surface. The feelings are readily accessible and, in fact, family members often report they are deluged with emotion. The visual representation of this state is provided in Figure 4.1.

The Coping/Adaptation Process   With time, the development of support systems, the outside circle, expands. As the outside circle's area becomes larger, its effectiveness as a buffer for the inner circle improves (see Figure 4.2). It now takes longer for a person to be affected by the emotional field. As this occurs, the family member becomes better able to cope with the stressors in his/her life.

The Impact of Stress   Family members of children with disabilities experience stressful feelings similar to those experienced by all families. There are predictable and periodic times of stress that occur within families containing children with disabilities (South Carolina Department of Disabilities and Special Needs, 1998). In relationship to the Hilton model, stress increases an individual's access to feelings. Stress can, in fact, undo the effects of support, understanding, and adjustment. When stress occurs, the family member returns for a period of time to a previous state where a variety of feelings and emotions rapidly enter. In these situations, feelings of lack of control, emotional instability, and emotional devastation return. Usually this state of emotional deluge is transient and the family member returns to a state of emotional stability similar to that prior to the onset of the stress. In terms of the Hilton model, the circle returns to a state similar to Figure 4.1.

Another way that a family member may be affected by stress is when the inner circle becomes offset within the outer circle, making the feelings located on that side of the circle more accessible (see Figure 4.3). When this occurs, the family member under

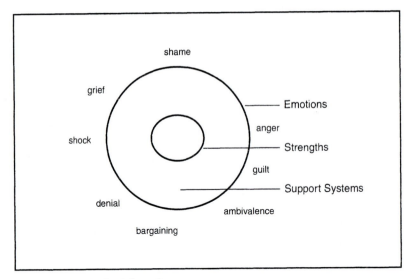

Figure 4.2 *Coping/adaptation.*
Source: From "A Multidimensional Model for Understanding and Working with Families of Children Who Have Disabilities," *by* A. Hilton, 1998, *in* A. Hilton & R. Ringlaben (Eds.), Best and promising practices in developmental disabilities (*pp.* 275–286), Austin, TX: Pro-Ed.

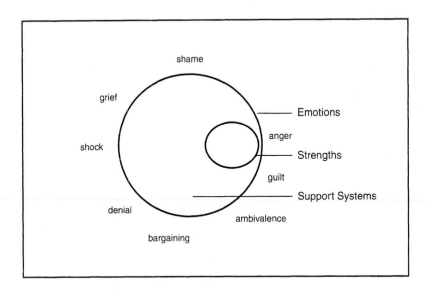

Figure 4.3 *The impact of stress.*
Source: From "A Multidimensional Model for Understanding and Working with Families of Children Who Have Disabilities," *by* A. Hilton, 1998, *in* A. Hilton & R. Ringlaben (Eds.), Best and promising practices in developmental disabilities (*pp.* 275–286), Austin, TX: Pro-Ed.

stress gravitates toward a certain feeling or group of feelings. An example is the family member who when under stress becomes angry for a period of time over a variety of activities such as the IEP process and school personnel.

It should be noted that individuals, professionals, and/or specific settings could cause unusual stress for a family member. This in turn causes the family member to focus upon one set of feelings when interacting with that specific person or in that specific setting. When a family member's feelings are off-center, seeking a friend, family member, or professional for support may help the family member become more centered. Family members may remain in this state for periods of time, although support systems and the passage of time may gradually help remove or lessen the impact of stress. An example of such a situation might be the time of transition from elementary to middle school. Feelings of fear and concern may surface until questions are answered and concerns are resolved. Again, feelings will vary depending on the personality and background of the family member. Read the scenario in Box 4.2 and analyze family dynamics and stress using the Hilton model.

Assumptions of the Hilton Model   If a professional is to effectively use the model provided by Hilton (1998), there are a set of assumptions the practitioner must recognize (see Table 4.5).

Although the previous discussions suggests actions and thoughts the professional should maintain when working with families, there are specific role definitions that are an outgrowth of this model. Hilton (1998) described the roles of the educator as follows:

1. Facilitating the family's understanding of stress and the role of support systems.
2. Helping parents recognize that the interaction of stress and emotional actions in a grieving process is normal and healthy.
3. Assisting parents in understanding the grieving process as an ongoing and dynamic process.
4. Empowering parents to act independently.
5. Developing and providing training to families concerning the components of the model.
6. Facilitating parents' interaction with other parents and professionals.
7. Avoiding roles that are beyond their responsibilities and training (for example, a teacher acting as a family counselor).
8. Helping families understand that each family member presents a unique set of needs and strengths based on personal attributes, access to support systems, and individual reactions to stress.
9. Recognizing that some parents and at some times other professionals may interact more effectively. (p. 293)

By keeping these roles in mind the professional can more effectively understand and work with family members of children with disabilities.

Table 4.5   Issues/assumptions practitioner must recognize.

---

1. Grieving is an ongoing process. Feelings related to grief and loss often are experienced for long periods of time or a lifetime.
2. Grieving is a natural and healthy activity. It is a totally normal process.
3. The extent of emotional impact that affects their lives varies based primarily on the unique individual factors.
4. Grieving is not a static process. Stress, time, knowledge, and support systems all play a major role in causing change.
5. Intervention has to be focused based on the needs of the family as the family members perceive those needs.
6. Effective professionals working with parents should discuss with the family members personal strengths, support systems, and feelings.
7. Using family member input, the model can then be completed. Ongoing interaction between professionals and parents should include focusing on the changes that have taken place over time.
8. The professional must be careful not to judge change or lack of change, but use that information to identify support options from which the parent may choose.

Box 4.2   *STRESS FOR THE FAMILY*

Bob and Susie have been married for 13 years. They have four children, ages 2, 5, 8, and 11. Mike, the 11-year-old, was diagnosed with Asperger's syndrome when he was 8. Since Mike's diagnosis, the family has come together and provided support for Mike. However, recently this extra time for Mike has started creating problems. Mike's siblings are beginning to resent the time that their parents spend on Mike's issues. Occasionally they will have their playmates over to play and Mike will be disruptive and cause problems. Some of the other children's friends don't want to come to their house to play any more. Bob's job may be moved to another community, about 14 hours away. The family will have to deal with this move if Bob is asked to go to the other location. Bob and Susie's marriage is having some ups and downs. Seems like they are blaming each other for more and more of the family problems and rarely get the chance to spend quality time alone together.

SUMMARY

Both the literature and parent input clearly indicate that for families and professionals to work together, it must be from a multidimensional perspective. Individual parents experience different feelings at different times and enter the process with differing feelings and abilities to cope with the impact of the issues resulting from the birth or identification of a child as having disabilities. Furthermore, family members continue to experience feelings of grief or loss for extensive periods of time. Family members have consistently reported that these feelings return during periods of stress. Professionals must recognize that it is quite difficult to understand the emotional reactions of individual family members using a linear model that has a precise beginning and end. An approach that uses stages through which individuals must advance to ultimately reach resolution does not match or explain what family members actually experience. A different model based on concentric circles provides the professional and parent with an alternative view of family coping and the sources of support that are important to the family.

QUESTIONS FOR DISCUSSION

1. Turnbull and Turnbull (2001) have identified four critical stages of the family life cycle. The four stages of this model are based on the child's age and include early childhood, school age, adolescence, and adulthood. Describe the role of family members with each stage and how this impacts the way school personnel interact with families.

2. Stage theory supports the notion that families go through distinctive stages of reaction after finding out that their child has a disability. Describe these stages and issues that school personnel must consider when families are in a particular stage. Are there stages where school personnel can be more helpful than others? Describe your response.

3. Discuss the similarities and differences between the family systems theory and the Hilton Coping model. Describe the role of school personnel within each theory or model.

REFERENCES

Ainge, D., Covin, G., & Baker, S. (1998). Analysis of perceptions of parents who have children with intellectual disabilities: Implications for service providers. *Education and Training in Mental Retardation and Developmental Disabilities* 33, 331–341.

Allen, R. I., & Petr, C. G. (1996). Toward developing standards and measurements for family-centered practice in family support programs. In G. H. S. Singer, L. E. Powers, & A. L. Olson (Eds.), *Redefining family support: Innovations in public-private partnerships* (pp. 57–86). Baltimore: Brookes.

Bailey, D. V., Skinner, D., Rodriquez, P., Gut, D., & Correa, V. (1999). Awareness, use, and satisfaction with services for Latino parents of young children with disabilities. *Exceptional Children*, 65, 367–381.

Beckman, P. J. (1991). Comparison of mothers' and fathers' perceptions of the effect of young children with and without disabilities. *American Journal on Mental Retardation*, 95, 585–595.

Bennett, T., Lee, H., & Lueke, B. (1998). Expectations and concerns: What mothers and fathers say about inclusion. *Education and Training in Mental Retardation and Developmental Disabilities*, 33, 108–122.

Birenbaum, A., & Cohen, H. J. (1993). On the importance of helping families: Policy implications for a national study. *Mental Retardation*, 31, 67–74.

Bronfenbrenner, U. (1990). Discovering what families do. In D. Blankenhorn, S. B. Ayme, & J. B. Elshtain (Eds.), *Rebuilding the nest: A new commitment to the American family* (pp. 27–38). Milwaukee, WI: Family Service American.

Dyson, L. L. (1997). Fathers and mothers of school-age children with developmental disabilities: Parental stress, family functioning, and social support. *American Journal on Mental Retardation*, 102, 267–279

Ellis, J. B. (1989). Grieving for the loss of the perfect child: Parents of children with handicaps. *Child and Adolescent Social Work*, 6, 259–270.

Erin, J. N., Rudin, D., & Njoronge, M. (1991). Religious beliefs of parents of children with visual impairments. *Journal of Visual Impairments and Blindness*, 85, 157–162.

Garber, M. (1992). Helping families with developmentally delayed children: POP as a model of parental involvement. In L. Kaplan (Ed.), *Education and the family* (pp. 41–53). Boston: Allyn & Bacon

Gargiulo, R. M., & Graves, S. B. (1991). Parental feelings. *Childhood Education*, 67, 176–178.

Gargiulo, R. M., & Kilgo, J. (2000). *Young children with special needs: An introduction to early childhood special education*. Albany, NY: Delmar Publishers.

Hadley, M. B., & Hanzlik, J. R. (1990). A comparison of perceived competence in child-rearing between mothers of children with Down syndrome and mothers of children without delays. *Education and Training in Mental Retardation*, 25, 132–141

Hancock, K., Wilgosh, L., & McDonald, L. (1990) Parenting a visually impaired child: The mother's perspective. *Journal of Visual Impairment and Blindness*, 84, 411–413.

Hanline, M. R. (1991). Transitions and critical events in the family life cycle: Implications for providing support to families of children with disabilities. *Psychology in the Schools*, 28, 53–59

Hilton, A. (1998). A multidimensional model for understanding and working with families of children who have disabilities. In A. Hilton & R. Ringlaben (Eds.), *Best and promising practices in developmental disabilities* (pp. 275–286). Austin, TX: Pro-Ed.

Hilton, A., & Henderson, C. J. (1993). Parent involvement: A best practice or forgotten practice? *Education and Training in Mental Retardation*, 28, 199–211

Hintermann, M. (2000). Children who are hearing impaired with additional disabilities and related aspects of parental stress. *Exceptional Children*, 66, 327–332.

Hodapp, R. M., Freeman, R. M., & Kasari, C. L. (1998). Parental educational preferences for students with mental retardation: Effects of etiology and current placement. *Education and Training in Mental Retardation and Developmental Disabilities*, 33, 342–349

Horwath, A. (1998). Empowering family members to work as partners with professionals. In A. Hilton & R. Ringlaben (Eds.), *Best and promising practices in developmental disabilities* (pp. 287–293). Austin, TX: Pro-Ed.

Hughes, R. S. (1999). An investigation of coping skills of parents of children with disabilities: Implications for service providers. *Education and Training in Mental Retardation and Developmental Disabilities*, 34, 271–280.

Jaffe, M. L. (1991). *Understanding parenting*. Dubuque, IA: W. C. Brown.

Karpel, M. (Ed.). (1986). *Family resources: The hidden partner in family therapy*. New York: Guilford.

Kubler-Ross, E. (1969). *On death and dying*. New York: Macmillan.

Lambie, R., & Daniels-Mohring, D. (1993). *Family systems within educational contexts: Understanding students with special needs*. Denver: Love.

Linn, S. (2000). Coping and adaptation in families of children with cerebral palsy. *Exceptional Children*, 66, 201–218.

Lustig, D. C., & Akey, T. (1999). Adaptation in families with adult children with mental retardation: Impact of family strengths and appraisal. *Education and Training in Mental Retardation and Developmental Disabilities*, 34, 260–270.

Lyon, S. R., & Lyon, G. (1991). Collaboration with families of persons with severe disabilities. In M. Seligman (Ed.), *The family with a handicapped child* (2nd ed., pp. 237–268). Boston: Allyn & Bacon.

Marsh, D. T. (1993). *Families and mental illness*. New York: Praeger.

Mary, N. (1990). Reactions of black, Hispanic and white mothers to having a child with handicaps. *Mental Retardation*, 28, 1–5.

Mayer, J. A. (1994). From rage to reform: What parents say about advocacy. *Exceptional Parent*, 49–51

Meyer, E. C., & Bailey, D. B. (1993). Family-centered care in early intervention: Community and hospital settings. In J. L. Paul & R. J. Simeonsson (Eds.), *Children with special needs: Family, culture, and society* (2nd ed., pp. 181–209). Fort Worth, TX: Harcourt Brace Jovanovich.

Nadler, A., Lewinstein, E., & Rahav, G. (1991). Acceptance of mental retardation and help-seeking by mothers and fathers of children with mental retardation. *Mental Retardation, 29*, 17–23.

Olshansky, S. (1962). Chronic sorrow: A response to having a mentally defective child. *Social Casework, 43*, 190–194.

Palmer, D. S., Borthwick-Duffy, S. A., & Widaman, K. F. (1998a). Influences on parent perceptions of inclusive practices for their children with mental retardation. *American Journal on Mental Retardation, 103*, 272–287

Palmer, D. S., Borthwick-Duffy, S. A., & Widaman, K. F. (1998b). Parent perceptions of inclusive practices for their children with significant cognitive disabilities. *Exceptional Children, 64*, 271–282.

Parette, H. P., & Petch-Hogan, B. (2000). Facilitating culturally/linguistically diverse family involvement. *Teaching Exceptional Children, 33*, 4–10.

Paul, J. L., Porter, P. B., & Falk, G. D. (1993). Families of children with disabling conditions. In J. L. Paul & R. J. Simeonsson (Eds.), *Children with special needs: Family, culture, and society* (2nd ed., pp. 3–24). Fort Worth, TX: Harcourt Brace Jovanovich.

Raghavan, C., Weisner, T. S., & Patel, D. (1999). The adaptive project of parenting: South Asian families with children with developmental delays. *Education and Training in Mental Retardation and Developmental Disabilities, 34*, 281–292.

Roach, M. A., Orsmond, G. I., & Barratt, M. S. (1999). Mothers and fathers of children with Down syndrome: Parental stress and involvement in childcare. *American Journal on Mental Retardation, 104*, 422–434.

Robbins, F. R., Dunlap, G., & Plienis, A. J. (1991). Family characteristics, family training, and the progress of young children with autism. *Journal of Early Intervention, 15*, 173–184.

Ronnau, J., & Poertner, J. (1993). Identification and use of strengths: A family system approach. *Children Today, 22*, 20–23.

Sandler, A. G. (1998). Grandparents of children with disabilities: A closer look. *Education and Training in Mental Retardation and Developmental Disabilities, 33*, 350–356.

Seligman, M. (1991). Grandparents of disabled children: Hopes, fears, and adaptation. *Families in Society, 72*, 147–152.

Seligman, M. (2000). *Conducting effective conferences with parents of children with disabilities.* New York: Guilford Press.

Seligman, M., & Darling, R. B. (1997). *Ordinary families, special children.* (2nd ed.) New York: The Guilford Press.

Serafica, F. C. (1990). Counseling Asian-American parents: A cultural-developmental approach. In F. C. Serafica, A. I. Schwebel, R. K. Russell, P. D. Isaac, & L. B. Meyers (Eds.), *Mental health of ethnic minorities.* New York: Praeger.

Simeonsson, R. J., & Simeonsson, N. E. (1993). Children, families, and disability: Psychological dimensions. In J. L. Paul & R. J. Simeonsson (Eds.), *Children with special needs: Family, culture, and society* (2nd ed., pp. 25–50). Fort Worth, TX: Harcourt Brace Jovanovich

Simpson, R. L. (1996). *Working with parents of exceptional children and youth* (2nd ed.). Austin, TX: Pro-Ed.

Smith, C. (1993). Cultural sensitivity in working with children and families. In J. L. Paul & R. J. Simeonsson (Eds.), *Children with special needs: Family, culture, and society* (2nd ed., pp. 113–121). Fort Worth, TX: Harcourt Brace Jovanovich.

Sontag, J. C & Schacht, R. (1994). An ethnic comparison of parent participation and information needs in early intervention. *Exceptional Children, 60*, 422–433.

South Carolina Department of Disabilities and Special Needs (SCDDSN). (1998) *Working with professionals: A guide for families of children with developmental disabilities.* Retrieved January 3, 2004 from www.state.sc.us/ddsn/pubs/pros/pros.htm.

Spidel, J. (1995). Working with parents of the exceptional child. In E. H. Berger (Ed.), *Parents as partners in education* (4th ed.). Englewood Cliffs, NJ: Merrill.

Stewart, J. C. (1986). *Counseling parents of exceptional children* (2nd ed.). Columbus, OH: Merrill.

Stoneman, Z., Brody, G. H., Davis, C. H., Crapps, J. M., & Malone, D. M. (1991). Ascribed role relations between children with mental retardation and their younger siblings *American Journal on Mental Retardation, 95*, 537–550.

Thomas, D. D. (1993). Minorities in North America: African-American families. In J. L. Paul & R. J. Simeonsson (Eds.), *Children with special needs:*

Family, culture, and society (2nd ed., pp. 122–138). Fort Worth, TX: Harcourt Brace Jovanovich.

Thompson, R. J., & Gustafson, K. E. (1996). *Adaptation to chronic childhood illness*. Washington, DC: American Psychological Association.

Turnbull, A. P., Turbiville, V., & Turnbull, H. R. (2000). Evolution of family-professional partnership models: Collective empowerment as the model for the early 21st century. In J. P. Shonkoff & S. L. Meisels (Eds.), *The handbook of early childhood intervention* (2nd ed.). New York: Cambridge University Press.

Turnbull, A. P., & Turnbull, H. R. (2001). *Families, professionals, and exceptionality: Collaborating for empowerment* (4th ed.). Upper Saddle River, NJ: Merrill/Prentice Hall.

Waggoner, K., & Wilgosh, L. (1990). Concerns of families of children with learning disabilities. *Journal of Learning Disabilities, 23,* 97–98, 113.

Wang, T. M. (1993). Families in Asian cultures: Taiwan as a case example. In J. L. Paul & R. J. Simeonsson (Eds.), *Children with special needs: Family, culture, and society* (2nd ed., pp. 165–178). Fort Worth, TX: Harcourt Brace Jovanovich.

Webb-Mitchell, B. (1993). Hope in despair: The importance of religious stories for families with children with disabilities. In J. L. Paul & R. J. Simeonsson (Eds.), *Children with special needs: Family, culture, and society* (2nd ed., pp. 97–110). Fort Worth, TX: Harcourt Brace Jovanovich.

Whitechurch, G. G., & Constantine, L. L. (1993). Systems theory. In P. G. Boss, W. J. Doherty, R. LaRossa, W. R. Schumm, & S. K. Steinmetz (Eds.), *Sourcebook of family theories and methods: A contextual approach* (pp. 325–352). New York: Plenum.

CHAPTER 5
Working with Families: Respecting Diverse Backgrounds

●○●○●○●○●○●○●○●○●○●○●○○○○

Objectives

After reading this chapter, you will:

- Know the characteristics that merge to form one's culture
- Understand the meaning of *diversity*
- Know how to identify cultural values of different groups

- Understand the basic principles for working with culturally diverse families
- Understand your own culture
- Know how to work with families with linguistic diversity
- Know how to increase family involvement of families from diverse cultures
- Understand how to involve families from diverse cultures in conferences
- Know basic issues related to making home visits
- Understand the importance of and how to organize parent advisory committees

A culture is the "attitudes, values, belief systems, norms, and traditions shared by a particular group of people that collectively form their heritage" (Gargiulo, 2003, p. 81) that is transmitted from generation to generation. A culture influences how a person perceives and interprets what is happening and determines how the person behaves, initiates, and reacts in various situations (Gollnick & Chinn, 2002). According to Turnbull, Turnbull, Shank, and Smith (2004), culture "influences our rituals; determines our language; shapes our emotions; and is the basis for what we determine is right or wrong about ourselves, others, and society" (p. 93). Gollnick and Chinn (2002) present a listing of characteristics that merge to form one's culture, including:

- Gender
- Ethnicity
- Race
- Class
- Geography
- Age
- Exceptionality
- Religion
- Language

Diversity is a word that has been used increasingly over the past several decades in the discussion of differences that exist among all individuals. *Diversity* can be defined as "the fact or quality of being different" (Sparks, 1998, p. 180). People are diverse in many ways, including size, skin color, language, gender, and temperament. Diversity, when used in the context of discussions about cultural and linguistic diversity, may include differences in cultural characteristics, cultural expectations, cultural experiences, cultural diversity, and linguistic diversity. However, a caution should be offered at this point. The professional should not respond to students and their families based on a diversity-based assumption (Smith, Polloway, Patton, & Dowdy, 2004). For example, one should not assume that a second-generation Korean American has the same beliefs as a recent immigrant or that all non-English-speaking persons have the same cultural beliefs or even the same language. The length of time that the student has been in the country, his/her age, and the proximity of other family members also can influence the individual's culture (Gollnick & Chinn, 2002). Because of the external factors encountered in daily life, the culture of students may differ from the culture of the parents or grandparents, which further complicates issues when attempting to build family-school partnerships.

CEC 1

Foundations

TEACHER TIP 5.1

Make sure that generalizations about individuals from various culturally diverse groups are not made; all individuals and all families should be viewed as unique. Overgeneralizing about families from similar cultural backgrounds can be as harmful as ignoring all aspects of cultural diversity.

UNDERSTANDING CULTURAL AND LINGUISTIC DIFFERENCES IN FAMILIES

Cultural and linguistic diversity is a reality in the United States as this is one of the more diverse countries in the world (Vaughn, Bos, & Schumm, 1997). The early belief in the United States as a melting pot in which all citizens were to be assimilated into one generic culture simply did not happen. In fact, rather than becoming more similar, in many ways the people who populate the United States have become more diverse (Gonzalez, Brusca-Vega, & Yawkey, 1997), with this diversity being reflected in the student population in public schools.

Although there are many benefits to this diversity, challenges and conflicts can result among individuals from such different backgrounds. These conflicts may occur because individuals from different cultures do not understand the nature of the "other" culture. Patton, Blackbourn, and Fad (1996) note that a primary reason for the occurrence of cultural conflict is that one culture, usually the majority culture, tries to achieve a "cultural fit" for everyone. In other words, conflict often occurs when one culture tries to "fit" all other cultures into its norms. The way to avoid or lessen cultural conflict is to gain a better understanding of the diverse cultures represented as opposed to expecting everyone to "fit" into the majority culture.

Thus, school personnel should develop an understanding of the cultures represented in their schools (Sparks, 1998). Without this understanding, cultural conflict is more likely to occur and the quality of education for children from diverse cultural and linguistic backgrounds will be negatively impacted. By understanding the cultural and linguistic backgrounds of students and parents, teachers and other school personnel are less likely to misinterpret actions and comments, less likely to have their own actions and comments misinterpreted, and more likely to meet the needs of students (Vaughn et al., 1997). Thus, mistakes/errors can often be avoided when school professionals have an understanding of their own culture and the culture of their students and their families. Different cultures often have different value systems even though they exist within a majority culture.

Warger (2001) suggests a method for developing an understanding of the cultures represented in schools through the use of "a two-way process of information sharing and understanding called Cultural Reciprocity" (p. 1). Through this process both partners learn to identify their own cultural values and beliefs and to share them with others. The steps of the process are:

Step 1: Identify the cultural values that are embedded in your interpretation of a student's difficulties or in the recommendation for service.

PRAXIS 1

Understanding Exceptionalities

CEC 9

Professional and Ethical Practice

CEC 2

Development and Characteristics of Learners

Step 2:   Find out whether the family being served recognizes and values your assumptions, and if not, how their view differs from yours.

Step 3:   Acknowledge and give explicit respect to any cultural differences identified, and fully explain the cultural basis of your assumptions.

Step 4:   Through discussion and collaboration, try to determine the most effective way of adapting your professional interpretations or recommendations to the value system of this family. (Warger, 2001, p. 2)

In order to enhance the success of family-school partnerships, parents and professionals both should consider any barriers such as language, culture, and so on that may impact, positively or negatively, on their relationship. By using the process of Cultural Reciprocity, school personnel and family members have an opportunity to learn more about each other and to develop a deeper relationship with one another, a relationship based on knowledge and mutual respect.

TEACHER TIP 5.2

School personnel should make an effort to understand all cultures represented in their schools. Having representatives from various cultures make brief presentations to school staff might be a helpful beginning.

WORKING WITH FAMILIES FROM CULTURALLY AND LINGUISTICALLY DIVERSE BACKGROUNDS

CEC 10

Collaboration

Working with families from culturally and linguistically diverse backgrounds can be very challenging. School personnel must remember that there are great variations both within and among cultural and linguistic groups. For example, the Hispanic culture and language is significantly different from that of the Asian culture and language. But at the same time, there are many differences in the language spoken and in the beliefs within each culture. The extensiveness of diversity found among students and their families means that school personnel must often work very hard to learn more about diverse cultures along with ways to work with families from these cultures. Taking an attitude of "everyone should be like us" and really meaning "everyone should be like me" is very damaging to family-school relationships.

PRINCIPLES FOR WORKING WITH CULTURALLY DIVERSE FAMILIES

Although each cultural and linguistic group reflects unique characteristics and needs, there are several general principles that should be used to guide professionals when working with families from any diverse cultural and linguistic group. These general principles, along with considerations for specific groups, will facilitate successful strategies by school personnel. See Table 5.1 for general principles (Cross, Bazron, Dennis, & Isaacs, 1989).

When families from diverse cultural and linguistic groups are involved in school activities for their children with disabilities, many different areas are affected, including

Table 5.1 General principles for working with culturally diverse families.

1. The family, as defined by each culture, is the primary system of support and preferred point of intervention.

2. The system must recognize that minority populations have to be at least bicultural and that this status creates a unique set of mental health issues to which the system must be equipped to respond.

3. Individuals and families make different choices based on cultural forces that must be considered if services are to be helpful.

4. Practice is driven in the system of care by culturally preferred choices, not by culturally blind or culturally free interventions.

5. Inherent in cross-cultural interactions are dynamics that must be acknowledged, adjusted to, and accepted.

6. The system must sanction and in some cases mandate the incorporation of cultural knowledge into practice and policymaking.

7. Cultural competence involves determining a client's cultural location in order to apply the helping principle of starting where the client is and includes understanding the client's level of acculturation/assimilation.

8. Cultural competence involves understanding cultural preferences in order to support client self-determination.

9. Cultural competence functions with the recognition that in order to provide individualized services, clients must be viewed within the context of their cultural group and their experience of being part of that group.

10. Cultural competence functions with the acceptance of a client's culture as it really is, without judgment, and adapts service delivery to fit the context within which the client functions.

11. Cultural competence involves working in conjunction with natural, informal support and helping networks within the minority community, for example, neighborhoods, churches, spiritual leaders, healers, and so on.

12. Cultural competence extends the concept of self-determination to the community. Only when a community recognizes and owns a problem does it take responsibility for creating solutions that fit the context of the culture.

13. Culturally competent services seek to match the needs and help-seeking behavior of the client population.

14. Culturally competent services are supported and enhanced when the system of care functions as an integrated support network.

(continued)

Table 5.1   *Continued*

15. Community control of service delivery through minority participation on boards of directors, administrative teams, and program planning and evaluation committees is essential in the development of effective services.

16. An agency staffing pattern that reflects the makeup of the potential client population, adjusted for the degree of community need, helps ensure the delivery of effective services.

17. Culturally competent services incorporate the concept of equal and nondiscriminatory services, but go beyond that to include the concept of responsive services matched to the client population.

Note: From *Towards a Culturally Competent System of Care* (pp. 52–54), by T. L. Cross, B. J. Bazron, K. W. Dennis, and M. R. Isaacs, 1989, Washington, DC: National Technical Assistance Center for Children's Mental Health, Georgetown University Child Development Center.

classroom management and the activities included in the special education process especially related to the development and implementation of the Individualized Education Plan (IEP). Some areas of the IEP process affected include: (1) sensitivity to over- and underrepresentation of students from diverse cultural and linguistic backgrounds in special education programs; (2) nondiscriminatory assessment practices; (3) inclusion of a language component in the student's IEP, if necessary; (4) attention to language development and English as a second language (ESL); (5) provision of instruction in the child's native language; (6) use of current ESL approaches; and (7) involvement of parents throughout the process using their native language or an interpreter (Garcia & Malkin, 1993). The development and implementation of the student's IEP requires family involvement and is the same for students from culturally and linguistically diverse backgrounds as it is for majority culture/language students. However, families from diverse cultural and linguistic backgrounds may require special considerations such as being sensitive to the needs of families and ensuring effective communication with family members.

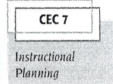

CEC 7

Instructional Planning

The student's culture and language should also be taken into consideration when implementing special programs. An activity as simple as communicating with family members about the progress being made by the student may be affected by cultural and linguistic diversity. Homework, study habits, and reading opportunities may also be affected by cultural and linguistic factors.

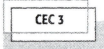

CEC 3

Individual Learning Differences

A third area impacted when working with students and families from diverse cultural and linguistic backgrounds is that of classroom management and discipline. Many teachers are unprepared for the cultural differences in terms of classroom behavior. Likewise, Neal, McCray, and Webb-Johnson (2001) found that the flexibility of some teachers paired with the inflexibility of others led to confusion concerning classroom expectations for children with diverse cultural and linguistic backgrounds. According to Yates, Hill, and Hill (2002), the root of the problem is the teacher's misunderstanding of the role of culture and language in the learning process. This may result in a mismatch of home and school cultures known as cross-cultural dissonance

CEC 5

Learning Environments and Social Interactions

(Harry, 1992a, 1992b). Examples of cross-cultural dissonance that can be perceived by teachers as classroom management problems and discipline issues include classroom expectations of competitiveness, requirement to look the teacher in the eye, requests to speak up and out, verbal response that include lengthy pauses, volunteering (perceived as showing off), or being quiet and obedient (Weinstein & Mignano, 2003). Such misunderstandings of cultural differences can lead to referrals for special education services (Artiles, Harry, Reschly, & Chinn, 2002). Therefore, teachers need to work to gain insight into such cultural issues and be cognizant of their potential ramifications.

TEACHER TIP 5.3

Before referring children from diverse backgrounds for special education services, school staff should ensure that the child's performance is not being negatively impacted by cultural issues, such as not speaking up and not being competitive with peers.

Understanding Your Own Culture

As Harris (1996) notes, an important prerequisite when working with individuals from different cultures is for school personnel to recognize and understand their own culture. Understanding their own culture and how it differs from the cultures of families with whom they are working will greatly facilitate collaborative relationships between school personnel and families (Hyun & Fowler, 1995). Without an understanding of one's own culture, it is very difficult to recognize and understand the unique needs that result from other cultural and linguistic backgrounds. Table 5.2 provides a list of questions that will help individuals understand their own cultural backgrounds.

Empowering Families

As noted in each chapter, in order for families of students with disabilities to be involved in their child's educational programs, they must feel empowered to take such an active role. This may be difficult since many individuals from different culturally and linguistically diverse backgrounds feel powerless in all areas. Empowering them in school activities may take an extra effort from school personnel. Two things that school personnel can do to help family members feel empowered are to encourage family involvement in their child's educational program and help them realize their legal rights and their need to be involved in decisions affecting their child (Horwath, 1998). Empowering families can occur through many different activities. Some general principles that school personnel need to consider when empowering families include:

1. Realizing that family members are the experts on their children;
2. Empowering family members to serve as the leader in activities for their child; and
3. Utilizing family issues and needs to motivate various activities. (Stodden & Horwath, 1993, p. 4)

Table 5.2   Cultural self-awareness questions.

1. What is my definition of culture?
2. Of what cultural group am I a member?
3. What is the status of my cultural group among other groups?
4. What are characteristics of my cultural group?
5. How do I meet the general characteristics of my cultural group?
6. What are stereotypes of my cultural group?
7. How do I meet the stereotypes of my cultural group?
8. How fair are the stereotypes of my cultural group?
9. Which stereotypes of my cultural group do I agree with and which ones do I disagree with?
10. What stereotypes of my cultural group would I change if I could?
11. If I were not a member of my cultural group, to which cultural group(s) would I want to belong and why?
12. If I were not a member of my cultural group, to which cultural group(s) would I not want to belong and why?
13. Of all cultural groups I encounter on a regular basis, which ones have fair stereotypes and which ones do not have fair stereotypes?
14. What are the cultural groups represented in my class/school?
15. How do I meet the unique needs of culturally different children in my class/school?
16. Do I let inappropriate stereotypes interfere with providing appropriate educational opportunities to my students?

Additionally, when working with families from culturally and linguistically diverse backgrounds, school personnel should be sensitive to factors unique to these families, such as language differences and cultural values (Sparks, 1998). Without this sensitivity, many parents will simply assume that teachers and other school staff are condescending or insensitive to their beliefs and values. This misconception can create a significant barrier to family empowerment and effective parent-school collaboration and the end result may be the development and implementation of programs that are less effective. Table 5.3 provides suggestions for working with families from several diverse cultural and linguistic backgrounds.

Working with Families with Linguistic Diversity

Working with families who speak languages other than English, or who speak a dialect very different from the teacher, presents unique challenges. Because IDEA requires communication with families to be in their native language, fully involving families who speak languages different from the teacher's may be difficult. Family members who speak a non-majority language may feel alienated when they cannot fully understand

CEC 6

Language

Table 5.3   Suggestions for working with culturally diverse families.

1. Conduct a self-assessment to understand your knowledge of cultural diversity.
2. Use a range of culturally sensitive instructional methods and materials.
3. Use interdisciplinary units.
4. Use instructional scaffolding.
5. Use journal writing.
6. Establish a classroom atmosphere that respects individuals and their cultures.
7. Foster an interactive classroom learning environment.
8. Employ ongoing and culturally aware assessments.
9. Collaborate with other professionals and families.

Note: From "Creating Culturally Responsive, Inclusive Classrooms," by W. Montgomery, 2001, *Teaching Exceptional Children, 33,* 4–9. Copyright 2001 by the Council for Exceptional Children.

what school personnel are saying. This lack of understanding may add to an already existing atmosphere of distrust, making close collaboration very difficult.

Because few special education personnel are bilingual, this adds to the language dilemma, making communication with family members with diverse languages more difficult (Gersten & Woodward, 1994). In situations where school staff are not proficient in the native language of the home, specific steps may need to be taken to overcome any language differences and assure that family members feel they are an integral participant in the educational process for their children. There are numerous strategies that professionals can use to help overcome language issues, including (1) adopting a philosophy that diverse languages represent a strength in our society and not a burden, (2) using interpreters and translators, and/or (3) making an attempt to learn as much about the language and culture as possible (Sparks, 1998). When school personnel make an attempt to understand the family's language, family members are more likely to believe that the school cares about their child and is interested in the family's involvement in the student's educational program. On the other hand, if parents think that school staff are insensitive to their language diversity and are condescending to their culture, the family may be less likely to cooperate and participate fully in the process.

A beginning point for school personnel working with families who have a different language is to attempt to understand the language and communication patterns of different cultural groups. By learning simple words in the family's language and adopting greetings that are culturally appropriate, school personnel convey a level of cultural sensitivity to the family that assists in establishing trust and obtaining their support. When school personnel make no attempt to learn even the most rudimentary phrases in the language, such as greetings, family members feel that school personnel really do not care about their diverse language or problems that result from it. Read the teachers' lounge conversation in Box 5.1 and reflect on the different attitudes of the two teachers regarding language diversity.

TEACHING TIP 5.4

Before meeting with family members from diverse linguistic backgrounds, school staff should make an effort to learn a few words of the family's language. Even words of greeting make family members feel like you respect their language and culture and that you are making a strong effort to work with their children.

Box 5.1

Ms. Murry and Mr. Greenwood are in the teachers' lounge during the first week of the school year. Ms. Murry states that she wishes she knew how to speak Spanish because she has three children in her second-grade classroom who are non-English speakers. She says "I think I am going to ask Ms. Blake at the high school to tutor me in Spanish. I really want to learn some basic Spanish so I can at least have a general understanding of what my three kids are saying. I think they would feel much more at home if I could say a few words in Spanish." Mr. Greenwood, the sixth-grade teacher responds, "They need to learn English. I don't think we should have kids in our classes if they can't understand the language. They need to go to a special class, learn English, then they can come into our classes. I do not think I should have to learn a foreign language just to talk to students." Ms. Murry responds, "But don't you think we should at least make an effort? I know my kids' parents don't speak English, and I think they would feel much more comfortable if I at least made an effort to speak and understand their language. Even if I just said hello in Spanish." Mr. Greenwood, sounding very frustrated, says, "Well, you learn Spanish if you want to; personally, I don't want these kids if they can't speak the language everyone else uses, and if their parents are working and making money here, then they need to learn English too."

Using Language Interpreters and Translators

Despite developing some minimal skill in a family's primary language, there are times in which the only way to communicate effectively with the family members is through an interpreter or a translator. Translators concentrate on communicating written materials, whereas interpreters concentrate on oral communications (Turnbull et al., 2004). Interpreters are critical in allowing family members and school personnel to communicate effectively. Interpreters make it feasible for family members and school representatives to discuss student issues to a degree impossible without language assistance. Interpreters also ensure the family's understanding of due process requirements and allow for a discussion of the issues rather than simply presenting the translated contents of documents and requesting that the family members sign at the appropriate places. Using an interpreter allows both parties to ask and answer questions and allows for a more effective partnership.

Despite the benefits gained from the use of interpreters, working with them may present challenges for educators. One challenge concerns the necessary qualifications of interpreters. For example, should interpreters be knowledgeable in special education, or simply be conversant in the language and have interpretation skills? Although there is no requirement for interpreters to have a special education background, having some knowledge about the field can assist the interpretation process. Without some knowledge of special education, the interpretation of some of the terminology specific to special education may be difficult for interpreters. In addition, they may have a difficult time understanding parts of the process.

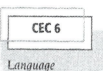

CEC 6

Language

A second challenge relates to the role of interpreters. For example, should interpreters be allowed to meet with family members to interpret materials without other school personnel present to explain the contents of the information, or should they simply be allowed to directly translate information provided by other school personnel? This challenge also concerns in part the first challenge related to the knowledge of interpreters about special education. If interpreters understand the special education process, allowing them to interpret materials might be appropriate. On the other hand, interpreters who are not knowledgeable about the special education process should limit their interpretation to what special education professionals present.

Using interpreters effectively requires skill in understanding the role of the interpreter. School personnel need to remember that the skill level of interpreters will vary with each interpreter. Generic recommendations will always need to be tailored for specific individuals. See Table 5.4 for guidelines for working with interpreters.

TEACHING TIP 5.5

Because interpreters with some general knowledge about special education will be in a better position to interpret to families, school staff should provide opportunities for interpreters to learn about the special education process so they can be more knowledgeable interpreters.

Table 5.4 Guidelines for working with an interpreter.

- Introduce the interpreter to all individuals present at the meeting.
- Talk to the person you are addressing, not the interpreter. (Remember, you are talking with the individual with a language barrier, not the interpreter.)
- Maintain eye contact with the individual with the language barrier, not the interpreter, when both talking and listening.
- Do not talk too fast; make sure you break your comments into translatable phrases.
- Do not interrupt the interpreter when she/he is in the middle of a translation.
- Make sure you frequently ask the individual if he or she understands or wants to comment on something.
- Always close the meeting by thanking the interpreter.
- Make sure that any interpreter is aware of confidentiality issues.

INCREASING FAMILY INVOLVEMENT

The involvement of family members in the education of all children is important; however, for children with disabilities, especially those from diverse cultural and linguistic backgrounds, family involvement may be even more critical (Gonzalez et al., 1997). This is because children from diverse cultural and linguistic backgrounds may experience academic difficulties, or may be at risk for experiencing problems as a result of these differences. Unfortunately, just as families from majority cultures are often not involved in the education of their children with disabilities, many families from culturally and linguistically diverse backgrounds are also not involved. The same reasons for noninvolvement exist for all families. Unfortunately, some educators may believe that these families from diverse cultures are not involved because they lack trust in the system, are apathetic, live stressful lives, and disagree with the special education placement of their child (Harry, 1992a, 1992c). Such beliefs reflect a strong bias against families and children from culturally and linguistically diverse backgrounds. In fact, the beliefs noted above may not be true, as families from diverse cultural and linguistic backgrounds have legitimate reasons for their limited involvement, including:

- Family level of acculturation
- Prior experiences with discrimination
- Structure of the family
- Disciplinary strategies (Salend, Dorney, & Mazo, 1997)

With so many children from diverse cultural backgrounds involved in special education programs, increasing participation of family members is an important consideration.

One of the first actions that school personnel can take to increase family involvement is to get to know the students better. By getting to know students, school personnel are in a better position to understand individual cultural backgrounds, parents, and home interactions. Vaughn et al. (1997) suggest the following general areas with questions that teachers and other school personnel can use when finding out more about students and their cultures:

- **Time:** How do students perceive time? How is timeliness regarded in their cultures?
- **Space:** What personal distance do students use in interactions with other students and with adults? How does the culture determine the space allotted to boys and girls?
- **Dress and Food:** How does dress differ by age, gender, and social class? What clothing and accessories are considered acceptable? What foods are typical?
- **Rituals and Ceremonies:** What rituals do students use to show respect? What celebrations do students observe, and for what reasons? How and where do parents expect to be greeted when visiting the class?
- **Work:** What types of work are students expected to perform, and at what age, in the home and community? To what extent are students expected to work together?
- **Leisure:** What are the purposes for play? What typical activities are done for enjoyment in the home and community?
- **Gender Roles:** What tasks are performed by boys? By girls? What expectations do parents and students hold for boys' and girls' achievements, and how does this differ by subject area?

- **Status:** What resources (e.g., study area and materials, study assistance from parents and siblings) are available at home and in the community? What power do parents have to obtain information about the school and to influence educational choices?
- **Goals:** What kinds of work are considered prestigious or desirable? What role does education play in achieving occupational goals? What education level does the family and student desire for the student?
- **Education:** What methods for teaching and learning are used in the home (e.g., modeling and imitation, didactic stories and proverbs, direct verbal instruction)?
- **Communication:** What roles do verbal and nonverbal language play in learning and teaching? What roles do conventions such as silence, questions, rhetorical questions, and discourse style play in communication? What types of literature (e.g., newspapers, books) are used in the home and in what language(s) are they written? How is writing used in the home (e.g., letters, lists, notes) and in what language(s)?
- **Interaction:** What roles do cooperation and competition play in learning? How are children expected to interact with teachers? (p. 278)

In addition to getting to know students better, school personnel can use several other strategies to increase the participation of families, including those from cultural and linguistic diverse backgrounds. Some areas for parent participation are:

INTASC 10

School and Community Involvement

- Conferences
- Home visits
- Family liaisons
- Parent advisory committees
- Family education workshops
- Print media
- Volunteers (Gonzalez et al., 1997)
- Cultural events at school
- Cultural awareness days/weeks
- Programs that honor diversity

Conferences

Conferences are a primary method for involving parents of students with disabilities. Conferences provide an opportunity for school personnel to sit down with parents, spend time getting to know the family, and gather information that will help them develop and implement programs for children. It also gives parents an opportunity to get to know school personnel better. Conferences, when conducted properly with family members participating as full members, can greatly facilitate trust between school personnel and parents. Unfortunately, it is sometimes difficult to get parents to attend conferences. In a study of 24 families of African American children in preschool special education programs, Harry, Allen, and McLaughlin (1995) found that as their child ages, the family often becomes less involved in conferences. This may result from their perception that professionals become less accessible over time.

Professional actions were found to sometimes serve as active deterrents to family involvement in conferences. Many parents in the study felt that notices of meetings were often sent too late for them to make arrangements for work or childcare. Also, the notices suggested that the meeting would have to be held at a particular time and place, without regard for parents' needs. A second problem reported by many parents was the limited amount of time available for conferences. Many parents felt that they were rushed, with only 20 to 30 minutes set aside for conferences.

Parents also reported that school personnel often focused on documents that were available rather than active participation by those in attendance. According to Harry et al. (1995), "When parents were asked how they perceived their role in the conferences, the majority consistently replied that their main role was to receive information about their child's progress and to sign the documents" (p. 371).

Parents also felt that too much professional jargon was used during the conference, often making it difficult for them to understand what professionals were saying about their child. Finally, parents indicated that the entire structure of many of the meetings placed them at a distinct disadvantage. Many parents felt as if they were simply there to read and hear reports by professionals about their child, not to take an active role in discussing appropriate educational options (Harry et al., 1995).

All of the concerns expressed by parents in Harry et al.'s 1995 study can be addressed. School personnel can easily schedule conferences well in advance, with parental input regarding their schedules; allow more time for conferences to ensure that all parties feel like their concerns and input were heard; reduce the use of professional jargon; emphasize real parental participation; and orchestrate the meeting so that parents do not feel like they are powerless and are only there to listen and agree.

Several specific actions can convey to family members that their presence and involvement is genuinely sought. In order to use conferences as a positive means of increasing family involvement, professionals should (1) let families know through nonverbal mannerisms, verbal statements, and how meetings are planned and conducted that cultural and linguistic diversity are valued; (2) hold conferences when they are needed and desired by either party, not simply because they are "due"; and (3) ensure that conferences are an opportunity for two-way communication where parents' ideas and values are "acknowledged, genuinely accepted, and acted upon" (Gonzalez et al., 1997, p. 200).

One action that schools can do to ease parents' fears and make them more likely to participate in conferences is to indicate to them that they are welcome to bring an advocate or someone with them. Often, for parents from different cultural and linguistic backgrounds bringing an advocate who understands their cultural and linguistic background is reassuring. Schools might even suggest a particular individual who could serve as an advocate if they are aware of someone in the community (Yates & Ortiz, 1995).

Families who attend conferences should feel as if they are accepted as equal partners in the process. For families from diverse cultural and linguistic backgrounds, developing the belief of equal partnership may require school personnel to increase efforts in demonstrating the acceptance of the family as a partner. Understanding the cultural and linguistic backgrounds of the families helps school personnel interact with family members and provides a sound basis for the family members to feel comfortable and accepted within the school. How family members are addressed, to whom questions are directed, and how the family is viewed as a unit are all important

CEC 6

Language

INTASC 3

Diverse Learners

considerations for school personnel before, during, and after conferences. Some general considerations during conferences include the following:

- Establish an agenda for the meeting.
- Greet the parent(s) respectfully using appropriate forms of address (do not say Mom, Dad).
- Introduce everyone present at the meeting and their role with the child.
- Set the purpose of the meeting.
- Avoid professional jargon.
- Do not overwhelm the parents with large numbers of school personnel who are not required by regulations.
- Be active in bringing parents into the conversation.
- Make sure that positive things are said about the child.
- Ensure that parents understand what school personnel are saying; restate comments in understandable terms without condescension.
- Suggest an advocate for the parents if one would be helpful.

Even though these suggestions may not be effective with all families, their implementation will usually increase the participation of family members.

TEACHING TIP 5.6

School staff should ensure that parents feel they are an integral part of the conference proceedings. They should be brought into the discussion about their child and given the opportunity to add information that the school may not have.

Home Visits

Home visits can be an incredible opportunity to help parents feel as if their participation in their child's educational program is valued and appreciated (Sparks, 1998), and that they are respected as equal partners in the educational process. Too often, parents are told that meetings about their child will be held at a particular location, on a particular day, and at a particular time. Even if parents can arrange to attend the meetings, it is often not very convenient. Because of inconvenience or simply an inability to make appropriate arrangements, many parents do not attend meetings. The school may read this as a message that parents are not interested and do not care to become involved. However, what the lack of parental participation may show is that the way parents were invited to attend the prearranged meetings made them perceive that their involvement is really not very valued by school personnel. Home visits can result in benefits for the child, family, and the school (see Table 5.5 for a list of possible benefits).

When making home visits, it is very important for school personnel to understand that they are guests in the home. Even if the home is not similar to the one in which the school professional lives, it is still a home. Size of the home, location, customs, scent, and decor should not result in actions by the professional that indicate

Table 5.5 Benefits of home visits.

1. Professionals and family members can interact more readily and genuinely in homes than in classrooms.
2. Home visits are less threatening and intimidating than classroom visits because family members are in familiar environments.
3. Home visits offer professionals opportunities to observe family-child interactions and effectively match, model, and use these positive interactional styles with their students for effective results.
4. Home-visit formats can be easily adapted to particular cultural and linguistic variations to include special components that mesh with and support these variations.
5. Professionals come to know the home settings of their students, the values of their family, and the materials common to the home that might be used in the home training of family members.
6. Understandings, skills, and attitudes of students in the home can be identified and used as the bases for successful work in the school.
7. Home programs provide firsthand observations of the effects of the educational programming on students and family members.
8. By developing and sharing common understandings and visions through home programs, family members and professionals realize that they are working toward the best results with the same individual—the student.

Note: From *Assessment and Instruction of Culturally and Linguistically Diverse Students with or At-Risk of Learning Problems* (p. 200), by V. Gonzalez, R. Brusca-Vega, and T. Yawkey, 1997 Boston: Allyn & Bacon. Copyright © 1997 by Pearson Education.

discomfort to the family members. For example, some families remove their shoes before crossing the threshold and entering the home. Making home visits should be viewed as a unique opportunity for the school person to learn about the culture of the family of the child and to demonstrate respect for the family and its members.

Following are some general considerations when making home visits: (1) always be on time; (2) dress comfortably and professionally, but not in a manner that would make the host family feel uncomfortable; (3) sit where the host family indicates, without hesitation; (4) when offered refreshments, always remember that the family is the host and use good judgment, with the goal being "give no offense"; (5) do not talk down to the parent or other family members; (6) always seek input from the parent; (7) never act as if you are in a hurry; (8) use an interpreter when visiting a home in which the native language is different from your own; (9) ask parents' permission before you visit and permission for other visitors who may be accompanying you; and (10) remember to include positive information.

School personnel should always schedule visits at the family's convenience with the understanding that the time requested by the parent may be based on others who the family wishes to have attending. For example, in some cultures, the grandparents are the ones who make decisions, so any visits should coincide with their availability. School personnel should ask parents if they wish to invite extended family members or advocates. The amount of time required for the meeting should also be discussed with the parents in order to assure that sufficient time can be allotted to address the goals of the meeting. School personnel should also remember that in some instances the family does not wish to meet with the school personnel in their home and that if home visits do occur, they may increase the stress within the family (see discussion in Chapter 4).

When the home visit occurs, the school personnel should be aware of culturally appropriate behaviors. Additionally, the home visit should be planned so that its goals can be met in the time allotted. Following is a discussion of some areas of possible concern.

Greeting the Family   Because the greeting sets the stage for the entire visit, this is a critical part of the home visit. School personnel should greet all adults first. Next, greet children if they are present. The attitude of school personnel should be one of pleasure in being a guest in the home as opposed to an attitude of required attendance. Sensitivity to cultural and linguistic differences is important. If an interpreter or translator is present, this individual should greet family members and be introduced as the person who will be available for interpreting. In addition, the parent should decide where in the home the meeting is to occur. This can be the living room, den, kitchen, or any other room where the parent feels comfortable. Additionally, any cultural mores should be remembered when entering the family's home such as removal of shoes at the door, greeting the family with both hands not just one, using appropriate titles when greeting the family, and so on.

TEACHING TIP 5.7

When making home visits, remember to be comfortable and be cognizant of cultural mores that should be followed. For example, in some cultures, the father figure makes key decisions for the family. In this situation, make sure that the father is the family member who is addressed most during the meeting.

Follow-up on Last Visit or Contact   At the beginning of the visit, it is appropriate to take a few moments to establish or reestablish rapport with family members. This time may be used to review previous meetings or contacts. Sometimes, small talk may help all individuals who are present feel more comfortable. The school person should never act as if time is short and that the meeting must be hurried. Therefore, when planning meetings, school personnel should schedule ample amounts of time for the visit.

Establish the Purposes of the Meeting   It is important for most families to have an understanding of the purpose of the meeting. Although this may have been indicated in previous conversations and correspondence, the school person making the visit should restate the purpose to ensure that family members understand. If the purpose of the meeting is to become better acquainted with the family, then state that. On the other hand, if information is needed for an assessment, then the school person should indicate that the purpose of the visit is to gather information to determine how best to help the child. The purpose should be stated in plain, understandable terms.

Complete the Purposes of the Meeting   School personnel should take a leadership role in the meeting, unless it is obvious that a family member wants to take the lead. If the meeting becomes sidetracked, the school person should try to refocus the discussion back to the purpose. While not wanting to rush through the meeting, or keep family members from injecting comments, it is very important to stay on task and to focus on the original purpose of the meeting. If it becomes necessary, the school person may indicate that another meeting can be scheduled if other issues keep arising.

Summarize the Meeting   It is always a good idea to summarize the meeting as it is coming to an end. Highlighting the key points that were discussed and any specific actions that were taken or will be taken is important. Always ask family members if they concur with the summarized points to ensure that both parties have the same impressions from the meeting. In some cases, a formal written record of the meeting may be important. School personnel can summarize the meeting on multicopy paper, sign a copy, have a family member sign, and leave a copy with the family member. This results in a written account of the meeting and any agreement or actions that result from the meeting.

Establish the Next Meeting Time   There may be a need to establish another meeting time, or it may be that another meeting will be established later. In either case, the

Table 5.6   Home-visit checklist.

Before the visit:
1. Have you scheduled the home visit around the family's needs?
2. Did you send any materials home for family members to review before the home visit?
3. Did you explain to family members the purpose of the home visit?
4. Do you have good directions on how to get to the house?
5. Do you have other school staff making the home visit with you?
6. Are you familiar with the family situations (e.g., number of children, employment status, composition of family)?
7. Are you appropriately dressed for the home visit (professional but not in a way to make family members feel uncomfortable)?

During the meeting:
8. Did you arrive on time?
9. Did you make family members feel comfortable?
10. Did you provide structure to the meeting (e.g., time, topics, etc.)?
11. Did you provide a summary of the meeting at the end?
12. Did you appropriately respond to offers of food/drink?

After the meeting:
13. Did you provide some follow-up information to the family after the meeting?
14. Did you schedule another meeting, if necessary?

Box 5.2   *Home Visit*

Ms. Smith feels strongly that home visits are an excellent means of connecting with families, especially culturally diverse families. She needed to go to Daniel's house for a home visit, because she could not get his mother to complete any paperwork for special education services, and she desperately wanted to get Daniel in special education. She also thought that the home visit would help establish a positive relationship between Daniel's parents and the school. She was able to get Ms. Brown, the school counselor, to go with her. Daniel is 10 years old and in Ms. Smith's third-grade classroom. Although he has never been a very good student, Ms. Smith has decided that he might be able to benefit from special education and has therefore initiated a special education referral. Ms. Smith called Daniel's mother on Tuesday and told her of her concerns for Daniel, and asked if she and Ms. Brown could stop by on Wednesday to discuss some interventions they might be able to implement for Daniel. Both Ms. Smith and Ms. Brown thought the visit could result in some positive services for Daniel. They told Daniel's mother they would be by between 3:00 and 3:30, and arrived about 3:20. They went to the door and were greeted by Daniel's mother, who invited them in. Both Ms. Smith and Ms. Brown dressed professionally, but not too dressy because Daniel was from a poor home. When Daniel's mother asked them to sit down, they did so, and indicated "yes" when Daniel's mother asked them if they would like a glass of tea. Both Ms. Smith and Ms. Brown started the conversation with positive comments about Daniel and made sure to invite Daniel's mother to contribute throughout the conversation. Eventually they told Daniel's mother that a referral for special education might result in Daniel's receiving some services that would be very helpful to him. They described the special education process and eventually left after about 45 minutes, with all paperwork signed. Daniel's mother had been very cooperative and even asked if Ms. Smith and Ms. Brown would come back in a few weeks and give her a progress report on Daniel.

school person should discuss the need for the next meeting and obtain information for use in scheduling.

Good home visits do not just happen. In order to be effective, they should be well planned, structured, and at a time that is set by mutual agreement and is convenient for both parties (Gonzalez et al., 1997). Schools should develop a home visit checklist to ensure that proper planning has been accomplished and that considerations have been made to assure home visit success. Table 5.6 shows an example of such a checklist. Read the scenario in Box 5.2 and use the home-visit checklist to evaluate whether proper planning occurred.

Family Liaisons

Some programs require a home-based intervention program. This is a routine service delivery approach for young children served through Part C of IDEA, but it also may be the service model used for older children, particularly those with certain kinds of health problems who may be served in their home setting periodically. When using this model, individuals who go into the home setting to provide services should have the skills necessary to develop and maintain a positive working relationship with family members. These skills may include being able to speak and write the native language of the home, or having an interpreter present; having the interpersonal skills necessary to establish a working relationship with family members; and being sensitive to cultural routines and practices (Gonzalez et al., 1997).

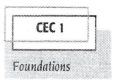

CEC 1

Foundations

Teachers who visit the home to develop and implement home-based programs should follow many of the guidelines suggested for general home visits. They should always remember that they are visiting in the home of a family whose child is receiving special assistance. Acting as a guest is an important thing to remember. Being on time, having plans and appropriate materials for the session, and explaining what is being accomplished are all important guidelines when providing home-based services.

Parent Advisory Committees

INTASC 10

School and
Community
Involvement

Parent advisory committees are an excellent mechanism for getting families with diverse cultural and linguistic backgrounds involved in educational programs. If these committees are to be effective, they should be more than mere rubber-stamping groups. Committee members need to be respected for their opinions and school personnel need to honor their recommendations with genuine consideration. Members of the parent advisory committees and school personnel should develop a trusting relationship with each other. As the trust develops for both parties, the parents will begin to feel as if their ideas are being better received, and school personnel will begin to feel as if parents' suggestions are valid and should be considered (Gonzalez et al., 1997).

Membership on parent advisory committees is an important consideration for school personnel. Volunteers are important, but there are also likely candidates who might not want to volunteer. School personnel familiar with families in the district should discuss the strengths of various parents and invite those who would likely make a strong contribution. Stacking a parent advisory committee with "friendly" parents is not a good way of developing effective committees. Often, the most vocal critic of a school district may become its greatest supporter if serving on a parent advisory committee.

TEACHING TIP 5.8

Make sure that parent advisory committees are used and not just constituted to make an appearance of family involvement. Have the advisory committee provide recommendations to a variety of issues that school staff should address.

Family Education Workshops

Family education workshops are growing in popularity as a method for increasing family participation in educational programs for children with cultural and linguistic differences. These workshops are most effective when parents have been involved in their planning and development. This gives parents ownership and helps schools focus on what parents feel they really need rather than schools telling them what they need. Unfortunately, many schools do not involve parents in selecting workshop topics. They simply schedule topics in which they think parents would be interested and want assistance. Researchers have determined that as a result many family members do not attend workshops because they focus on topics of little interest to them. Involving parents in planning workshops will help prevent this (Gonzalez et al., 1997).

One method of establishing a family education workshop program is to organize a committee composed of parents and school staff to determine topics and develop programs. Begin the school year with a parent survey asking if they would be interested in serving on such a committee and the topics that they think would be of interest. The survey should be printed in the native languages of the families in the district or an interpreter should be available. The committee could help prioritize identified topics, contact speakers, and set times and dates for workshops. The time and the date of workshops are very critical because parents may not be able to attend workshops during the day because of work. Therefore, parent schedules should be considered when establishing the workshop schedule.

Print Media

Newsletters, community notes, personal notes, newspaper clippings, and handouts are forms of print media that are used to solicit parental involvement. These have been found to be effective means of communicating with parents. For parents of students with cultural and linguistic differences, school personnel should take into consideration language when using print media (Gonzalez et al., 1997). Information sent home using print media should be written in the native language of the home. This is important because it enables parents to read and understand the content of the information. Second, it indicates to parents that school personnel are sensitive to their cultural and linguistic needs and are willing to take steps to facilitate communication.

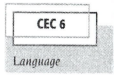

CEC 6

Language

Volunteers

Using parents of students with diverse cultural and linguistic needs as volunteers helps engage them in school activities. As volunteers, they may be able to communicate better with other families with similar cultural and linguistic backgrounds than other school staff from a different background. Their cultural and linguistic differences may be a commonality that helps establish and maintain communication between the school and family. As tutors, parents from cultural and linguistic diverse backgrounds may be better able to work with students from those backgrounds than other tutors. When parents from different cultural and linguistic backgrounds see other parents from similar backgrounds volunteering in the school, it may increase their trust in the school and they may view the school as a place where their children are welcome.

The development of new roles for families of children with disabilities from diverse cultural and linguistic backgrounds is important. Currently there are only two roles that are provided for these families: consent giver and educational planner. Typically, consent giver is the only role that is offered to family members. New roles could include: (1) parents as assessors, (2) parents as presenters of reports, (3) parents as policymakers, and (4) parents as advocates and peer supports (Harry, 1992a). These new roles would not only encourage parents to participate more in their child's educational program, but would also provide specific opportunities for this participation.

TEACHING TIP 5.9

When using parents of students with diverse cultural and linguistic needs, remember that these parents are volunteers. It's easy to ask willing parents to do more and more, and parents may burn out if they are asked to do too much.

Training for Professionals

CEC 9

Professional and Ethical Practice

Professionals involved in providing services to children with disabilities from diverse cultural and linguistic backgrounds should develop an understanding of the culture and language of the children served, as well as a general understanding of how to provide services to these children and their families (Yates & Ortiz, 1995). Without this knowledge, the best-intentioned program may be unsuccessful. Unfortunately, there are few training opportunities for professionals to develop the skills that are necessary in working with this population (Sexton, Lobman, Constans, Snyder, & Ernest, 1997).

Because of limited training opportunities, schools may need to be creative in preparing staff development activities. Ford (1992) suggests the following to assist special educators in providing services from a multicultural framework:

- Engaging teachers in self-awareness activities to explore their attitudes and perceptions concerning their cultural group and beliefs—as well as the effects of their attitudes on students in terms of self-concept, academic abilities, and educational opportunities.
- Exposing teachers to accurate information about various cultural ethnic groups (e.g., historical and contemporary contributions and lifestyles, value systems, interpersonal-communication patterns, learning styles, and parental attitudes about education and disabilities).
- Helping educators explore the diversity that exists between, as well as within, cultural ethnic groups.
- Showing teachers how to apply and incorporate multicultural perspectives into the teaching-learning process to maximize the academic, cognitive, personal, and social development of learners (e.g., assessment; curriculum; and instructional management, strategies, and materials).
- Demonstrating the effective interactions among teachers, students, and family members.
- Providing special education teachers with opportunities to manifest appropriate applications of cultural information to create a healthy learning climate. (p. 108).

SUMMARY

In summary, without parental involvement, school personnel are hampered in their efforts to provide appropriate programs for students with disabilities (Hilton, 1998). Because of the disproportionate number of students from culturally and linguistically diverse backgrounds in special education programs (MacMillan & Reschly, 1998; Patton, 1998; Patton et al., 1996), the close collaboration between parents of these children and school personnel is critical. Research has shown that families of children from diverse cultural and linguistic backgrounds are less likely to participate in the education of their children than other families (Sontag & Schacht, 1994).

This chapter has focused on families with children with disabilities who come from diverse cultural and linguistic backgrounds with an emphasis on family-school collaboration. It was noted that a starting point in understanding diversity in families is to understand one's own culture. Cultural and linguistic sensitivity were discussed, along with specific strategies for working with families with linguistic diversity. Considerations for working with language interpreters were also discussed.

Finally, challenges to increasing school involvement and strategies to ameliorate this concern were discussed. These strategies included conferences, home visits, family liaisons, print materials, parent advisory committees, and family education workshops. Finally, ways to provide staff development for school personnel related to cultural and linguistic diversity were provided. It was also noted that school personnel should be trained in working and collaborating effectively with students and family members from diverse backgrounds if cross-cultural dissonance is to be avoided and true family-school partnerships are to be secured.

QUESTIONS FOR DISCUSSION

1. The early belief in the United States as a melting pot in which all citizens were to be assimilated into one generic culture simply did not happen. Describe society today in terms of diversity. Is it better or worse to have a diverse society than one where different cultures melt into one? Why or why not?

2. What are some of the problems encountered by schools when interacting with families from different cultural and linguistic backgrounds? What are some strategies that can be used to overcome these problems?

3. Increasing family involvement is an issue with all families of children with disabilities. How does cultural and linguistic diversity create more of a challenge to increase family involvement? What are some things the school can do to facilitate increased involvement among families with diverse cultural and linguistic backgrounds?

REFERENCES

Artiles, A. J., Harry, B., Reschly, D. J., & Chinn, P. C. (2002). Over-identification of students of color in special education: A critical review. *Multicultural Perspectives, 4*, 3–10.

Cross, T. L., Bazron, B. J., Dennis, K. W., & Isaacs, M. R. (1989). *Towards a culturally competent system of care* (Volume 1 A monograph on effective services for minority children who are severely emotionally disturbed). Washington, DC: National Technical Assistance Center for Children's Mental Health, Georgetown University Child Development Center.

Ford, B. A. (1992). Multicultural education training for special educators working with African-American youth. *Exceptional Children, 59*, 107–114.

Garcia, S., & Malkin, D. (1993). Toward defining programs and services for culturally and linguistically diverse learners in special education. *Teaching Exceptional Children, 26*, 52–58.

Gargiulo, R. M. (2003). *Special education in contemporary society: An introduction to exceptionality.* Belmont, CA: Wadsworth/Thompson Learning.

Gersten, R., & Woodward, J. (1994). The language-minority student and special education: Issues, trends, and paradoxes. *Exceptional Children, 60*, 310–322.

Gollnick, D. M., & Chinn, P. C. (2002). *Multicultural education in a pluralistic society* (6th ed.). Upper Saddle River, NJ: Merrill/Prentice Hall.

Gonzalez, V., Brusca-Vega, R., & Yawkey, T. (1997). *Assessment and instruction of culturally and linguistically diverse students with or at-risk of learning problems*. Boston: Allyn & Bacon.

Harris. K. C. (1996). Collaboration within a multicultural society. *Remedial and Special Education*, 17, 355–362.

Harry, B. (1992a). *Cultural diversity, families, and the special education system: Communication and empowerment*. New York: Teachers College Press.

Harry, B. (1992b). Developing cultural self-awareness: The first step in values clarification for early interventionists. *Topics in Early Childhood Special Education*, 12, 333–350.

Harry, B. (1992c). Restructuring the participation of African-American parents in special education. *Exceptional Children*, 59, 123–131

Harry, B.. Allen, N., & McLaughlin, M. (1995). Communication versus compliance: African-American parents' involvement in special education. *Exceptional Children*, 61, 364–377

Hilton, A. (1998). A multidimensional model for understanding and working with parents and families. In A. Hilton & R. Ringlaben (Eds.), *Best and promising practices in developmental disabilities*. Austin, TX: Pro-Ed.

Horwath, A. (1998). Empowering family members to work as partners with professionals. In A. Hilton & R. Ringlaven (Eds.), *Best and Promising Practices in Developmental Disabilities* (pp. 287–293). Austin, TX: Pro-Ed.

Hyun, J. K., & Fowler, S. A. (1995). Respect, cultural sensitivity, and communication. *Teaching Exceptional Children*, 28, 25–28.

MacMillan, D. L., & Reschly, D. J. (1998). Overrepresentation of minority students: The case for greater specificity or reconsideration of the variables examined. *Journal of Special Education*, 32, 15–24.

Montgomery, W. (2001). Creating culturally responsive, inclusive classrooms. *Teaching Exceptional Children*, 33, 4–9.

Neal, L. T., McCray, A. D., & Webb-Johnson, G. (2001, January). Teachers' reactions to African American students' movement styles. *Intervention in School and Clinic*, 36, 168–174.

Patton, J. M. (1998). The disproportionate representation of African Americans in special education: Looking behind the curtain for understanding and solutions. *Journal of Special Education*, 32, 25–31.

Patton, J. R., Blackbourn, J. M., & Fad, K. (1996) *Exceptional individuals in focus* (6th ed.). Columbus, OH. Merrill.

Salend, S. J., Dorney, J. A., & Mazo, M. (1997). The roles of bilingual special educators in creating inclusive classrooms. *Remedial and Special Education*, 18, 54–64.

Sexton, D., Lobman, M., Constans, T., Snyder, P. & Ernest, J. (1997). Early interventionists' perspectives of multicultural practices with African-American families. *Exceptional Children*, 63, 313–328.

Smith, T. E. C., Polloway, E. A., Patton, J. R., & Dowdy, C. A. (2004). *Teaching students with special needs in inclusive settings*. Boston: Allyn & Bacon.

Sontag, J. C., & Schacht, R. (1994). An ethnic comparison of parent participation and information needs in early intervention. *Exceptional Children*, 60, 422–433.

Sparks, S. (1998). Multicultural practice in mental retardation and developmental disabilities. In A. Hilton & R. Ringlaben (Eds.), *Best and promising practices in developmental disabilities*. Austin, TX: Pro-Ed.

Stodden, R., & Horwath, A. (1993). *Integrating a family focus within a University Affiliated Program*. Honolulu: Hawaii University Affiliated Program.

Turnbull, R., Turnbull, A., Shank, M., & Smith, S. (2004). *Exceptional lives: Special education in today's schools* (4th ed.). Upper Saddle River, NJ: Merrill/Prentice Hall.

Vaughn, S., Bos, C. S., & Schumm, J. S. (1997) *Teaching mainstreamed, diverse, and at-risk students*. Boston: Allyn & Bacon.

Warger, C. (2001). Cultural reciprocity aids collaboration with families. Retrieved January 4, 2004, from http://library.adoption.com/Special-Needs-Cultural-Reciprocity-Aids-Collaboration-with-Families/article/928/3.html.

Weinstein, C. S., & Mignano, A. J. (2003). *Elementary classroom management: Lessons from research and practice* (3rd ed.). Boston: McGraw Hill.

Yates, J. R., Hill, J. L., & Hill. E. G. (2002, February) "A vision for change" but for who? A personal response to the National Research Council report. *DDEL News*, 11, 4–5.

Yates, J. R., & Ortiz, A. J. (1995). Linguistically and culturally diverse students. In R. S. Podemski, G. E. Marsh, T. E. C. Smith, & B. J. Price, *Comprehensive administration of special education* (2nd ed.). Upper Saddle River, NJ: Merrill/Prentice Hall.

CHAPTER 6
Working with Families: Communicating to Overcome Challenges and Develop Solutions

○ ○

Objectives

After reading this chapter, you will:

- Understand the basic components of communication
- Understand the importance of conferences for communicating with families

- Understand the key considerations in making conferences successful
- Know specific issues that arise before, during, and after conferences
- Know how to use grade report conferences with parents of students with disabilities
- Understand the different forms of communication with family members through the year
- Know how to address inappropriate parental behaviors
- Understand common problems in meetings and how to solve them
- Understand how family stress can impact communication

Foundations

Effective schools need to communicate effectively with the families of their students. The Individuals with Disabilities Education Act (IDEA) mandates encouraging family involvement and participation in the special education process. Effective communication is essential in meeting this mandate. As a result, special educators must learn and use effective communication strategies, thus allowing families and professionals to communicate successfully.

Legal and Societal Issues

AN OVERVIEW OF COMMUNICATION

Communication is "the process of exchanging knowledge, ideas, opinions, and feelings through the use of verbal or nonverbal language" (Smith, 2004, p. 153). For communication to occur, there must be at least two people: a sender and a receiver. The sender has a thought, idea, or feeling to be shared. The thought, idea, or feeling is the message. Then the sender translates the message into a code that the sender can understand. Communication can occur only when the receiver understands the message that the sender intends to send.

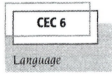

Language

Receiving Messages

To receive a message, one must listen. Decker (1994) has suggested that good listening involves listening to what *is* being said, listening to what *is not* being said, and listening to what people *want to say* (not how they say it). Three components to receiving information effectively are: (1) communicating the desire to understand the message, (2) understanding the message, and (3) interpreting the sender's ideas, position, and/or feelings. Effective receiving, or listening strategies are based on research in the areas of nonverbal communication and active listening. Effective listening requires that the receiver provides the sender with information indicating involvement in the listening process and demonstrates that the information from the sender is being processed.

Nonverbal Approach   Nonverbal communication involves the use of the body, arms, hands, face, and voice. Through the use of nonverbal communication, the receiver conveys that attention is focused on the sender and that there is interest in the message being sent. See Table 6.1 for positive indicators of nonverbal communication in two-way communication.

Table 6.1   Positive indicators of nonverbal communication.

Area	Positive Indicators
Body	Turn and face sender.
	Relax your body.
	Lean slightly forward toward the person.
	Move slowly.
	Limit repetitive movements (e.g., moving a leg up and down).
Head	Nod to express your understanding.
	Tilt or turn an ear slightly toward the sender to help indicate you are listening.
Face	Look at the person but be aware of their comfort.
	Smile frequently.
	Show expression of interest (e.g., amazement).
Arms	Keep arms relaxed and open.
	Rest arms on the table or the arm of your chair.
Hands	Keep hands open with palms up.
	Touch the person gently.
	Use gestures of understanding.
Voice	Use a soft tone of voice.
	Reduce verbiage.

The goal of nonverbal communication is to put the other person at ease while receiving information. By nonverbally expressing an open and positive attitude toward the sender, the receiver increases the security and comfort of the sender, leading to a supportive and collaborative atmosphere in which goals may be met.

Verbal Approach   The receiver has the responsibility of reporting to the sender what he/she has heard and understood. When used skillfully, verbal communication approaches can facilitate problem solving, assist in mutual understanding, and advance team building among professional(s) and family member(s). Verbal approaches can be grouped into seven categories: (1) getting started, (2) obtaining information, (3) encouraging continuation, (4) repeating or reflecting information or feelings, (5) probing for information, (6) conveying understanding, and (7) summarizing. Examples of each of these are found in Table 6.2.

Three specific verbal communication techniques that fit into several of the categories in Table 6.2 are paraphrasing, echoing, and perception checking. Because of their usefulness, they warrant further discussion.

Paraphrasing   Paraphrasing is the restating of the sender's ideas. The purpose of paraphrasing is to ensure that the receiver has correctly understood the message. Paraphrasing can encourage the sender to expand on the message or to correct the

Table 6.2 Effective verbal communication techniques.

Category	Examples
Getting Started	"What are your concerns?"
	"Where shall we start?"
	"As I remember from our last meeting . . ."
Getting Information	"When did this first start?"
	"And?"
	"How often does this occur?"
Encouraging Continuation	"Please continue"
	"Tell me more"
	"Thank you for that explanation"
Repeating or Reflecting	"You would like him to . . ."
	"So you are seeing . . ."
	"You are mad about how I am . . ."
	"You said Tom frightens you when . . ."
Probing for Information	"What are your ideas concerning this issue?"
	"Do you see these problems at home?"
Conveying Understanding	"I think you are telling me . . ."
	"Correct me if I am wrong, but you feel . . ."
Summarizing	"The things you want me to do are . . ."
	"So you are concerned about . . ."

receiver's interpretation of the message if it was incorrectly restated. Paraphrasing can be used to encourage communication, solicit more information, demonstrate understanding, and summarize the result of the conversation. With a little practice professionals can effectively use paraphrasing to facilitate two-way communication.

Echoing   Echoing is a method of letting the sender know that what was said was received. When the sender clearly describes an emotion, the idea is reiterated in the speaker's own words. For example:

Family Member (Sender): "I feel intimidated at IEP meetings and can't state my opinions clearly."

Teacher (Receiver): "You feel somewhat uncomfortable at IEP meetings and can't state your opinions clearly."

Echoing then becomes a tool that the professional can use at any point when emotions are shared. Echoing, if not overused, lets the sender know that the receiver is listening and attempting to understand the speaker's feelings. It encourages both the sender and the receiver to continue and can be used to gain a focus on particularly important feelings.

Perception Checking   Perception checking, on the other hand, is used to check the subtext of a message. Perception checking often is used to describe what the receiver believes to be the sender's feelings. To use perception checking, the listener needs to carefully interpret nonverbal clues, including facial expression, tone of voice, body position, and gestures. For example:

Family Member (Sender):   "You are planning to place Mary in that kind of class?"

Psychologist (Receiver):   "Are you are upset with the proposal to place Mary in an inclusive classroom?"

Important guidelines that need to be followed when using verbal techniques during the early stages of communication include: (1) not expressing approval or disapproval, (2) not expressing personal feelings, (3) avoiding interpretation or explanation of causes, and (4) not adding to the sender's message without the sender's approval. A rule the receiver of a message needs to remember is that personal ideas or feelings can be expressed only after the ideas and feelings of the sender have been restated accurately to the sender's satisfaction.

TEACHER TIP 6.1

Remember to be an active listener with parents. Parents know if you are really paying attention to them or not. Focus not only on verbal communication but also any non-verbal communication used by the parent.

Sending Messages

Professionals who are interested in achieving the best for students desire positive communication with family members and send messages home consistently and often. Effective transmittal of information is not complicated, but there are strategies that may increase the clarity of the message. These strategies include: (1) taking responsibility for message ownership, (2) being complete and specific in the message, and (3) repeating the message in alternative but consistent forms to enhance understanding.

INTASC 6

Communication and Technology

Ownership   By using the pronouns "I" or "my" the sender acknowledges that the feelings, observations, or opinions that follow are his/her own. It is important that family members and professionals identify the ownership of the content as that of the sender and not messages from or for others.

Completeness and Specificity   For messages to be understood, they must be complete and specific. To do this, the sender should provide enough background information so that the receiver can understand the situation or problem. Then the receiver can evaluate the importance of the information and more effectively assist in developing possible solutions.

Repetition of the Message   Research is clear that when a message is repeated it is more likely to be understood. Repetition can be accomplished by repeating important words or phrases; summarizing the important points or issues; using pictures, charts, or data; or having a second person summarize or restate the information presented.

When employing these strategies, several additional considerations can further ensure the success of the communication process. First, during the initial phase the message should not include blame and is not to be evaluated or interpreted. Second, when describing feelings it is important to provide the receiver with a clear statement of the specific feeling the sender is experiencing (e.g., "I am angry"). Third, information concerning the student needs to be reported by the professional as an observer, rather than as an emotional response to the situation. Fourth, the professional's non-verbal communication needs to be monitored to ensure it is providing the listener with a message consistent with the verbal message. Finally, the professional needs to remember that communicating effectively is the responsibility of both the sender and the receiver; however, the professional has the regulatory and ethical responsibility to ensure effective communication with families of children with disabilities.

COMMUNICATION THROUGH CONFERENCES

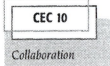

INTASC 6

Communication
and Technology

CEC 10

Collaboration

Conferences are an important means by which school personnel and parents communicate. However, conferences are often one of the less effective methods of communication. Two types of communication can occur during conferences: one-way and two-way. One-way communication occurs when one person sends a message without expecting a response from the receiver. Educators often employ one-way communication in the form of informational letters and newsletters. One-way communication such as letters or notes demonstrates to families and students that the school is attempting to keep them advised of school activities, but unfortunately, the person sending messages does not know whether the message is received and understood or received and misunderstood or misinterpreted.

Educators should avoid using one-way communication when family members are present. For example, teachers report that parents who do attend parent conferences often sit and listen but ask no questions, only nodding occasionally, thus resulting in one-way communication. When this occurs, school personnel should first determine if the behavior is a result of cultural dissonance or mismatch. If the behavior is not related to culture, then the educator can encourage quiet or nonresponsive family members by asking them if they have any questions, asking them to share their thoughts or opinions, or inviting them to offer solutions or alternatives to what has been discussed. Teachers should actively avoid the one-way communication trap by working to remove the risk for the family member in their communication by establishing supportive relationships prior to the meeting. Another alternative is to provide training opportunities for family members on the IDEA, on self-advocacy skills, and on effective group communication.

School personnel should strive to use conferences as venues for two-way communication. In two-way communication, information and ideas flow in all directions. Two-way communication is necessary for building effective working relationships between the family and the school personnel because each participant should understand the other participant's position or idea. Two-way communication may take more time than one-way; however, effective two-way communication often reduces potential communication problems, leads to more effective problem solving, and assists in building cooperation and collaborative partnerships. Such benefits greatly outweigh any investment of time, particularly because conferences are an important method of transmitting information concerning the student and essential in developing family-school partnerships.

> **CEC 10**
>
> *Collaboration*

TEACHER TIP 6.2

Solicit communication from parents and other family members. If family members are only listening to you, utilize some strategies to get them to talk. It's easy to just tell your side, but effective communication should be a two-way street.

Conferences can be separated into two categories: mandated conferences and nonmandated conferences. Mandated conferences are meetings required under federal and state laws and regulations, such as IEP conferences. Nonmandated conferences are those activities or meetings that may be required by the school or the district but are not required under law or regulation. They may be required of both special education and general education teachers and are practices that are implemented by effective educators. According to Strudder (1993), several considerations that increase the effectiveness of both mandated and nonmandated conferences are:

- Make early contact with families to introduce oneself and start to develop rapport
- Send home positive messages to develop positive communication prior to conferences
- Start conferences on a positive note
- Have examples and samples to share
- Remain objective in all reporting to families
- Practice active listening
- Make reflective responses
- Provide families with suggestions and alternatives
- Respond to the meaning and concern in the message even if the message seems aggressive or angry
- Deliver what you promise
- Contact parents after meetings
- Continue to send home positive information after conferences

Decker (1994) provides an additional set of tips for professionals to enhance effective communication during conference. These tips include:

- Eliminate distractions
- Focus on the main points
- React to ideas not to the person
- Focus on the positive
- Listen for what is not said
- Learn to tolerate silence
- Ask for clarification instead of making assumptions
- Contemplate the communication, not the speaker

The following is a set of suggestions for both mandated and nonmandated conferences. Following these suggestions should improve the effectiveness of both types of conferences.

Before the Conference   Preparation prior to the meeting is essential to the effective use of time, building of rapport, effective communication, and achievement of the goals of the conference. To do these things the professional should confirm the meeting as early as possible either by telephone or by return mail. A meeting time should be established that is mutually satisfactory based on family needs and demands and on the availability of school personnel. When possible, a reminder should be sent to the family that includes directions to the location of the meeting; a tentative, flexible agenda that includes, when appropriate, questions family members may want to ask; and other meeting-related materials. It is the responsibility of school personnel to arrange for a mutually agreeable meeting place in pleasant surroundings where seating arrangements are available that put all parties on an equal basis. In some instances transportation, childcare services, and translators may be necessary and should be arranged by school personnel. In essence it is the responsibility of both parents and school personnel to be prepared for the meeting, but the physical arrangements are the sole responsibility of the school.

TEACHER TIP 6.3

Before the conference begins, make sure you have introduced yourself to the family members. Make sure you say some positive things about their child; all parents like to be proud of their children's accomplishments.

During the Conference   The role of all participants is to focus on the needs of the child. However, a pleasant environment can assist in reducing possible stress and increase communication. To do this, if at all possible, refreshments may be provided. Eating or drinking together is often an effective manner of decreasing stress and increasing rapport. Additionally, refreshments offer an opportunity for informal discussions prior to the formal meeting and thus may help break the ice. However, prior to choosing or offering refreshments, cultural preferences and religious dietary restrictions should be considered.

At the start of the meeting, a positive experience or story relating to the student can be shared with the family in order to begin the meeting on a positive note. Begin by stating an appreciation for the unique, interesting, and fun qualities of the child. A substantial portion of the meeting should be devoted to a discussion of the family member's concerns, ideas, information, and potential solutions. A folder with examples of the student's work, notes concerning issues to be discussed, and questions that are of importance should be compiled prior to the meeting. This folder will be used as a resource during the discussion of student efforts and progress.

The meeting should close on a positive note by summarizing the actions to be taken and the roles of the family and school personnel in the child's program. The professional coordinating the meeting should thank the family members for their efforts and concerns and encourage follow-up meetings or discussions when necessary.

After the Conference   Often, one of the most neglected areas is the follow-up after the conference. Post-conference activities should include a telephone call or note to the parents to thank them for their participation, to ask them if they have additional thoughts or ideas to share, and to underline a commitment to action. Documentation of the outcome of the conference and the plan of action to be taken should also be sent to all participants. As soon as possible, recommendations and actions developed at the conference should be implemented and notification sent to the conference participants, thereby demonstrating the commitment to collaborating for the "best" education for the child.

Mandated Conferences

Mandated conferences were discussed from a legal and regulatory stance in the previous chapters on the legal bases and the special education process. In this chapter, mandated conferences will be discussed from the stance of effective communication. For example, following IEP meetings, parents state that they feel they have been put on the spot—having been given little support and often having no knowledge of what is expected of them. These meetings are often threatening for parents; however, professionals report that they are nonthreatening and provide an excellent opportunity to meet with school personnel rarely seen at the school. This difference in perception of meetings may lead to tension and stress for the participants, thus reducing the ability of the members to communicate and lessening the effectiveness of the conference. The following activities implemented before, during, and after the meeting can be used to enhance communication between parents and school personnel and lead to more effective collaboration as members of the family-school partnership.

Before the Meeting   Working with family members prior to the IEP meeting is an excellent way to defuse potential problems. Teachers may meet with parents at least 1 week prior to the IEP meeting to secure information and to identify questions and

INTASC 10

School and Community Involvement

CEC 1

Foundations

PRAXIS 2

Legal and Societal Issues

INTASC 10

School and Community Involvement

issues. Teachers should also encourage parents to bring information to the IEP meeting about the child's performance and behaviors at home. Ask the parents to bring their child's folder of materials (discussed in an earlier chapter) and a list of possible goals. In some cases, teachers may provide parents with inventories to complete concerning their child's performance in the home and the community. This approach is useful as it assists the parents in bringing valuable information to the IEP meeting.

During the Meeting   The manner in which the meeting begins is very important in securing the parents' involvement during the IEP meeting. Parents should not be made to wait for the meeting to begin. If delays in beginning the meeting should occur, a professional who has had contact with the family should explain the delay and make sure that family members are as comfortable as possible.

The use of an agenda has proven to be an efficient and effective tool to ensure that parent concerns will be discussed. By asking at the beginning of the meeting if there are other issues that need to be included on the agenda, an opportunity is provided for parents to mention additional concerns and have them placed on the agenda. At this time the team leader should present the focus of the meeting. It is important to present information concerning what the student *can* do, not only what the student *cannot* do. Parents report being devastated by the feeling that their child is helpless or so far behind that institutionalization is imminent. Additionally, it is important that during the meeting the participants' understanding of the issues and discussion is periodically checked. In order to make sure terms and concepts are clear to all participants a team member may be assigned to request clarification of terms or discussion topics.

After the Meeting   Interviews with parents have noted concerns with what actions or changes occur or do not occur after the meeting. Some parents have reported that after the IEP meeting, they remember important information that should have been discussed and they do not know how or to whom they should communicate. To a lesser degree, parents report feelings of sorrow for their child, the feeling that they have not done enough, or the feeling that they have signed away the rights of the child. Post-meeting is a critical time that provides an excellent opportunity for follow-up communication with parents. At the conclusion of the meeting, one of the team members should reassure the parents that the IEP can be changed or modified through the use of addendum forms that do not require every member of the team to be present. Also, a member of the team should state that someone from the team will be contacting the family within the next week to check to see if the family has questions or concerns about the IEP after reviewing it at home. The family should also be reminded that they may call the school if they have questions or concerns prior to that contact. Both actions leave the lines of communication open and provide parents with clearly defined options if concerns develop.

Parette and Petch-Hogan (2000) have provided a list of additional concerns for professionals when working and communicating in conferences with families who are culturally/linguistically different. These include:

- Using trained translators when necessary
- Having flexibility when working with diverse family members

- Scheduling meetings with family members in their homes prior to the IEP meeting
- Identifying local support groups to help the family with the process
- Discussing specific cultural issues with other professionals working with this family for information and advice

Nonmandated Conferences

Parent-teacher conferences and school open houses are the main types of nonmandated conferences. These events allow for casual parent-teacher contact. Some schools schedule such conferences in the evening or on noninstructional days or when substitutes can be hired. Although principals and teachers agree that the involvement of all parents in the school process is an appropriate goal, they would say that during parent-teacher conference times or school open houses, there is not enough time for conferencing with all the families who attend. Generally, these encounters are limited at best and do not allow adequate time for problem solving. However, such arrangements do offer time for educators to meet and extend their relationships with families.

> **CEC 10**
>
> *Collaboration*

In fact, establishing a problem-solving relationship with a family often requires multiple meetings. The following example demonstrates how a series of short meetings may be used to accomplish this goal of developing an educator-parent problem-solving relationship.

Meeting One:	Get acquainted and begin to develop initial relationship. Identify the issue(s) under examination and related factors.
Meeting Two:	Review the issues under examination. Brainstorm solutions. Select possible solution(s) and develop an implementation plan including assigning responsibility for implementation and data collection. Set a date to discuss the result of the plan and to plan for future steps.

For some students, meeting one might be preceded by a telephone conversation. For the first meeting with a family, MacFarlane (1996) has listed some essential considerations to address for the educator to be successful in increasing family involvement and attendance at meetings (see Table 6.3).

TEACHER TIP 6.4

It is important to establish a positive rapport with family members. To do this, family members need to trust school personnel. Therefore, take some time, as much time as necessary, to establish this sense of trust and make family members know that you really care about their child.

Table 6.3   Strategies for encouraging family attendance at conferences.

Consideration	Strategy
Make the family members feel comfortable.	Select a more comfortable setting than the classroom. Offer snacks and drinks.
Be aware of transportation concerns or issues.	Hold meetings close to or at the home of the parents. Provide transportation.
Be aware of need for babysitting and arrange if necessary.	Check for funds. Check local scout troops. Check with the home economics teachers. Check background information before hiring.
Be aware that parents are busy or overwhelmed.	Do not waste time during the meeting. (Have an agenda.) Do not be late to meetings. Help families prioritize. Meet on Saturdays or at the parents' home.
Be aware that parents may have little confidence in their ability to participate in meetings concerning their child.	Reassure parents of their capabilities in participating in meetings. Use positive reinforcement when they take risks.
Identify whether family members do not read or speak English.	Arrange tutoring for family members. Identify whether siblings may be able to teach family members. Arrange for interpreters for communication.
Be aware that cultural differences may exist.	Help educate the parents about their potential role and importance of the meeting. Arrange peers from the community to help them understand the school. Emphasize the importance of partnership.

Note: From "Reaching Reluctant Parents," by E. McFarlane, 1996, *The Education Digest, 61*(7), 7–12.

School Conferences and Open Houses   Often school districts and/or specific schools require teachers to hold one or two parent meetings per year. Such meetings may include school socials, open houses, carnivals, career counseling sessions, and individual academic advisement meetings.

As with other meetings involving parents, teacher preparation is essential. When planning a meeting, the parents should be apprised of the goals of the meeting. An estimation of the amount of time the family members feel that they may need to address issues and concerns should be discussed so that sufficient time may be allotted for the conference. The parents and other participants should be contacted well in advance of the meeting date so that any additional necessary arrangements can be made. All participants should be provided a conference-planning sheet that outlines the agenda for the meeting and provides pertinent information including examples of questions that they might want to ask.

It is essential that professionals prepare for conferences by planning an agenda, scheduling sufficient time, having work samples available, and arranging the room prior to the meeting. Effective teachers often have their students develop a portfolio of their work, which is made available to family members. This material should be dated and organized to demonstrate progress or lack thereof.

Another communication tool that can be used prior to conferences is a short letter to parents addressing the positive aspects of the student. Box 6.1 provides an example of a positive letter prepared by a kindergarten teacher. The positive letter accomplishes several important communication goals. It provides a sizable amount of information in a short time, explains the academic activities of the classroom, demonstrates teacher concern, and starts the conference on a positive note. When a positive letter is supplemented with work samples, the teacher can efficiently communicate important information concerning the student in a relatively short time while beginning to develop a relationship with family member(s).

Educators should also have informational materials available for distribution to parents who have questions concerning issues related to behavior management, teaching children, and so on. These materials should be available in the parent's primary language and can be distributed to parents at conferences. Information concerning education and disability-focused websites should also be available.

At the conclusion of the conference, the teacher should summarize the outcomes and thank the family members for their support and attendance. Additionally, the next meeting, family activity, and/or communication should be discussed.

CEC 7

Instructional Planning

INTASC 6

Communication and Technology

Box 6.1   *Example of a Letter Prepared by a Kindergarten Teacher*

Parent Conference—Jason

November 21

Jason is a delightful child with a sensitive, caring nature. He has overcome his initial apprehensions and is very much at ease in the group. He has made friends and is really enjoying his school experiences. Jason is able to choose activities and stay with them to completion. He is a bit of a perfectionist, but has learned to relax because of our noncompetitive environment. He knows that no one will get upset if mistakes are made, that he can always start again, and that perfection is not part of the curriculum.

Jason has a very positive attitude toward learning and is an active participant in all reading activities—Superkids, key words, writing class books, and large group language experience. He is able to write several letters of his name now.

Jason is doing very well and enjoying the math activities. He understands and applies patterns and is working on numeral writing.

I enjoy having Jason in my classroom.

Teacher's Signature

Parent-Teacher Grade Report Conferences   One of the mandatory obligations of the professional is the reporting to the parents of educational progress of all students, usually in the form of grades. Often this obligation is met through a nonmandated conference known as a parent-teacher conference. These often occur at scheduled times throughout the school year and provide a brief time for parents and teachers to discuss academic and behavioral progress.

Even though grade reporting is generally straightforward for students who do not have disabilities, it is less so for students with disabilities. Report cards or progress reports are designed to provide parents information on academic progress and, in some cases, on behavior. With the advent of computerized systems, reporting has become more structured. However, such structure may prevent the flexibility that is necessary for reporting results of academic, social, self-help, behavioral, and/or vocational objectives that appear in an IEP. To solve this problem, some districts have developed a supplemental report card that is attached to the report card. A supplemental report card allows for comments concerning specifics related to the IEP (see Figure 6.1 for an example).

Although the supplemental report card method is superior to using the standard grade or progress card, it still may fall short in communicating to families of students with disabilities the exact measures of performance required in the IEP. One alternative is a letter to the family providing a narrative description of how their son or

---

X Valley Public Schools

Report Card Supplement (Year)

School Comments

_____

Name of Student

_____

Teacher(s)

_____

Grading Period #1

_____

Grading Period #2

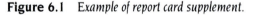

Figure 6.1   *Example of report card supplement.*

IEP Update	
Name Jason	Date 12-13-96

Objective	Comments
1.1 Will increase reading rate of fifth-grade materials	
1.2 Will be able to answer comprehension questions at 80%	
1.3 Will spell vocabulary words found in reader at 80%	
2.1 Will add fractions with unlike denominators at 90%	
2.2 Will subtract fractions with unlike denominators at 90%	

Figure 6.2   *Example of IEP update template.*

daughter is progressing toward IEP goals. This allows the teacher to add personal notes and comments concerning effort and motivation along with progress. This approach, although it is personal, may be difficult for those teachers who have a large number of students.

A template report sheet is another alternative method by which to communicate progress on IEP goals. The template reflects a short version of the IEP goal and provides space to discuss progress and add personal notes. If these sheets are prepared on the computer or copied prior to initial use, they can be used each grading period or more if needed. (See Figure 6.2 for an example of this approach.) In Figure 6.2 the teacher has shortened the goals but still provides the family with enough information to identify the objective or to reference it in their copy of the IEP. Using this approach, it is possible for the teacher to send reports to families more frequently than the required 10- or 11-week reports. In fact, some teachers use similar forms to provide updates to families on a monthly basis.

COMMUNICATION THROUGHOUT THE YEAR

To build and maintain close relationships with parents, ongoing communication is essential. Although effective teachers use many approaches for communicating with parents, all communicate whenever possible with the families of all class members. When communicating with parents, a good rule for teachers to follow is "more is better."

INTASC 6

Communication and Technology

CEC 10

Collaboration

Weekly Visits

Meetings between parents and teachers do not always have to be formal or necessitated because of crisis situations. Some teachers have established weekly visits or meetings if needed by family members of children with intense needs or for families that request additional support or clarification. These meetings are time limited and may include others, such as therapists or specialized service personnel. Sicley (1993) points out that such meetings may help build the partnership between the teacher and the family and increase communication concerning effectiveness of strategies and materials.

Daily Correspondence

Communicating with families on a daily basis can be an effective manner in which to support a family's efforts to work with the school. Cartledge, Kea, and Ida (2000) suggest that sending home daily notes relating to instruction is an effective tool to increase home-school collaboration. They suggest that this increased level of collaboration with family members might be achieved by using notes to indicate social skills and behavior issues that need to be monitored or reinforced by family members.

Often, daily correspondence is achieved when the student carries a notebook or log to and from school. The teacher writes in the notebook and the family responds. When the family has concerns or information for the teacher, the parent writes in the book for the teacher to respond. In some cases, only a single-page memo is necessary, but in other cases a rating system for academics and behavior may be useful. Teachers with small classes may choose to use this daily approach with all of their students and teachers with larger classes may do this only with specific students on an "as needed" basis (Sicley, 1993).

Gartland (1993) provides several suggestions for using daily correspondence. These are:

- Decide with the parents whether they will respond with written comments daily or just sign each day that they have seen the report.
- Structure the system to reflect the domains (academic, behavioral, social) that are to be addressed.
- Design a system that will provide clear information and be as minimally time-consuming as possible for parents and teachers.
- Use positive comments.
- Involve the student in the system if at all possible.
- Fade the use of the system when it is appropriate.

It may be helpful to discuss the implementation, effectiveness, or discontinuance of daily communication at conferences or during other less frequent communication. Parent conferences should include a plan when negative reports are sent home. Be aware of their potential impact. Possibly include the statement "I am sending you this information to keep you informed, but I have taken care of the situation at school." In some situations when parents cannot read communications from the teacher, even "Happy Grams" or "Good News Notes" can result in a difficult situation for the child. Again, the development of a plan may reduce difficulties for both the child and the parents.

TEACHER TIP 6.5

The use of e-mail to communicate regularly with some families is becoming an excellent means to maintain contact. For families that have computers and use e-mail, teachers may want to establish a weekly or regular "note" home about the child's progress.

Weekly Folder

Sicley (1993) also describes the value of the weekly folder, a manila folder that contains the student's work for 1 week, teacher notes concerning the child and school-related activities, and a comment sheet with room for brief notes. This form of communication is sent home on Fridays and returned to school the following Monday. The comment sheet allows for several weeks of responses from both the teacher and the family. In this manner, the teacher and the family are able to communicate efficiently concerning homework, class work, and student behavior.

Periodic Correspondence

Throughout the year effective teachers periodically correspond with the families of students. This correspondence may be scheduled (formal) or unscheduled (informal) in nature and might go to specific families or to the families of all students in the class. Periodic correspondences include informative notices, surveys and questionnaires, class newsletters, personal notes, e-mail messages, postcards, school newsletters, or telephone messages.

Informative Notices   Informative notices are sent periodically to families of students with disabilities to advise them about the completion of special homework assignments or projects (Sicley, 1993). These notices may be in letter or memo form and include special requirements, additional materials that might be needed, and/or opportunities for family members to assist in school activities. Sicley (1993) provides the following guidelines for making these notices successful:

- Address only one project or assignment per notice.
- Develop summary sheets that indicate the critical issues and include them with the notice.
- Distribute notes when other material is expected.
- Send notes at least 5 days in advance of the activity to allow parents to act.

Surveys and Questionnaires   Teachers sometimes send surveys or questionnaires to families of enrolled students to gather information and to identify opportunities for family involvement. These surveys and/or questionnaires might include the following:

- The type of volunteer activities in which family members would like to take part
- The family needs and priorities concerning information or training
- The student's functioning in the home and community
- The family's evaluation of the year's activities

In order to increase the return of useful information from surveys and questionnaires, teachers should make sure that the reading level is appropriate so that questions will be understood. In general, a fifth-grade reading level is acceptable. The number of questions should be limited to fit on two pages or less. When non-English-speaking families are to receive the survey/questionnaire, it should be translated into their native language. Additionally, teacher-designed questionnaires/surveys should be field-tested by individuals who will not be receiving the material to discover potential problems in format or with the questions. Surveys and questionnaires can be useful when gathering large amounts of information and involving parents in the educational process.

Newsletter   School newsletters are an effective method for communicating with groups of parents. When preparing written materials such as newsletters for distribution, follow the guidelines prepared by Decker (1994):

- Publications should be designed for easy reading.
- Written materials should be supplemented with art and other forms of graphic design.
- Readable type size (10–12 point) should be used.
- Headlines should incorporate action words.
- Writing style and reading level should match the readers for whom it is intended.
- Key points of articles should be noted in the first paragraph with general information in later passages.
- Headlines and leads should be developed that indicate the copy that follows.

The class newsletter is a scheduled type of communication that most often occurs on a weekly, monthly, or quarterly basis. Class newsletters can be teacher produced, student produced, or a combination of both. According to Decker (1994), such communications should be:

- Attractive, appropriate, and brief
- Easy to read, requiring little time and effort
- Published regularly, frequently, on schedule
- Fresh, timely, informative, entertaining
- Important
- Able to convey the spirit and tone of the agency or organization (p. 105)

Newsletter topics are infinite but Gartland (1993) suggests the following topics for inclusion:

- Classroom or school news and events
- Home activities to supplement classroom activities
- Instructional techniques for the home
- Question-and-answer column
- Reading and resource lists
- Activities available during vacations
- Parent-teacher conference tips
- Lists of community and regional resources (p. 42)

Additionally students could prepare items for publication, such as:

- Outstanding papers on a current issue
- Lists of interesting words and definitions
- Drawings
- Class stories that the teacher transcribes from each student's input
- Parent or student interviews (if the subject is informed and gives permission)
- Stories about field trips
- Questions and answers
- Messages from students to their families
- Greetings for the holidays, resolutions for the New Year, valentines, and other holiday wishes
- Holiday wish lists

This list can be expanded depending on the creativity of the teacher. It is suggested that items developed for a newsletter should relate to a classroom project, and that work selected for inclusion should represent the work of as many students as possible. Over the course of the year, an opportunity for all students to have material appear in the newsletter should be provided.

Parent Postcards   Sending postcards to parents is another type of periodic correspondence. It is a quick and easy way to remind parents of events such as early school registration, back-to-school orientation, back-to-school night, and class plays, as well as a way to communicate information with individual families or the parents of the class as a whole. Postcards can also be sent as a reminder to families who have volunteered for special activities. Postcards have the advantage of being cheaper than letters and easily developed either with the computer or by hand. When using postcards, remember that you should never include information of a personal nature because of the "open" nature of the communication.

CEC 10

Collaboration

INTASC 6

Communication and Technology

Personal Notes   Personal notes are periodic forms of correspondence that are given a variety of names by teachers including "Good News Notes," "Happy Grams," and "Unslips" (Berger, 1995, p. 166). Sending these short, positive notes to parents on a periodic basis provides them with information concerning the successes experienced by their child. Use of the personal note communicates to the parents that teachers wish to share in their child's success, and provides the teacher with an opportunity to express admiration or pleasure at the student's progress. It also provides an answer to that daily question, "So what happened at school today?" Frequent personal notes defuse the complaint that is often voiced by parents that teachers only contact them when there is a problem.

E-mail   An increasing number of teachers use e-mail to send messages to families who have computers. Any of the forms of correspondence previously mentioned can be transmitted in this manner. Two shortcomings of this approach are that some families do not have access to a computer and that cultural or linguistic issues may limit the effectiveness of technology as a communication tool (Parette, 1998; Parette & Petch-Hogan, 2000).

Telephone Correspondence An additional unwritten form of periodic correspondence occurs when teachers contact parents by telephone. The general approaches and rules for communication and conferencing apply to telephone communication, but teachers should remember that such unscheduled telephone conversations may be disruptive to family structures or daily activities. Gartland (1993) offers guidelines for teachers who use telephone correspondence to communicate with parents:

- Call parents within the first few days of the school year. At this time it is often advisable to survey parents about good times to call and how they would like to be addressed (Mr., Mrs., Dr., etc., or first name, if given permission).
- Call family members at work only in case of an emergency unless given permission.
- Identify oneself at the beginning of the call and ask if it is a convenient time for the parent to talk.
- Have a pencil, paper, and calendar at hand when calling.
- Leave messages on answering machines, but remember that the message may not be received.
- End the conversation with a positive statement and always thank the family member for spending time talking with you.

Read the telephone conversation scenario in Box 6.2. How could the teacher have made the conversation more positive?

Box 6.2   TELEPHONE CONVERSATION

Ms. Johnson: Hello.

Teacher: Hello, Ms. Johnson, this is Billy's teacher, Ms. Johanson. I wanted to call and let you know that Billy is not doing very well. Lately he has been misbehaving a lot, not doing his homework, and generally, not being a good student.

Ms. Johnson: Well, this is a surprise. His father and I thought he was doing well. When did he start having difficulties?

Teacher: Oh, I would say he has been having problems since school started, four months ago. I just assumed that you would know he wasn't doing well by the grades I was giving him on his papers. Didn't you see his homework grades? The grades for the first 9 weeks' grading period were not that good.

Ms. Johnson: We thought maybe his grades would have been better on his report card, but we assumed that you would have called us if you thought there was a problem.

Teacher: Well Ms. Johnson, I have 24 other children in my class and I simply can't call every parent if I think their child is doing poorly or is beginning to fail. I just assume that parents will be keeping up with their child's work at home and figure out that the child is not doing well.

Ms. Johnson: Well, I am sorry we didn't notice that. We probably should have realized that Billy wasn't doing as well as he should be doing; again, we thought you would contact us.

Teacher: Well, now I am contacting you and I think we should consider Billy for special education. Now I don't think that he's retarded, or anything like that, but I do think he is having some problems that should be addressed.

Ms. Johnson: Oh no, you really don't think he is mentally retarded, do you?

Teacher: No, like I said, I don't think that he is, although we really won't know until we get him tested. We have some specialists who really know about these kinds of disabilities and they will let us know.

Ms. Johnson: Well, is there anything we can do at this point?

Teacher: No, just let our experts test Billy and we'll get a better handle on his problems and let you know.

Ms. Johnson: Well, thank you for calling, and please let us know if we can help.

Teacher: I don't think so at this time. I'll let you know when we have a meeting to talk about Billy. It will probably be during the school day, and even though we would like for you and/or your husband to attend, you really don't have to.

Ms. Johnson: Well, we want to be there; please let us know.

Teacher: I will. Good bye.

Some schools have voice mail systems that allow for teachers to leave messages for parents or family members concerning homework or the next day's activities. Some teachers also tell parents that they can contact them by telephone and establish hours when parents can call them at school. It is not generally advisable to encourage families to call teachers at home, but it has worked effectively in some cases. There are a number of reasons for not receiving calls at home including the possibility of distractions, confidentiality issues, and difficulty in maintaining documentation. Some teachers may institute a secondary telephone line with an answering machine to screen calls and take messages. The advantages of telephone communication are obvious in that (1) most people do have a home telephone and (2) verbal communication is quick, easy, and effective in providing immediate timely two-way communication. Thus, it remains an effective method of communication between the school and the family.

TEACHER TIP 6.6

Call parents just to give them good news. Most telephone calls to parents are about problems. Teachers should make it a point to call at least one family each week with only good news about their child.

CHALLENGES TO EFFECTIVE COMMUNICATION

Working with families, even when conducted effectively, can occasionally be fraught with challenges and problems. Often, factors beyond the control of the educator will impact the process. Such factors include employment problems and family issues that may be carried over into working with schools. Past experiences with schools including personal educational experiences may also shape how family members

CEC 10

Collaboration

interact with school personnel. Additionally, Epstein, Rudolph, and Epstein (2000) point out that the current referral process requires professionals to label and describe students in terms of deficits, problems, and pathology, which can cause stress and pain to the family members involved in the process. Family members then may choose a defensive negative role, becoming hostile or angry, or withdraw from most forms of communication with school personnel. Educators need to be prepared for such reactions, taking steps to ensure that the best outcomes are achieved for the student with disabilities for whom the communication was designed. By remaining cognizant of the uniqueness of individual families and individual needs of the student, the professional can better provide support for both.

Negative Roles Assumption

It is not unusual for family members or school personnel to assume negative roles when communicating with each other. These behaviors most often appear during conferences, but may occur during other meetings or in conversations between individuals. In such interpersonal situations, the following types of unproductive behaviors may appear.

- Aggressive (hostile)—Behaviors that criticize, blame others, or focus on personal status
- Blocking—Behaviors that employ the use of tangents, arguments, personal attacks, or rejection of other's ideas
- Competitive—Behaviors that take issue with or dispute others or others' ideas
- Complaining—Behaviors that find fault with everyone and everything
- Explosive—Behaviors that use sudden and often unpredictable tantrums or forceful speech
- Indecisive—Behaviors that convey hesitation, irresolution, and inconsistency typified by the participant refusing to make a decision and being undependable in performing agreed-upon tasks
- Kidding/Joking—Behaviors that use clowning or mimicking to disrupt the communication process
- Know it all—Behaviors that convey the belief that a participant knows everything and puts forth sustained effort to convince everyone of that fact
- Pleading—Behaviors that attempt to justify personalities, projects, or goals and are revisited at each meeting despite the goal of the meeting or group
- Withdrawing (silent)—Behaviors that include silence, nonparticipation, or retreat from the communicative process
- Monopolizing—Behaviors that dominate the conversation or meeting by continued talking in a self-absorbed manner without regard for the other participants

These behaviors often are used in an effort to control or direct the behavior of others and strategies will need to be developed to defuse such situations. Table 6.4 provides a list of strategies for working with difficult communicative behaviors.

Table 6.4   Coping strategies for working with difficult family members.

Behavior	Coping Strategy
Aggressive	Ask the person if they know what they are doing.
	Present your ideas with force.
	Refuse to argue.
	Be friendly.
Blocking	Seek support from other group members.
	Be directive.
Competing	Prevent domination by soliciting others' opinions.
	Provide recognition of good ideas.
Complaining	Ask for them to write down the facts.
	Move rapidly to problem solving.
	Do not agree with them.
Explosive	Attempt to reduce fears and tensions.
	Help them regain self-control.
	Talk with them separately in a monitored environment.
Indecisive	Listen and acknowledge their fears.
	Make sure they understand the importance of proposals and actions.
	Encourage and support decision making and follow-through.
Kidding/Joking	Ignore joking.
	Encourage joking as a release of tension.
	Focus on the problem seriously.
Knowing It All	Be sure your facts are correct.
	Use questions to express disagreement.
Pleading	Use questions to direct the person away from his or her topic.
	Use and acknowledge their knowledge on this subject.
Withdrawing/Silent	Use open-ended questions.
	Use summaries of what they do say.
Monopolization	Encourage important information sharing.
	Draw others into the conversation.

TEACHER TIP 6.7

Regardless of your efforts, negative and unproductive behaviors may be exhibited. If you realize that communications have hit this snag, make every effort to turn things back in a positive direction. Always remember that the child's needs and services should be foremost in mind for all parties.

Emotionally Upset Behaviors of Family Members   It is not uncommon for family members to become emotionally upset during meetings or conversations relating to their child with disabilities. These family members are displaying an emotional reaction to the challenges presented by students with disabilities. Such behaviors often accompany feelings of frustration and hopelessness concerning the situation. When working with an upset family member, professionals need to listen carefully and allow the person to express their feelings without interrupting or offering solutions. Simpson (1982) provides several special considerations for professionals who are encountering upset family members. Some of these include:

- Examine your own feelings concerning emotional reactions so you can comfortably support others.
- Use effective listening techniques.
- Allow talk without interruption or offering solutions; provide only emotional supportive statements.
- Do not attempt to talk them out of their feelings or help them deny feelings.
- Do not patronize, discount, or refute feelings.

By employing these concepts, the professional can support family members during the stressful and difficult times that will occur.

Angry and Hostile Behaviors   Seligman (2000) notes that parents may become angry with the teacher, the school, or the curriculum. He also notes that the parents' anger may be related to past experiences or totally unrelated to school issues. Regardless, teachers must anticipate and be prepared for parents who are or become angry or hostile during meetings or any communication opportunity including telephone calls and home visits. Professionals need to be prepared to reduce the anger and hostility in order to identify and address the family member's concerns.

Margolis and Brannigan (1990) reported that most teachers are not trained to respond in productive ways when faced with parents' anger. To address this lack of preparedness, professionals have suggested numerous strategies and approaches for dealing with hostile or angry family members. Table 6.5 organizes many of those approaches based on the place in the process when it occurs.

Even those proficient in using the previously mentioned methods may encounter times when it is necessary to terminate a conference. When closing a conference, no new issues should be introduced. A simple statement should be made that it is time to close the discussion until the next meeting. If there has been hostility, verbal abuse, or threats during the meeting, then a statement may be simply spoken that the meeting cannot be held when these behaviors are present. Set a date for the next meeting and leave.

Further, Simpson (1982) suggests that if there have been problems with inappropriate behavior during previous conferences, it would be prudent and appropriate to ask a colleague to attend the conference. Other strategies might include:

- Requesting a colleague to walk by the meeting site to monitor the climate of the conference
- Keeping the door open or cracked for ease of monitoring

Table 6.5 Strategies for working with angry and hostile family members.

Place in the Conference	Suggested Strategy for the Professional
Preparation	Review active listening strategies (previous chapter).
	Organize the setting and have pertinent materials.
	Attempt to relax and remove hostility from your feelings.
	Remind yourself that anger may be useful in problem solving (Simpson, 1982).
Beginning	Demonstrate confidence.
	Do not allow yourself to be intimidated.
	Establish ground rules.
	Empathize with concerns and fears (Margolis & Brannigan, 1990).
	Establish a nonthreatening environment for discussion.
During	Allow discussion without interruption and exhaust any list of concerns (Margolis & Brannigan, 1990; Simpson, 1982). Ignore personal attacks, threats, or generalizations (Simpson, 1982).
	Avoid personal reactions and arguing (Simpson, 1982).
	Attempt to not assume responsibility or ownership for problems (Simpson, 1982).
	Use silence to buy time, think, and de-escalate (Simpson, 1982).
	Monitor your body language (Simpson, 1982).
	Keep focused on the problem at hand and attempt to record concerns (Simpson, 1982).
	Provide periodic summaries (Margolis & Brannigan, 1990).
Reaching Resolution	Attempt to redirect personal attacks and generalizations (Simpson, 1982).
	Do not discount family members' feelings (Simpson, 1982).
	Have family offer their criteria for solutions (Margolis & Brannigan, 1990).
	Brainstorm solutions (Margolis & Brannigan, 1990).
	Attempt to become an ally by problem solving and offering solutions (Seligman, 2000).
	Provide productive and doable solutions (Margolis & Brannigan, 1990).
	Ask clarifying questions.(Seligman, 2000).
	Develop a plan (Margolis & Brannigan, 1990).
After the Meeting	Regularly evaluate the plan (Margolis & Brannigan, 1990).
	Maintain communication with the family.

- Developing a plan for emergency intervention including a code word used to alert the person providing backup
- Sit near the door for ease of exit

Anger management and professional counseling can do much to assist in overcoming inappropriate displays of anger. There is also a set of techniques that enable people to choose alternatives to anger. Below are a few techniques that can be easily implemented to reduce the escalation of anger and allow for more effective communication. Teachers may want to share these when it is appropriate.

- Take a breath and tell yourself that what is said is not personal.
- Ask for a time-out or a little break.
- Ask for a second to organize your thoughts.
- Substitute humor for anger.
- Refuse to allow personal statements in the discussion.
- Postpone the discussion to a specific future time.
- Ask to meet the individual in private.
- Ask others to mediate the situation.

By using these techniques, angry exchanges often may be avoided, thus preventing the breakdown of communication and enabling achievement of the goals set for students with disabilities.

TEACHER TIP 6.8

Always focus on the child and encourage family members to focus on the child. Never be afraid to apologize to family members if something has been said that is hurtful or is perceived as hurtful. Focusing on the child can help resolve differences encountered by school personnel and family members.

There may be a time when dealing with family members who are angry or upset, that it becomes necessary to move from active listening to information gathering or problem solving. In some cases, the situation may be so out of control that the time to move on to information gathering or problem solving is the next meeting. However, signs indicating that it may be appropriate to move from active listening to another step should not be overlooked. These signs may include the use of inquiring or questioning statements, the acknowledgement of being stuck or at wit's end, or the request for help. These verbal signs will probably be accompanied by other nonverbal signs such as a calmer demeanor, straightening clothing, worrying about makeup or appearance, and shifting positions, orientation in seating, or correcting posture. In any case, meeting with the individual in private may put you at risk. Be certain to select an easily monitored environment for all meetings.

Once the educator has identified readiness of the angry or upset family member to move on, some statements that could help in this transition include:

- "I think I have a picture of the problem. It is . . . Are we ready to work on it now?"
- "How can we address this problem?"
- "Do you think you have given us all the information that is necessary for us to begin to plan for dealing with it?"
- "Is there anything else?"

If the answers to these or similar questions are affirmative, then the meeting or conference may move to problem solving and, ultimately, a specific solution.

Common Problems in Meetings

A set of common problems that are often encountered in meetings can be avoided if recognized. Kohm (1985) has summarized these problems. One major problem is that too many ideas are presented at one time. Only two or three ideas should be addressed during a meeting with the remaining time used to increase the understanding of these concepts by the family members rather than introducing new ideas. Lecturing by the professional is another problem that often occurs during conferences. The professional should remember never to talk for more than 10 minutes without asking for a reaction from the group or requesting group member participation.

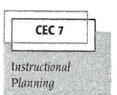

CEC 7

Instructional
Planning

Often the professional who may be serving as group leader tries to "rescue" people; that is, he or she attempts to help people who don't need to be helped or who don't want to be helped. To remedy this situation, the professional should attempt to see family members as strong and capable rather than weak and vulnerable. This can be done by focusing on the individual's strengths and expecting that person to behave in a strong, capable manner.

Many times members of the group have had previous meetings where they became angry. If this is the case, the family and/or the group leader may have concealed their anger. If this has occurred, then the expectations for the current meeting should be clearly and fully discussed during the first session. If group members do not comply or meet the expectations set, then the leader should address the "bits and pieces" of anger before they accumulate and circumvent the goal of the meeting. In addition, sometimes a member of the group may not like or approve of another member of the group. In this case, the leader will need to focus on the development of a "positive regard" for all group members by all group members. This is accomplished by focusing on each member's strengths and by attempting to understand what it would be like to "walk in their shoes."

In some instances, the family members may not agree on plans for their child. The professional should be very careful not to align him- or herself with one parent against the other. All participants should be encouraged to discuss any issues or problems with each other and with the group before making decisions. Before giving any advice, the professional should ask each family member about feelings and opinions, as well as both their family histories. It is advisable to follow the rule that no advice should be given unless it is requested. To ensure that general advice is not

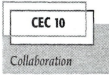

CEC 10

Collaboration

given without request, only open-ended questions should be used (e.g., "What will you do now?") with short advisory comments following (i.e., no more than two or three sentences). Before continuing with further questions or advice, the professional should wait for a response from the family member.

Although disagreements during meetings are to be expected, a clear set of rules should be established upon which all parties can agree. This reduces the chances of disagreements, enhances the ability of group members to discuss issues, and lessens the concern that family members are just "rubber-stamping" a decision made by the professional. This rule making should occur during the first session. If problems arise, then the rules should be restated and followed so that problems do not accumulate and escalate.

TEACHER TIP 6.9

When disagreements occur during meetings, make sure parents understand that you have the interests and needs of the child in mind, and that you know family members feel the same way. Always explain your positions in terms that family members can understand, without being condescending.

In some instances, the professional leading the meeting may attempt to usurp power from the parents or from the other members of the group. To decrease this problem, the conferences should be structured so that parents can develop their own solutions to problems, and not have the group membership tell them what they should do. In the same manner, group members should be encouraged to provide information and support for each other. For example, instead of answering individual questions, the professional could ask for opinions from the group.

In an attempt to meet the needs of the family, the discussion may veer away from the goals of the conference. To reduce the chances that this will occur, a general outline or agenda for the conference should be developed. This outline should be specific enough to cover the main points with enough time to discuss the issues raised. If concerns or ideas that are not on the agenda arise during the meeting, refocus the discussion by using phrases such as: "That sounds like another whole discussion." or "Let's save it for next time." or "We don't have time to discuss that now, but you might want to think about what this would mean to your child."

Professionals who wish to become effective group leaders should guard against these common mistakes. Any educator who is planning to facilitate or lead family groups should recognize that in conferences with parents and other professionals, these are adults and should be treated as such.

COMMUNICATION AND FAMILY STRESS

CEC 10

Collaboration

As previously discussed, stress is an element in any family that includes a child with a disability. In times of stress, family members may have more difficulty communicating their needs to school personnel. Additionally, professionals can unsuspectingly increase stress through communicative actions. Therefore, the professional should be aware of stressful times and work with the family to keep the lines of communication open.

Divorce and Separation

Separation and divorce are significant events in the lives of families. During these times communication problems often develop. For example, when under marital stress, parents may be concerned less with the schooling of their children than the emotional impact caused by the events that are occurring at home. Communication with the parents is also difficult because the role of the parents is now tangled with the role of the custodial parent versus the role of the parent who may have recently lost legal rights to decision making. Educators need to recognize that family-related issues will and do influence the outcome of the educational program of the student. It is not unusual for both parents to want information concerning the child's progress, and at times it may be necessary to hold separate conferences with each parent. Professionals should not fall into the trap of contacting only the parent with whom the child is living and assuming that the parents have worked out communication between the two homes. If both homes choose to stay involved, teachers should do the following:

INTASC 6

Communication and Technology

PRAXIS 1

Understanding Exceptionalities

- Obtain current telephone numbers and addresses of both parents.
- Contact both parents regarding critical issues concerning educational progress and decision making.
- Mail two sets of materials such as newsletters and volunteer request forms.
- Provide the opportunity for separate conferences and meet separately with parents/families prior to IEP meetings.

Along with these suggestions, educators need to keep in mind that parental custody and educational decision making often shift during this time. Both parents need to be offered the opportunity to stay involved. It is also important for professionals to keep open communication with both parents to ensure that neither family feels the professional is taking sides or making judgments concerning the situation.

TEACHER TIP 6.10

A variety of family variables will impact communication. Stress resulting from divorce and other marital problems may create substantial barriers to effective communication. Always focus on the child, and encourage the family member to do likewise. Hashing out family problems may not be useful in developing appropriate programs for the student with disabilities.

Death

Death is a topic many individuals in our society have difficulty handling both emotionally and communicatively. On the other hand, the death rate of special education students with health concerns is higher than that of general education students and, therefore, needs to be addressed as a communication issue. Religious and social-cultural beliefs play a major role in the expression of grief. When communicating with families concerning death, the educator should be cautious and avoid offending. Within the classroom, all students who are impacted by a death should be monitored and, when needed, families should be offered assistance through the resources available within the school or educational community.

Death of a Family Member   Death within a family can adversely impact communication between the school and home. The loss of a family member is stressful to all family members and especially the children. Teachers should call or send a card or a note of condolence to the family. When appropriate, the teacher might provide information concerning behaviors common to children who lose a loved one so that the parents might be better prepared to meet these needs. For example, children who lose a family member often suffer from bouts of guilt and fear that other family members may also be taken away. Behavior and/or academic problems may increase due to the stress caused by the loss of a family member. Students who have lost a family member may display an increase in crying, distractibility, aggressiveness, acting out behaviors, poor academic work, depression, or other behaviors. Classroom teachers should talk with students and, when necessary, with their families concerning the connection of feelings and changes in behavior. If such behaviors do occur, then contact the parents immediately and offer to refer the child to the school counselor or social worker.

Loss of a Classmate   Often classmates become as dear to the students as a family member. Therefore, when a class member dies, it is essential that the families be notified and provided the appropriate information to assist them in apprising their child of the situation. This is particularly true if the death is due to a suicide or an act of violence. The school district may have a grief counselor available, and the teacher should seek these services whenever they are available. If there is no grief counselor, then the teacher may wish to seek assistance from the school counselor. Parents should also be advised when such personnel are actively involved in the classroom. Educators and counselors can play an important role in helping families understand the impact of the death of a classmate may have on their children, just as family members can provide information concerning the needs of the child as the healing process occurs.

SUMMARY

In order for an appropriate education to be provided to all students, including those with disabilities, educators should communicate with parents and family members effectively. There are parent-teacher meetings, which can be either legally mandated (e.g., IEP meetings) or district mandated (e.g., parent-teacher conferences). For these meetings to be effective, it is essential that educators and families communicate clearly. There are numerous methods for communicating in a timely and appropriate manner including student-delivered notes, e-mails, newsletters, and so on. The method of communication chosen should depend on the age of the student, the comfort level of the teacher, and the reason for the communication. With continuing communication between the educator and the family member, the goal of success in school for the student with a disability is more likely to be achieved.

The causes of communication difficulties are varied. Professionals who feel uncomfortable when communicating with family members or when dealing with conflict should seek to increase their skills in this area through professional training opportunities (see Bennett, DeLuca, & Bruns, 1997; Hilton & Henderson, 1993). Dealing with difficult situations often requires substantial patience and effective communication skills, skills that should be developed by those who wish to effectively serve students with disabilities and their families.

QUESTIONS FOR DISCUSSION

1. Sometimes the message gets destorted when a group of individuals are talking. When parents are involved in a discussion with school personnel about their child, the school staff may think they conveyed some information in a particular way and the parents may have "heard" it very differently. What are some things that school staff can do to avoid this miscommunication?

2. Mandated and non-mandated conferences can be useful in communication between family members and school staff. What are the advantages and disadvantages of both types of conferences? How can school staff overcome the problems found in both types of conferences. When establishing successful communication with family members, which form of conference is better and why?

3. Often, when communicating with family members about a child with a disability, anger and hostility must be dealt with. What are some reasons family members might be angry with the school and develop hostility toward staff members. How can school staff defuse some of these situations? Give some specific examples of why family members might become angry and hostile and steps school staff can take to refocus efforts on behalf of the child.

REFERENCES

Bennett, T., DeLuca, D., & Bruns, D. (1997). Putting inclusion into practice: Perspectives of teachers and parents. *Exceptional Children, 64,* 115–131.

Berger, E. H. (1995). *Parents as partners in education* (4th ed.). Upper Saddle River, NJ: Merrill/Prentice Hall.

Cartledge, G., Kea, C. D., & Ida, D. J. (2000). Anticipating differences—Celebrating strengths: Providing culturally competent services for students with serious emotional disturbance. *Teaching Exceptional Children, 32*(3), 30–37.

Decker, L. E. (1994). *Home-school-community relations: Trainers manual and study guide.* (ERIC Document Reproduction Service ED371822)

Epstein, M. H., Rudolph, S., & Epstein, A. A. (2000). Strength-based assessment in transition planning. *Teaching Exceptional Children, 32,* 50–54.

Gartland, D. (1993). Teacher-parent partnerships: Effective communication strategies. LD *Forum,* 18(3), 40–42.

Hilton, A., & Henderson, C. J. (1993). Parent involvement: A best practice or forgotten practice? *Education and Training in Mental Retardation, 28,* 199–211.

Kohm, B. (1985). *Promoting powerful parents: A model for parent discussion groups and classes.* Paper presented at the Biennial National Training Institute, Washington, DC (ERIC Document ED264959).

MacFarlane, E. (1996). Reaching reluctant parents. *The Education Digest*, 61(7), 7–12.

Margolis, H., & Brannigan, G. (1990). Calming the storm. *Learning*, 18, 41–42.

Parette, H. P. (1998). Assistive technology effective practices for students with mental retardation and developmental disabilities. In A. Hilton & R. Ringlaben (Eds.), *Best and promising practices in developmental disabilities* (pp. 205–224). Austin, TX: Pro-Ed.

Parette, H. P., & Petch-Hogan, B. (2000). Approaching families. *Teaching Exceptional Children*, 34, 4–9.

Seligman, M. (2000). *Conducting effective conferences with parent of children with disabilities.* New York: Guilford Press.

Sicley, D. (1993). Effective methods of communication: Practical interventions for classroom teachers. *Intervention in School and Clinic*, 29, 105–108.

Simpson, R. L. (1982). *Conferencing parents of exceptional children.* Rockville, MD: Aspen.

Smith, D. D. (2004). *Introduction to special education: Teaching in an age of opportunity* (5th ed.). Boston. Pearson/Allyn & Bacon.

Strudder, R. (1993). Doesn't he have beautiful blue eyes? Tips for a successful parent-teacher conference. *Preventing School Failure*, 37(3), 11–13.

CHAPTER 7
Working with Families: The Legal Bases for Family Involvement

○ ○

Objectives

After reading this chapter, you will:

- Understand the legal requirements of IDEA for family involvement
- Know the steps in the special education process and how parents can participate in each step

- Understand due process rights of parents and actions to avoid due process hearings
- Understand the relevant components of Section 504 and its requirements for family involvement
- Understand school responsibilities under Section 504
- Know the relevant components of the Americans with Disabilities Act (ADA)

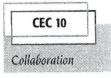

CEC 10

Collaboration

There are many reasons why family members should be involved in the education of children with special needs. The first reason is that the education of children is enhanced with family involvement and support (Smith, Polloway, Patton, & Dowdy, 2004). For no other reason than this, professionals should support the development of family-school partnerships in educational programs for children with special needs.

The second reason is the legal requirements for involving families of students with disabilities. Public Law 94-142, passed in 1975 and subsequently reauthorized as the Individuals with Disabilities Education Act (IDEA), requires schools to involve parents. Likewise, Section 504 of the Rehabilitation Act of 1973, which is increasingly a basis for special services for children with disabilities who are ineligible for services under IDEA (Streett & Smith, 1996), requires schools to involve families in the education of their children with disabilities. The Americans with Disabilities Act (ADA) also addresses the needs of individuals with disabilities and impacts secondary and post-secondary students with disabilities by providing legal access to full citizenship in the community and workplace. This chapter provides basic information on IDEA, Section 504, and ADA and how these legislative acts relate to families of children with disabilities.

PRAXIS 2

Legal and Societal Issues

IDEA AND FAMILY INVOLVEMENT

In 1975, Congress passed Public Law 94-142, the Education for All Handicapped Children Act. This law, which was reauthorized in 1990 as the Individuals with Disabilities Education Act (IDEA) and most recently reauthorized in 2004, revolutionized collaboration between schools and parents in educating children with disabilities. Prior to the passage of the act, school personnel often made educational decisions based solely on the school's view of student needs, and often without informing parents of their actions. Not only were parents not invited to participate in educational decisions, but sometimes school personnel attempted to avoid parental participation. Following are four reasons school personnel often chose not to include parents in the educational process:

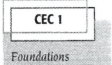

CEC 1

Foundations

- School personnel thought that they knew best what actions should be taken regarding a child with a disability.
- School personnel thought that parents would only complicate attempts to provide appropriate services.
- School personnel encountered difficulties in soliciting and securing the involvement of parents.
- School personnel routinely excluded children with disabilities from all services in public schools.

Although these were not the only reasons why parental participation was limited, they were often the bases for limiting collaboration between parents and school personnel.

An underlying premise of IDEA is to provide families with the right to participate in the education of their children with disabilities. School personnel need to understand the requirements of IDEA in order to protect the rights of children and to ensure legal compliance by the schools. The following is a brief explanation of the requirements of IDEA concerning the involvement of the family in the education of their child.

> **CEC 9**
>
> *Professional and Ethical Practice*

Child Find

Many parents are unaware of services available for their children. Therefore, school personnel are required to provide parents with information concerning the referral process for children who may need special education services. Notice may be provided through radio and television announcements, newspaper advertisements, school Internet bulletin boards, and/or flyers or letters sent to all parents residing in the district. Figure 7.1 provides an example of notice that could be sent home informing parents of IDEA services that are available.

TEACHER TIP 7.1

Learn about IDEA so that you can refer children who are having difficulties and may be eligible for IDEA services. Make sure you know what forms to complete and where to send the forms. Carefully follow the procedures and timelines.

Evaluation

IDEA requires schools to provide a comprehensive evaluation of students who may be eligible for special education services. This evaluation must be performed in a nondiscriminatory manner that includes the administration of tests in the language

---

> Parents of the Alzette School District
>
> The Alzette School District offers special education and other services to help students who are having difficulty in a wide variety of areas. Children with learning problems, behavior problems, vision or hearing problems, or physical problems may be eligible for these special services. The services are free for children who meet eligibility criteria. If you have a child who you believe could benefit from special education and other support services who may be eligible, please contact Mr. John Davis at 555-5555, or e-mail him at **jdavis@aaaa.edu.**

Figure 7.1   *Example of a parental notice.*

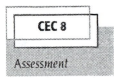

Assessment

most likely to yield accurate information on what the child knows and can do academically, socially, and functionally, unless it is not feasible to do so (IDEA, 2004). Schools are also required to ensure that parents understand the evaluation process and to obtain parental consent prior to beginning the evaluation process. Following the evaluation, the results and an interpretation of results are to be provided to the parents in a manner that assures their understanding. Given the complexities of the assessment process and the number of professional terms used, this can prove difficult. Table 7.1 provides definitions of assessment terms that may be used to increase understanding by reducing the use of professional jargon and terminology during school meetings with parents.

Parents are essential to successful completion of the assessment process. After all, they typically have different knowledge concerning their child than school personnel (Dunlap, Newton, Fox, Benito, & Vaughn, 2001). Schools should tap into parents' knowledge about the child, thus developing a more holistic picture of abilities and needs than a structured, norm-referenced assessment can provide. If parents do not give consent for an initial evaluation, the school cannot conduct an evaluation without pursuing due process (IDEA, 2004).

TEACHER TIP 7.2

When students in your classroom are having difficulties, make notes about their behaviors and academic performance on a daily basis. This information can be very useful if the student is referred for special services. Trying to re-create notes several days after the fact is very difficult.

Table 7.1 Professional jargon and terminology related to assessment.

Jargon	More Easily Understood Terminology
IQ, Intelligence quotient	Intelligence score
Standard score	Score compared to other students
Percentile rank	Percentage of other students who did as well as or better
Quartile	General performance compared to other students
Norm-referenced	Tests that can be used to compare him to other students
Criterion-referenced	Tests that can be used to see his specific gains
Norm group	Group to which we will compare him
Ceiling	The maximum level he performed on the test

Eligibility

Following a comprehensive, nondiscriminatory evaluation of a child, a determination must be made regarding the eligibility of the student for services under the IDEA. In order to be eligible, a student must meet the definitional requirements of one of the specified disabilities and must need special education services. Under IDEA, there are 13 disability categories. Students who do not meet the criteria for eligibility for services under IDEA are determined ineligible to receive services under the umbrella of IDEA. But if the child has been determined to have a disability, he or she may be eligible for services under Section 504 of the Rehabilitation Act. The 2004 reauthorization of IDEA noted that a child shall not be determined eligible under IDEA if the determinant factor for such a determination is because of (a) a lack of appropriate instruction in reading, (b) lack of instruction in math, or (c) limited English proficiency (Section 614 |b||5|).

CEC 1

Foundations

Parents are essential partners in the decision concerning eligibility. Although there is a legal requirement to obtain parents' signatures on eligibility paperwork, there is an additional reason for obtaining their involvement. Parents who understand and agree with the eligibility decision are more likely to want their child to receive special services and to support intervention efforts. Parents should have access to information on eligibility issues and an opportunity to present their views on eligibility decisions. If parents do not consent to placement of a child in special education, then the school may not place the student, nor can the school pursue the issue through due process (IDEA, 2004).

Appropriate Services/Placement

After children have been identified as eligible for special education services, schools are required to provide appropriate services, with parental consent. Appropriate services have been determined by the U.S. Supreme Court in *Board of Education of Hendrick Hudson Central School District v. Rowley* (1982) as the student's IEP that was developed through the special education process. This case made clear that appropriate services were not the very best services, but sufficient so that the child could progress from grade to grade successfully. Every student receiving special education and related services must have an IEP prepared by a multidisciplinary team that includes the child's parents or surrogate parents.

Thus, by law, school personnel must solicit parental participation in the IEP process. Simply inviting parents to participate is inadequate, and schools need to develop strategies for developing successful family-school partnerships. The reasons parents give for lack of participation are varied. Some parents may feel inadequate, others may believe that they have nothing worthwhile to contribute and prefer to leave this activity to school personnel, and others may lack transportation or childcare. Parents in some cultures actually think that school professionals should handle educational issues and they will handle home issues. Schools, therefore, need to support parental participation during this process. Parents who feel inadequate or feel that their participation has less meaning than that of school personnel might benefit from information sessions regarding the special education process or support from other parents or parental groups. School personnel or parent support groups might provide materials such as a pre-meeting outline, a meeting agenda, a list of possible questions that parents might ask or be asked, or materials that might be important to bring so that parents will feel prepared to make a contribution. If needed, transportation should be provided by the school. If childcare is an issue, then schools should provide on-site childcare or meet at a site that is convenient to the family, parent, and child. School personnel should remain flexible in scheduling both locations and times of meetings using the convenience of the family as the primary standards.

PRAXIS 3

Delivery of Services to Students with Disabilities

TEACHER Tip 7.3

During a placement committee meeting, encourage parents to express their opinions about the child's placement. Parents sometimes prefer to allow school personnel to dominate the discussion, but teachers need to encourage parental input, which often is invaluable in making a good placement decision.

Full-time regular class—This is when your child is in the regular classroom all day. Your child may receive some special help from a support staff member.

Resource room—This is when your child is in the regular classroom most of the day, but may be pulled out for brief periods of intense instruction by the special education teacher in the resource room.

Special class—This is when your child is in a special education classroom most or all of the school day receiving instruction from a special education teacher. Your child may be included in some activities with nondisabled students, such as lunch, assemblies, or nonacademic classes.

Special school—This is when your child is at a special school that is designed solely for students with severe disabilities.

Institution or residential facility—This is when your child actually lives at a facility for children with severe disabilities. Your child receives all education and training at this same location.

Homebound—This is when your child receives educational services at home by a homebound instructor. The amount of time the homebound instructor is at your home depends on your child's IEP.

Figure 7.2 *Description of placement options for families.*

Due Process Requirements

The legislation and regulations of IDEA specify the due process rights of children with disabilities and the methods for protecting these rights. Table 7.2 summarizes due process requirements under IDEA.

Table 7.2   Due process requirements under IDEA 2004.

(1) An opportunity for the parents of a child with a disability to examine all records relating to such child and to participate in meetings with respect to the identification, evaluation, and educational placement of the child, and the provision of a free appropriate public education to such child, and to obtain an independent educational evaluation of the child;

(2) (A) Procedures to protect the rights of the child whenever the parents of the child are not known, the agency cannot, after reasonable efforts, locate the parents, or the child is a ward of the State, including the assignment of an individual to act as a surrogate for the parents, which surrogate shall not be an employee of the State educational agency, the local educational agency, or any other agency that is involved in the education or care of the child. In the case of

   (i) a child who is a ward of the State, such surrogate may alternatively be appointed by the judge overseeing the child's care provided that the surrogate meets the requirements of this paragraph; and

   (ii) an unaccompanied homeless youth as defined in section 725(6) of the McKinney-Vento Homeless Assistance Act, the local educational agency shall appoint a surrogate in accordance with this paragraph.

   (B) The State shall make reasonable efforts to ensure the assignment of a surrogate not more than 30 days after there is a determination by the agency that the child needs a surrogate.

(3) Written notice to the parents of the child whenever the local educational agency—

   (A) proposes to initiate or change; or

   (B) refuses to change;

   the identification, evaluation, or educational placement of the child. . . or the provision of a free appropriate public education to the child;

(4) Procedures designed to ensure that the notice required by paragraph (3) is in the native language of the parents, unless it clearly is not feasible to do so;

(5) An opportunity for mediation in accordance with subsection (e) of this section;

(6) An opportunity for any party to present a complaint

   (A) with respect to any matter relating to the identification, evaluation, or educational placement of the child, or the provision of a free appropriate public education to such child;

   and

   (B) which sets forth an alleged violation that occurred not more than 2 years before the date the parent or public agency knew or should have known about the alleged action that forms the basis of the complaint, or, if the State has an explicit time limitation for presenting such a complaint under this part, in such time as the State law allows, except that the exceptions to the timeline described in subsection (f) (3) (D) shall apply to the timeline described in this subparagraph.

(7) (A) Procedures that require either party or the attorney representing a party to provide due process complaint notice in accordance with subsection (c) (2) (which shall remain confidential)—

    (i) to the other party, in the complaint filed under paragraph (6), and forward a copy of such notice to the State educational agency; and

    (ii) that shall include—

        (I) the name of the child, the address of the residence of the child, (or available contact information in the case of a homeless child), and the name of the school the child is attending;

        (II) in the case of a homeless child or youth (within the meaning of section 725(2) of the McKinney-Vento Homeless Assistance Act (42 U.S.C. 11434a(2)), available contact information for the child and the name of the school the child is attending;

        (III) a description of the nature of the problem of the child relating to such proposed initiation or change, including facts relating to such problem; and

        (IV) a proposed resolution of the problem to the extent known and available to the party at the time;

  (B) A requirement that a party may not have a due process hearing until the party or the attorney representing the party, files a notice that meets the requirements of subparagraph (A) (ii).

(8) Procedures that require the State educational agency to develop a model form to assist parents in filing a complaint and due process complaint notice in accordance with paragraphs (6) and (7) respectively.

Schools are responsible for assisting parents in understanding these rights. Schools document compliance with this responsibility by having parents read and sign a list of parental rights. Schools should provide parents with a copy of due process rights a minimum of one time per year, plus when the child is initially referred for evaluation or if the parents request an initial evaluation, if a complaint is filed by the parents, or if parents request a copy. (IDEA, 2004). Unfortunately, this list of parental rights may be written in a manner that is not easily understood. Figures 7.3 and 7.4 include two different descriptions of parental rights.

TEACHER TIP 7.5

Make sure you know and follow due process procedures. If you have any questions about due process, always ask your special education supervisor. Asking is much better than making a due process mistake.

You have a right to:

- Be notified by the school about where your child is receiving his or her education before it is changed by the school

- See and get a copy of your child's records

- Give your consent regarding testing and deciding if your child needs special education

- Get an evaluation by someone you choose if you do not agree with the school's evaluation (you may have to pay for the evaluation)

- Participate in mediation prior to asking for a hearing if you and the school do not agree on your child's educational program; mediation is voluntary, does not prevent you from having a hearing, and attempts to resolve the issues by having a mediator assist in solving the problem through a discussion participated in by both the family and the school

- Have an impartial hearing conducted by a hearing officer who is objective and non-biased who will listen to your side and the side of the school and make a binding decision

Figure 7.3 *Example of parental rights notice (easy to understand).*

- Notice from the school

- Consent before the school conducts an evaluation or places your child in special education

- An impartial hearing

- Mediation

- Independent evaluation

- Opportunity to examine records

Figure 7.4 *Additional example of parental rights notice (not easy to understand).*

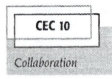

CEC 10

Collaboration

Ideally, school personnel and parents are expected to collaborate on the identification of students who need special education services and in the development of programs providing those services. However, instances occur when parents and school personnel disagree (Lake & Billingsley, 2000). When the disagreement concerns referral, identification, evaluation, placement, or programming issues, either party can request mediation and/or a due process hearing. Although either party can request a hearing, parents most frequently initiate hearings, and placement is the issue that is most often the subject of the dispute (Podemski, Marsh, Smith, & Price, 1995).

The IDEA amendments of 1997 required states to develop an optional system of mediation that could be used prior to requesting a due process hearing (Lake & Billingsley, 2000). Ideally, mediation would provide a private, informal process in which a third party would assist disputing parties to come to a reasonable resolution of the issue or issues. The IDEA amendments require that the mediation be voluntary for both parties and that the state assume the cost. If mediation fails to lead to a resolution of the issues, then a due process hearing may be requested. Because mediation is not binding, there is concern that it can be another barrier for parents to overcome before an appropriate education for their child may be obtained and be used as a delaying tactic (Murdick, Gartin, & Crabtree, 2002).

States and local education agencies may develop procedures to offer parents and schools not choosing to enter into mediation the right to meet with a disinterested party who will try to resolve the dispute. This disinterested party could be from a parent training and information center, community parent resource center, or an appropriate alternative dispute resolution entity (IDEA, 2004).

IDEA also requires states to have in place a system outlining the due process procedures. An impartial hearing officer (or hearing officer panel in some states) conducts the due process hearing. IDEA notes that this individual cannot be a state employee and should be impartial regarding the issue and both of the parties involved. Many states use attorneys as hearing officers, although this is not a requirement of IDEA.

The 2004 reauthorization of IDEA requires that within 15 days of the request for a due process hearing, the school district shall convene a meeting with the parents and members of the IEP committee for a resolution session to discuss and attempt to resolve the complaint, unless the school and parents agree in writing to waive such a meeting. In this meeting the school district may not have an attorney present unless the parent has an attorney. If a resolution is reached, a legally binding written document will be produced and signed by both parties. Either party may void this agreement within 3 days of its development.

If a resolution is not reached through mediation or the above described resolution session, a due process hearing will be held. Both parties to a due process hearing have certain rights, including:

- The right to a representative who may be an attorney
- The right to bring witnesses
- The right to examine and cross-examine witnesses
- The right to examine written evidence presented by the other side a minimum of 5 days prior to the hearing
- The right to require the presence of school personnel
- The right to a written or electronic verbatim record of the proceedings

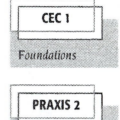

CEC 1

Foundations

PRAXIS 2

Legal and Societal Issues

In addition to these rights that both parties have, parents have the right to determine if the hearing is closed or open, and the right to have the child present. If parents request a closed hearing, then only individuals who have a need to be at the hearing may be present; but if the hearing is an open hearing, anyone may be present.

Hearings generally follow procedures similar to a court case. Because there are no directions in IDEA for the specific procedures to follow in due process hearings, each state develops its own guidelines. Generally these guidelines follow the following outline. After preliminary activities, the opening statements by both parties are given. Then each party has an opportunity to present evidence and question witnesses. Cross-examination of witnesses by the other party also occurs. Following the presentation of evidence and witnesses by both parties, both sides have an opportunity to present closing arguments. Although not required, many hearing officers following the hearing require both parties to prepare and submit briefs that include findings of fact and proposed resolution to the issues. After the hearing, hearing officers must arrive at a decision within the 45-day timeline required by federal regulations, unless both parties waive the time period. This time limit begins with the request for a hearing and ends with the submission of the written decision. The decision must be submitted in writing and must be implemented unless it is appealed. IDEA requires parties to engage in a due process hearing before either party may file suit in federal court.

Hearings often result in adversarial relationships. Regardless of the outcome, school personnel and parents must continue to work together to provide an appropriate educational program for the child, but cooperation increases in difficulty if adversarial relationships develop or deepen.

TEACHER TIP 7.6

If you are called as a witness in a due process hearing, don't panic. All you need to remember is to give honest, concise answers. You are allowed to bring data and notes to assist you in accurately answering questions. Keep in mind that due process hearings are intended to determine the appropriate services for students.

The cases presented in Boxes 7.1, 7.2, and 7.3 provide scenarios related to due process hearings. Read each case and determine how you would rule if you were the hearing officer. Hearing officers must interpret federal legislation and related case law in arriving at a decision, so it is possible that the same hearing heard by two or more hearing officers might result in very different decisions.

Services for Infants and Toddlers

In 1986, Congress passed Public Law 99-457, a reauthorization of Public Law 94-142 that made several changes to the original act. One important change was the addition of Part H, later known as Part C, which requires the provision of services to children with special needs who are ages 3 through 5. At the same time, the law provided financial incentives and program guidelines for states desiring to serve children ages birth through 2 years of age.

Part C requires agencies serving infants and toddlers to develop Individual Family Service Plans (IFSPs) for each eligible child with special needs. The fact that the individual plan is called a *family* plan indicates that the focus of services for this group of children is the family. In contrast to IEPs, IFSPs are to focus on the needs of the entire family. The underlying premise of this requirement is that it is necessary to meet

INTASC 10

School and Community Involvement

Box 7.1   Due Process Hearing Case

Name: Joe Drake
Age: 9 years
Hearing Date: December

Background information: Joe is a child with a learning disability and acting out behavior who receives special education in a resource room for 1 hour each day. Last year, in the third grade, Joe was suspended for a week because of an uncontrollable outburst. This school year, Joe has worked well in the fourth grade until 2 weeks ago when he was suspended again. The parents requested a hearing to determine the extent of the school responsibility to provide an education for their son.

Findings of Fact:

1. An IEP meeting was held in June to review Joe's IEP. It recommended that the parents seek therapy for their son at their own expense during the summer.
2. Another IEP meeting held in September concluded that Joe appeared to have controlled his outbursts but warned that further acting out behavior would result in another suspension.
3. On December 1, Joe hit his teacher during an argument.
4. Joe was immediately suspended by the principal in accordance with the recommendations of the IEP held the previous September.

Parent's Position:

1. Joe is not receiving a free appropriate public education in accordance with his IEP while he is on suspension.
2. The school has not provided adequately for Joe's special education needs.
3. Joe should be reinstated in his fourth-grade class immediately, an independent evaluation should be done at the school's expense, and an IEP meeting should be held to program appropriately for Joe.

School's Position:

1. Joe had been evaluated and appropriately placed to meet his educational needs in a resource room for students with learning disabilities.
2. Joe's behavior is such that the school cannot accommodate him in any of its programs.
3. Joe should be placed in a private day school for students with emotional disturbance at no cost to the parents.

Assignment: Review the facts of this case and make a ruling either in favor of the parents or school. Justify your ruling based on the requirements of IDEA.

the needs of the family in order to provide services to the child. The law requires that IFSPs include:

- A statement of the infant or toddler's present levels of physical development, cognitive development, communication development, social or emotional development, and adaptive development, based on objective criteria;

BOX 7.2   DUE PROCESS HEARING CASE

Name: Gail Baker
Age: 7 years
Hearing Date: December

Background Information: Gail is a 7-year-old child with multiple disabilities; she is functioning at a pre-school developmental level. She started in the local school at age 4 and was transferred to a regional program at 5 1/2 years when the IEP committee felt her needs could be better met there. Gail's parents disagreed and enrolled her in a private school where she has been for the past 2 years. The parents requested a hearing when the local school notified them that a program had been created in the local school for Gail.

Findings of Fact:

1. A previous hearing 2 years ago ordered that an adequate and appropriate placement be identified that would require no more than 2 1/2 hours travel time daily.
2. Five programs within the specified boundaries were explored but none was found to be satisfactory.
3. In the middle of this current year, an IEP meeting was held for Gail for the regional program for young children with moderate disabilities; the program is within 15 minutes from Gail's home.
4. Gail's parents would not approve the IEP because of a stated concern that the regional program was unable to implement the IEP and to provide the structure and one-to-one instruction.
5. The school district and regional program staff agreed to provide (a) extensive speech and language training, (b) another aide creating a 1 to 2 ratio, (c) a larger room with dividers, (d) additional support personnel, and (e) continue a special reading program.
6. The roundtrip travel time to the private school is 4 hours. This exceeds both state law (2 hours total) and the previous hearing agreement.
7. Gail has been on medication since January to control distractibility and increase attending; parents report that this has been helpful.
8. Parents and private school staff report that Gail is making satisfactory progress and enjoys school.

Parent Position:

1. Despite the travel time, Gail enjoys and is profiting from her placement in the private school.
2. Gail has unique educational needs, which can best be met in the present program at the private school.
3. Gail should be allowed to continue at the private placement at no cost to the parents.

School Position:

1. The school has no appropriate program with the district.
2. The regional program staff has developed an IEP to meet Gail's educational needs.
3. The regional program is an adequate and appropriate educational program and placement for Gail.

Box 7.3 *Due Process Hearing Case*

Name: Walter Smith
Age: 15 years
Hearing Date: August

Background Information: Walter was diagnosed as having mild mental retardation during the first grade and placed in a self-contained special class. Although no IEP meeting was held, Walter's parents agreed with that placement. A reevaluation conducted 9 years later indicated that Walter was a slow learner and did not have mental retardation. He was achieving on a third-grade level. The committee deemed Walter as no longer being eligible for special education services and recommended placement in the low track at the high school. Parents objected and requested a hearing.

Findings of Fact:

1. No formal assessments were conducted from grades 1 to 8.
2. A recent evaluation secured by the parents concurred with the school that Walter does not have mental retardation.
3. Test results show Walter to have a learning disability and emphasize the importance of special interventions and tutoring.
4. The high school principal testified that no special education program exists at the high school for students with learning disabilities. All students with special needs are served in the low academic track.
5. A wide range of vocational education programs are available at the high school for students who can pass entry exams.

Parent Position:

1. Walter has received special education throughout school and should continue to receive it.
2. Low track courses offered at the high school are not a substitute for special education.
3. The school should provide Walter with an appropriate special education program and access to vocational education.

School Position:

1. Walter was determined to be no longer eligible for special education.
2. Walter will be served in the low track courses to satisfy graduation requirements.
3. Walter will be allowed to take the entry exams for enrollment into the vocational education courses.

- A statement of the family's resources, priorities, and concerns relating to enhancing the development of the family's infant or toddler with a disability;
- A statement of the major outcomes expected to be achieved for the infant or toddler and the family, and the criteria, procedures, and timelines used to determine the degree to which progress toward achieving the outcomes is being made and whether modifications or revisions of the outcomes or services are necessary;
- A statement of specific early intervention services necessary to meet the unique needs of the infant or toddler and the family, including the frequency, intensity, and method of delivering services;

- A statement of the natural environments in which early intervention services shall appropriately be provided, including a justification of the extent, if any, to which the services will not be provided in a natural environment;
- The projected dates for initiation of services and the anticipated duration of the services;
- The identification of the service coordinator from the profession most immediately relevant to the infant's or toddler's or family's needs (or who is otherwise qualified to carry out all applicable responsibilities under this part). A statewide system described in section 1433 shall include, at a minimum, the following components for the implementation of the plan and coordination with other agencies and persons; and
- The steps to be taken to support transition of the toddler with a disability to preschool or other appropriate services. (20 U.S.C. § 1436 |d|)

Although the IFSP closely parallels the IEP in that it provides for a similar process and documentation, it differs in that it implements a family focus. The IFSP addresses both child and family needs including ways to deal with the stress inherent in parenting a child with special needs. The IFSP may also include the goal of assisting the parents in obtaining information concerning the child's disability. It may also include educational information concerning available services, ways to obtain services, and the legislative and procedural rights that they, as parents, and their child may possess (Hammitte & Nelson, 2001).

SECTION 504 AND FAMILY INVOLVEMENT

INTASC 10

*School and
Community
Involvement*

In 1973, Congress passed civil rights legislation for persons with disabilities. The legislation, Section 504, was a major component of the Rehabilitation Act, PL 93-112, which "grants the right to be free from discrimination to a diverse array of people." It specifically prohibits discrimination by entities that receive federal funds against individuals who meet the definition of disability in the act. This legislation originally targeted programs dealing with employment and the enhancement of employment for persons with disabilities but was amended in 1974 to "extend its protections to handicapped students seeking access to federally supported public schools" (Kortering, Julnes, & Edgar, 1990, p. 8). As a result of this extension, most school programs are covered by the law and its regulations.

Section 504 is a relatively small segment of the Rehabilitation Act being only one sentence long. Section 504 states that:

> No otherwise qualified individual with a disability   in the United States .   shall, solely by reason of her or his disability, be excluded from the participation in, be denied the benefits of, or be subjected to discrimination under any program or activity receiving Federal financial assistance . .   (29 U.S.C. § 794 |a|)

Primarily the Rehabilitation Act affects public schools in areas that focus on employment practices; program accessibility; and preschool, elementary, and secondary education. For parents, the focus is to ensure that schools do not discriminate against students with disabilities in educational and extracurricular programs and to ensure physical access for parents with disabilities (Smith, 2002).

Eligibility for Section 504

The definition of disability in Section 504 differs significantly from the one used in IDEA. Unlike the eligibility system in IDEA that is based on clinical categories of disabilities, eligibility for protections under Section 504 is based on a more functional model (Smith & Patton, 1998). Section 504 describes a person with a disability as one who:

    i. has a physical or mental impairment which substantially limits one or more major life activities,

    ii. has a record of such an impairment, or

    iii. is regarded as having such an impairment. (34 C.F.R. Part 104.3 |j| |1|)

A physical or mental impairment according to Section 504 is defined as:

    A. any physiological disorder or condition, cosmetic disfigurement, or anatomical loss affecting one or more of the following body systems: neurological; musculoskeletal; special sense organs; respiratory, including speech organs; cardiovascular; reproductive, digestive, genito-urinary; hemic and lymphatic; skin; and endocrine; or

    B. any mental or psychological disorder, such as mental retardation, organic brain syndrome, emotional or mental illness, and specific learning disabilities. (34 C.F.R. Part 104.3 |j| |2| |i|)

Although this definition does include some of the categories found in IDEA, it significantly expands the concept of disability. IDEA requires only that individuals have a categorical disability and that the disability results in the student's needing special education. Section 504 requires that the person have a disorder or condition that substantially limits one or more of the person's major life activities. Therefore, a child can be determined to have a disability under Section 504 without being included in any specific disability category.

    There are several points to keep in mind when comparing eligibility of students for Section 504 with eligibility under IDEA. Eligibility under Section 504 is not related to eligibility under other federal or state laws, such as IDEA. Section 504 regulations describe a qualified student with a disability as one who is:

- Of an age during which nonhandicapped persons are provided such services,
- Of any age during which it is mandatory under state law to provide such services to handicapped persons, or
- To whom a state is required to provide a free appropriate public education under Sec. 612 of the Education of the Handicapped Act. (34 C.F.R. Part 104.3 |k| |2|)

Because Section 504 defines disability differently than IDEA, different groups of students may be eligible for protections and services. A child with a disability ineligible for special education services under IDEA may be eligible for services under Section 504 (Smith & Patton, 1998). The result of the broad, functional definition and eligibility criteria of Section 504 is that a student may be eligible for services and protections under Section 504, but may not qualify for services under IDEA. Examples of students eligible for services under Section 504 and not IDEA include students with ADHD, those who are socially maladjusted, those who may be classified as slow learners, and even students with learning disabilities who do not meet IDEA eligibility criteria (Smith, 2002)

Just as some students are referred for IDEA services but may be found ineligible, a student may have a disability but be ineligible for Section 504 services. For example, a student could be diagnosed as having ADHD by a physician but be determined as not having a substantial limitation to learning or another major life activity. It is the school's responsibility, however, to make a determination of Section 504 eligibility. Specific actions for schools regarding referral, evaluation, and programming are included in Chapter 8.

Finally, similar to IDEA, schools are required to *find* students in their districts who may be eligible for protections under Section 504. Schools cannot wait for parents to refer their child for Section 504 services, but must actively seek and identify any child who needs assistance (Smith, 2002)

TEACHER TIP 7.7

Learn all you can about Section 504. Most school staff have a good understanding of IDEA; however, families are becoming more aware of 504 as a method of securing educational accommodations and modifications for their children who are not eligible under IDEA. All school personnel must be knowledgeable concerning 504 because it is an important means of securing services for both students and family members.

Additional Requirements of Section 504

The major focus on the nondiscrimination component of Section 504 is "equal opportunity" and "equal access." If nondisabled students have certain opportunities, then students with disabilities who would otherwise be qualified must also have that opportunity. For example, students with disabilities should be allowed to participate in all activities that are available for students without disabilities. These activities include the same academic curriculum as well as nonacademic extracurricular activities including health services, recreational activities, athletic events and participation, student employment, clubs, and field trips (Smith & Patton, 1998).

Section 504 mandates both physical and program accessibility. For students with physical disabilities, physical accessibility may be the primary consideration. For many students with other types of disabilities, program accessibility may be the major concern. Program access means that students have the opportunity to participate in a program and that the necessary modifications and accommodations are made for students with disabilities that enable them to be successful in the program (Conderman & Katsiyannis, 1995). Section 504 defines free appropriate public education (FAPE) somewhat differently than IDEA. IDEA says that FAPE means the provision of special and related services in the least restrictive setting as outlined in the IEP. Section 504 defines "free" and "appropriate" separately. Appropriate is defined in Section 504 as the provision of regular or special education and related aids and services that are designed to meet individual education needs of persons with a disability. Free in Section 504 is defined as the provision of educational and related services without cost to the person with a disability. The FAPE requirement under Section 504 is thus more broadly defined than under IDEA. Services can include education in general education classes, education in general education classes with supplementary aids, or special education and related services outside the general education setting (Jacob-Timm & Hartshorne, 1994). Accommodations or modifications should be individualized to meet the unique needs of students protected under Section 504.

Section 504, like IDEA, requires that students with disabilities be educated with their nondisabled peers as much as possible, unless it can be determined that the student's educational program cannot be achieved satisfactorily in the general education setting (Smith, 2002). A summary of the requirements in the Section 504 are shown in Table 7.3.

Providing education for students with disabilities who are ineligible for services under IDEA may require schools to develop a Section 504 Accommodation Plan that will specify modifications and accommodations (Conderman & Katsiyannis, 1995). This plan should be developed with input from the parents. The specific contents of a plan, known as a Section 504 Accommodation Plan, to address the educational as well as nonacademic activities of the qualified individual, are not specified in the act. However, the 504 Plan is designed to meet the needs of *individual* students and should result in a free appropriate public education for each. An example of a Section 504 Accommodation Plan is depicted in Figure 7.5.

PRAXIS 2

Legal and Societal Issues

Table 7.3   Requirements of Section 504.

- Location of all qualified individuals and notification of their parents or guardians (Section 104.32);

- Provision of a free appropriate public education to each qualified handicapped person, regardless of the nature or severity of the person's handicap (Section 104.33);

- Provide an education with persons who are not handicapped to the maximum extent appropriate to the needs of the handicapped person (Section 104.34);

- Establish nondiscriminatory evaluation and placement procedures to avoid the inappropriate education that may result from the misclassification or misplacement of students (Section 104.35);

- Establish procedural safeguards to enable parents and guardians to participate meaningfully in decisions regarding the evaluation and placement of their children (Section 104.36); and

- Afford handicapped children an equal opportunity to participate in nonacademic and extracurricular services and activities (Section 104.36).

Section 504 Accommodation Plan

Name: Jake Smith

School/Class: 11th grade—Central High School

Teacher: Pratt—History: Jordan—Literature   Date: 9/29/97

General Strengths: Jake is a bright student; he wants to learn and make good grades. He is very ambitious and wants to go to college and become an engineer.

General Weaknesses: Jake has been diagnosed with ADHD. His attention span is very short and he is easily distracted. He frequently gets out of his seat and walks around the room.

Specific Accommodations:

Accommodation #1

Class: History   Accommodation(s): Jake will be given extra time to complete his assignments. He will be given assignments divided into shorter objectives so that his progress can be checked sooner.

Person Responsible for Accommodation #1: Mr. Pratt—teacher

Accommodation #2

Class: History   Accommodation(s): Jake will sit at the front of the class.

Person Responsible for Accommodation #2: Mr. Pratt—teacher

Accommodation #3

Class: Literature   Accommodation(s): Jake will work with selected other students in cooperative learning arrangements.

Person Responsible for Accommodation #3: Ms. Jordan—teacher

Accommodation #4

Class: Literature   Accommodation(s): An assignment notebook will be sent home each day with specific assignments noted. Parents will sign the assignment notebook daily and return it to school.

Person Responsible for Accommodation #4: Jordan—teacher

Accommodation #5

Class: All classes   Accommodation(s): A behavior management plan will be developed and implemented for Jake for the entire day. The plan will include time for Jake to take Ritalin and will focus on positive reinforcement.

Person Responsible for Accommodation #5: Ms. Baker, Asst. Prin.

General Comments:

Jake's plan will be reviewed at the end of the fall term to ensure that it is meeting his needs.

Individuals Participating in Development of Accommodation Plan:

William Pratt—teacher   Fred Haynes—504 Coor.

Bonita Jordan—teacher   Hank Smith—father

Mary Baker—asst. prin.

Figure 7.5 *Example of a Section 504 Accommodation Plan.*
Note: *From* Section 504 and Public Schools (*pp. 50–51*), *by T. E. C. Smith and J. Patton,*
1998, *Austin, TX: Pro-Ed. Used with permission.*

Due Process Procedures and Section 504

Schools that serve students under Section 504 are required to establish and implement procedural safeguards related to the identification, evaluation, or educational
placement of children. These are mandated to ensure that the rights of children and
their families are protected. Procedural safeguards must include the right to notice,
the opportunity for parents or guardians to examine relevant records, the right to an
impartial hearing, and a specific review procedure for filing complaints. After a referral for Section 504 services, one of the first steps is that schools must inform parents
of their procedural rights. Table 7.4 summarizes the due process safeguards required
by Section 504 (Smith et al., 2004).

   Unlike IDEA, Section 504 does not require consent prior to the initial evaluation
of a child for Section 504 eligibility or for the development of the accommodation

> **PRAXIS 2**
>
> *Legal and Societal Issues*

Table 7.4 Due process rights under Section 504 regulations.

- Right to be informed by the district of specific due process rights
- Right for the child to have access to equal academic and nonacademic school activities
- Right for the child to have an appropriate education in the least restrictive setting, which includes accommodations, modifications, and related services
- Right to notice regarding referral, evaluation, and placement
- Right for the child to have a fair evaluation conducted by a knowledgeable person(s)
- Right to an administrative appeals process
- Right to examine and obtain copies of all school records

plan. However, it is preferred practice for the school to request such permission and for schools to follow the IDEA procedures related to notice and consent; the Office for Civil Rights (OCR) has stated on numerous occasions that consent should be obtained. This practice may result in schools doing more than mandated in Section 504, but it is an important task in the development of family-school partnerships.

Parents wanting to file Section 504 complaints must send them to the Office for Civil Rights in the region or the State Department of Education where the school district is located. The complaint must be sent within 180 days of the reputed violation of the act. Although it does not have to be on any particular form, it should include the following information:

- Name, address, and telephone number of the complaining party;
- Basis for the complaint, such as disability discrimination;
- Names of those who have been affected by the discrimination;
- Name and address of the discriminating agency, if known;
- Approximate date of the discriminatory conduct;
- Brief description of what happened;
- Signature of the complaining party. (Underwood & Mead, 1995)

After a complaint has been filed, an administrative investigation is conducted. Although IDEA requires a due process hearing before court action is instigated, the majority of courts permit parents to bring a Section 504 complaint directly to the court without first having a hearing (Underwood & Mead, 1995). However, the school district is required by Section 504 to have in place an impartial hearing process similar to the one required by IDEA. Thus, parents have the choice of action in Section 504 complaints (Underwood & Mead, 1995).

TEACHER TIP 7.8

Always try to resolve disagreements with family members. Even though schools cannot be required to do more than the law mandates, it is always better to attempt to reach a compromise with family members rather than go to mediation or due process. Also, remember to keep the child's best interests in mind. The child is the focus of all discussions.

Hearings are generally unpleasant for all involved. It is best when schools and families work together to provide an appropriate education to the children. Parents and schools can take the following actions in an attempt to avoid complaints and hearings:

1. Focus on the child. Be objective in reviewing the child's program. Work to ensure that an appropriate program is provided.

2. Have a positive attitude. Strive for a strong family-school partnership.

Name of Person Calling: _____

Date: _____   Time: _____

Who Initiated Call: _____

Purpose of the Call: _____

Length of the Call: _____

General Contents of the Conversation:

Figure 7.6   *Example of telephone documentation.*

Name of Person (s): _____

Date: _____   Time: _____

Length of Conversation: _____

Location of Conversation: _____

Circumstances of Conversation: _____

General Contents of the Conversation:

Figure 7.7   *Example of documentation of conversations.*

3. Provide information concerning the child to help with assessment. Include information on both strengths and needs.
4. Document. Proper documentation helps all parties keep events in perspective.
   - Document phone calls (see Figure 7.6).
   - Keep copies of letters and notices.
   - Make a record of all conversations (see Figure 7.7).
   - Send important material by registered mail.
5. Attempt to mediate. If negotiations are successful, it generally is better for all parties, especially the child.

THE AMERICANS WITH DISABILITIES ACT, PL 101-336

In 1990, Congress passed the Americans with Disabilities Act (ADA). ADA has three major components that focus on: (1) employment, (2) state and local governments, and (3) public accommodations. The ADA is similar to Section 504 in three ways.

CEC 1

Foundations

First, ADA uses the same broad, noncategorical definition of disability. Second, ADA is civil rights legislation for individuals with disabilities. Third, ADA does not have age restrictions. ADA expands the civil rights and nondiscriminatory protection provided in Section 504 to include private-sector employment, privately operated businesses that are open to the public, telecommunications, transportation, and state and local government activities and programs. Section 504 applies only to entities receiving federal funds, but the ADA applies to most public institutions, businesses, and activities, regardless of whether they receive federal funds or not (Smith et al., 2004).

Both Section 504 and the ADA apply to schools when parents have disabilities. For example, a parent may use a wheelchair or may require manual communication. Other parents may be visually impaired or have cognitive disabilities. In all of these examples, as well as other situations where adults have disabilities as defined by Section 504 and the ADA, schools must provide access. Therefore, if a parent using a wheelchair wants to observe his or her child in an inaccessible location, the school must take actions to make this observation possible. Another example is a parent with a visual impairment who cannot read print. Written communication from the school to home might need to be made available to the parent in Braille, or the school might have to ensure that the content of the information is made available through oral reading or audiotape. Specific accommodations or modifications would be determined on a case-by-case basis. Providing equal access is essential to developing family-school partnerships.

Consider possible challenges caused by the disabilities listed in Table 7.5. How can schools respond?

Table 7.5   Possible disabilities affecting parents and suggestions for ensuring equal opportunities.

Problem	Possible Accommodations
Parent with a hearing loss wants to attend PTA meeting	• School obtains the services of an interpreter for the meeting
Parent with a mobility impairment in a wheelchair wants to observe his or her child on the second floor of an inaccessible building	• Move the child's class to an accessible level so the parent can observe • Move the child's class to an accessible level for the entire school year
Parent with a visual impairment who cannot read print	• Call the parent to relay information that is not extensive • Arrange for material to be Brailled when it is sensitive or extensive
Parent with a mobility impairment in a wheelchair who wants to attend his/her child's graduation ceremonies in an inaccessible auditorium	• Move the graduation exercises to an accessible location

TEACHER TIP 7.9

When working with parents with disabilities, remember that they have civil rights under 504 and the ADA. Make certain that they are provided appropriate accommodations that will allow them to access school buildings and school activities.

SUMMARY

This chapter provides information related to the legal bases for family involvement. School personnel should involve parents not only because it is essential to the development of family-school partnerships, but also to comply with national legislation.

The Individuals with Disabilities Education Act (IDEA) provides a legal basis for parental involvement. IDEA provides the opportunity for parental involvement at every step of the IEP process, including referral, evaluation, program planning, and placement decisions. When parents and school personnel disagree concerning a child's educational program, either party can request mediation and/or a due process hearing.

Section 504 of the Rehabilitation Act provides educational access for children with disabilities who do not qualify for services under IDEA. Section 504, like IDEA, requires schools to provide parents of eligible students opportunities for involvement during the planning and implementation of Section 504 Accommodation Plan, which specifies the accommodations and modifications to be provided to the child. Parents have specific due process protections under Section 504 and legal access through both the courts and administrative hearings.

Finally, information is included regarding the responsibility of the schools under ADA and Section 504 in providing access to parents with disabilities. Because involving the families of children with disabilities is an essential part of the family-school partnership, professionals and families can use legislation to strengthen the partnership.

QUESTIONS FOR DISCUSSION

1. What are some reasons schools used to give for not involving parents in the education of their children? Can you support any of these reasons as valid? Given the time and circumstances of schools not involving families, were the actions justified or not?

2. Describe all the legal requirements for involving families in the education of their children with disabilities. Have laws gone too far in mandating family involvement? Why or why not?

3. Section 504 and the ADA are considered civil rights laws for individuals with disabilities. How can the involvement of families in the education of their children with disabilities be a civil rights issue? Should school personnel primarily follow IDEA or 504/ADA when dealing with parents? Why?

REFERENCES

Board of Education of Hendrick Hudson Central School District v. Rowley, 458 U.S. 176, 102 S.Ct. 3034, 73 L.Ed. 2d 690 (1982).

Conderman, G., & Katsiyannis, A. (1995). Section 504 accommodation plans. Intervention in School and Clinic, 31, 42–45.

Dunlap, G., Newton, J. S., Fox, L., Benito, N., & Vaughn, B. (2001). Family involvement in functional assessment and positive behavior support. Focus on Autism and Other Developmental Disabilities, 16, 215–221.

Hammitte, D. J., & Nelson, B. M. (2001). Families of children in early childhood special education. In D. J. O'Shea, L. J. O'Shea, R. Algozine, & D. J. Hammitte (Eds.), Families and teachers of individuals with disabilities (pp. 129–154). Boston: Allyn & Bacon.

IDEA. (2004). The Individuals with Disabilities Education Improvement Act. Washington, DC.: U.S. Government Printing Office.

Jacob-Timm, S., & Hartshorne, T. S. (1994). Section 504 and school psychology. Psychology in the Schools, 31, 26–39.

Kortering, L., Julnes, R., & Edgar, E. (1990). An instructive review of the law pertaining to the graduation of special education students. Remedial and Special Education, 11, 7–13.

Lake, J., & Billingsley, B. (2000). An analysis of factors that contribute to parent-school conflict in special education. Remedial and Special Education, 21, 240–251.

Murdick, N. L., Gartin, B. C., & Crabtree, T. (2002). Special education law. Upper Saddle River, NJ: Merrill/Prentice Hall.

Podemski, R. S., Marsh, G. E., Smith, T. E. C., & Price, B. J. (1995). Comprehensive administration of special education (2nd ed.). Upper Saddle River, NJ: Merrill/Prentice Hall.

Smith, T. E. C. (2002). Section 504: Basic requirement for schools. Intervention in School and Clinic, 37, 2–6.

Smith, T. E. C., Dowdy, C. A., Polloway, E. A., & Blalock, G. (1997). Children and adults with learning disabilities. Boston: Allyn & Bacon.

Smith, T. E. C., & Patton, J. (1998). Section 504 and public schools. Austin, TX: Pro-Ed.

Smith, T. E. C., Polloway, E. A., Patton, J. R., & Dowdy, C. A. (2004). Teaching students with special needs in inclusive settings (4th ed.). Boston: Allyn & Bacon.

Streett, S., & Smith, T. E. C. (1996). Section 504 and schools: A practical guide. Little Rock: The Learning Group.

Underwood, J. K., & Mead, J. F. (1995). Legal aspects of special education and pupil services. Boston: Allyn & Bacon.

CHAPTER 8
Working with Families: The Special Education Process

● ○ ○ ○ ○

Objectives

After reading this chapter, you will:

- Understand the barriers to family-school collaboration
- Recognize the role of parents in each step of the special education process
- Understand the different types of individual plans and the role of parents in the development of each plan

- Understand the factors involved in parent-school disagreements and ways to prevent them
- Know strategies for increasing family-school partnerships in the special education process

Research on family participation has identified numerous benefits for schools and students with disabilities. Academic development and successful outcomes for children have been found as a result of parental participation (Singh, Curtis, Wechsler, Ellis, & Cohen, 1997). In fact, parental participation has been found to positively impact student achievement, student test scores, student social skills, school attendance rates, dropout rates, student motivation, and student delinquency (Jayanthi, Bursuck, Epstein, & Polloway, 1997). It appears a safe assumption that when school personnel and parents and families can establish good working relationships, the school experiences of the children are enhanced (Smith, Polloway, Patton & Dowdy, 2004).

The goal of establishing family-school partnerships is theoretically sound; however, "parent-professional partnerships have been difficult to achieve in practice" (Guy, Goldberg, McDonald, & Flom, 1997, p. 166). Although many parents of children with disabilities are very involved in their child's education, others do not participate in their child's educational experiences, including the special education process. According to Nassar-McMillan and Algozzine (2001), specific barriers to participation encountered by parents include:

- Sometimes parents believe they are not smart enough to talk with teachers.
- Sometimes parents have had bad experiences with teachers.
- Sometimes parents believe they will not be treated fairly at school.
- Often parents believe teachers are better suited to work with their children.
- Often financial pressures override other areas of concern for some parents.
- Sometimes parents see schools as unsafe environments.
- Sometimes parents are unable to come to school because they lack access to transportation.
- Sometimes work prevents parents from participating in school activities. (p. 277)

Another reason that some parents may limit their participation is that an adversarial relationship has developed between them and school personnel. Such an adversarial relationship may make it very difficult for schools and parents to cooperate effectively (Lake & Billingsley, 2000). Because of the negative implications of limited parental participation, school personnel should engage in activities that will facilitate and reinforce parental participation in the educational process. Such actions may include home visits, assigning parent advocates, relocating meetings, changing meeting times, and training school personnel on how to develop better relationships with parents. From the parents' perspective, the key is that "meeting the child's needs is truly a shared concern and that input from family members will

INTASC 10

School and Community Involvement

be respected" (Dowdy, Patton, Smith, & Polloway, 1998, p. 175). If parents do not believe this can be accomplished, then their participation may be minimal and difficult to secure.

TEACHER TIP 8.1

Try to avoid adversarial relationships if at all possible. It is important to remember that after mediation, hearings, or even court cases occur, school personnel and parents must work together for the good of the child.

One of the most important reasons for parent participation is the parental desire to be involved in their child's education. Westling (1997) summarizes studies related to parental involvement and finds that parents of children with disabilities:

- Generally want more involvement in their child's education than parents of nondisabled children;
- Believe that they have more opportunities to influence their child's educational program than parents of nondisabled children;
- Want to be involved in their child's IEP process; and
- Want regular communication between themselves and school personnel.

Table 8.1 provides a list of what parents of students with learning disabilities want from schools. These items are similar to what most parents want. School personnel should realize that parent needs must be taken into consideration when attempting to establish a partnership. Parents who believe that school personnel understand their needs and attempt to meet those needs are more likely to participate in the child's program than parents who believe that school personnel are insensitive and unwilling to cooperate.

Table 8.1   What parents of students with learning disabilities want from schools.

- Communication without jargon
- Conferences held so both parents can attend
- Written materials that provide information to help them understand their child's problems
- A copy of the written report about their child
- Specific advice on how to manage specific behavior problems and how to teach them skills that they need
- Information about their child's social and academic needs

Note: Adapted from "Parents and Teachers: Can We Talk?" by C. L. Wilson, 1995, *LD Forum, 20*(2), pp. 31–33.

Early Childhood	School-Age Special Education
Referral by anyone	Referral by anyone
Family-focused assessment	Individual-focused assessment
Family-focused plan (IFSP)	Individual-focused plan (IEP)
Service coordinator	Teacher managed

Figure 8.1   *A comparison of the special education process for early childhood and school-age children.*

PARENTS AND THE SPECIAL EDUCATION PROCESS

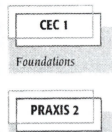

CEC 1

Foundations

PRAXIS 2

Legal and Societal Issues

The Individuals with Disabilities Education Act (IDEA 2004), as previously described, requires schools to take specific steps related to increasing opportunities for parental participation in all aspects of special education programs (Lake & Billingsley, 2000; Lytle & Bordin, 2001; Smith et al., 2004). The special education process includes procedures regarding the development and implementation of an education for children with disabilities (Smith et al., 2004). These procedures are the same regardless of age, although the focus of the intervention moves from family-centered interventions during the child's early years (birth to age 3) to child-centered interventions during the child's preschool and school-age years (see Figure 8.1).

An important facet, though, of all components of the special education process under IDEA is the focus on parental participation. IDEA reiterates at each level that parental participation is essential for the successful development and implementation of the specialized services (Lytle & Bordin, 2001). Although the school district may be in procedural compliance with IDEA requirements, it may not encourage parental participation. Schools, therefore, are challenged to develop and implement strategies that encourage, expand, and reinforce family-school partnerships at each step in the process. For each step of the special education process described next there are specific roles and activities for parental participation.

TEACHER TIP 8.2

When working with parents of students with disabilities, treat them like you would like to be treated if you were in their shoes. Parents have an interest and a right to be involved.

Prereferral

Before the legally mandated process begins, there is a step known as prereferral in which parents may participate if they choose. Prereferral is the identification and implementation of "modifications made in a student's general education program or classroom environment based on an analysis of screening information" (Murdick & Petch-Hogan, 1996, p. 172). These prereferral interventions (sometimes called Alternative Intervention Strategies) are designed to remedy concerns identified early in the student's educational career in order to prevent identification and placement in special education whenever feasible. IDEA 2004 permits schools to use up to 15% of their IDEA funds on prereferral interventions.

INTASC 1

Content Pedagogy

Many school districts (and some state departments of education) require the development and implementation of prereferral interventions prior to the referral of the student for an evaluation of eligibility to receive special education services. These activities may be designed by the classroom teacher or with the assistance of the Child Referral Team or Teacher Assistance Team. Most school district's Compliance Plan provides guidelines for development and/or a specific form for documentation.

Of course, prior to intervention, parents should be notified of any concerns that the teacher is having with the educational program for their child. There are no specific legal requirements, though, for parental consent for the initiation, change, or cessation of prereferral interventions or for parent participation in the development of prereferral activities as they are planned and implemented as part of a general education classroom program, nor are parents required to participate or attend meetings concerning prereferral activities.

Referral

Regardless of how well the prereferral interventions are planned and implemented, they may not result in the child's overcoming learning and behavior issues. If prereferral activities are not successful, then the next step would be to consider actions that will initiate the legally mandated special education process and indicate whether the child in question is eligible for services under IDEA. The first step of this process is known as "referral," which can be defined as a procedure by which an individual such as a doctor, nurse, teacher, other school personnel, parent, or family member seeks assistance in identifying the sources of problems the student is having with his/her educational program. Seeking services may be one of the more important actions that a parent can take. After identifying the possibility that a child may have a disability covered under IDEA, school personnel or parents must formally refer the child for consideration for special education and related services through completion of an approved form. During the referral process, it is determined whether the child might be eligible for services provided through IDEA. Simply referring a child does not guarantee that the child will be determined to be eligible for special education services. However, it is a first step in ensuring that children who are eligible will receive the appropriate education mandated by IDEA.

CEC 1

Foundations

PRAXIS 2

Legal and Societal Issues

If the parents are not the initiator of the referral, then the school district will notify them that a referral has been made. The school district will schedule and invite the parents to a referral conference, a meeting to determine if the child should be evaluated to determine eligibility for services provided through IDEA. This conference should be held at a time and place convenient to the parents. At the referral conference, individuals knowledgeable about the child, including the child's parents, discuss the issues that the child is experiencing and identify possible strategies to use. Additionally, at this meeting the evaluation process that is to follow the referral will be explained, specific assessment instruments to address the areas of the child's needs as outlined on the referral form will be described, the timeline for completion of the evaluation will be noted, and specific individuals who will complete the evaluations as part of the team will be listed.

It is very important for parents to participate in the referral step of the process. Parents are a valuable source of information concerning their child's behaviors, skills, work habits, and personal preferences as well as other factors that could be impacting school and school success. The parental view is essential to the process and some information may not be available to school personnel without parental input. Some parents may be concerned about this process as they may feel intimidated by school personnel, distrustful of school personnel, or simply not understand why their involvement is important.

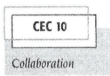

CEC 10

Collaboration

TEACHER TIP 8.3

Referral is one of the crucial points in which families should be involved. Family members are in a position to provide information critical in the referral decision about the student.

School personnel must go beyond the minimal legal requirements and actively seek parental participation. Actions that could be taken by school personnel to facilitate the participation of parents include:

- Making a home visit to explain the concerns of the school and the special education process
- Encouraging the parent to attend the referral conference to provide information
- Appointing a school person to serve as a mentor and support person for the parent during the conference
- Setting the referral conference at a time and location convenient to the parent
- Providing for any special needs of the parent during the referral process, such as accessibility issues, language issues, and any other supports that might be needed

CEC 10

Collaboration

Written communication with parents can also greatly affect the level of participation. Letters can be written that are warm and encourage participation, or letters can be written that do not encourage participation and sound as if parental participation is not desired. After receiving a letter that does not sound like a genuine invitation for participation, parents might be discouraged and choose nonparticipation. Read the letters in Box 8.1 to see how different letters inviting parental participation can sound. Even though such actions do not guarantee parental participation, they do indicate the desire for parents to be valued members of the committee.

The referral committee including the parents determines if it is likely that the child would be eligible for services under IDEA. If the referral committee decides that

Box 8.1 EXAMPLES OF LETTERS INVITING PARENTAL PARTICIPATION

Dear Ms. Samuel,

Your son, Johnny, has been referred for special education services. His academic work and behavior have been declining over the past several weeks. We will hold a referral conference on Friday, March 12, at 10:00 A.M. If you are not able to attend, we will go ahead and determine if we think Johnny should be tested for special education. Please let us know if you will attend or not.

Sincerely,

Ms. Brown

Dear Ms. Samuel,

Your son Johnny has been referred for special education services. We are concerned about his recent behavior and academic difficulties, and would like to meet to discuss how we can better meet his needs. We want you to attend this meeting and want to know when it is easiest for you to attend. Since you work during the day, would it be better if we scheduled the meeting for 4:30, after your workday ends? Please let me know so I can arrange a time when you can attend. If you need transportation, we can arrange that. Also, if you need childcare during the meeting, you can bring your children and we will have someone to look after them while we meet. Please contact me if you have any questions.

Sincerely,

Lauren Brown

---

the child is likely not eligible, then parents receive written notice of the decision and are provided information regarding due process rights and the appeal process if they should wish to appeal the decision not to evaluate the child. Again, involved parents will better understand the decision and its basis, their rights, and the subsequent actions that can be taken. If eligibility is a possibility, then the child is recommended for evaluation and parental permission is requested.

Evaluation

Under IDEA 2004 there are two primary purposes for the initial evaluation of children who are referred for special education services:

- To determine whether a child is a child with a disability
- Within 60 days of receiving parental consent for the evaluation, or, if the State establishes a timeframe within which the evaluation must be conducted within such timeframe; and
- To determine the educational needs of such child. (Section 614)

Prior to conducting an initial evaluation, schools must secure parental consent for evaluation. Most parents grant permission. However, when parents refuse to grant permission for schools to conduct initial evaluations, the school may continue to

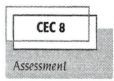

CEC 8

Assessment

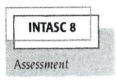

Assessment

pursue the evaluation only through mediation or due process hearings. Although this can legally occur, it is not a common response by the schools. School personnel will usually continue to work with the parents and attempt to persuade them to allow the evaluation to proceed.

Schools are charged with providing written notice to the parents of a child with a disability. This notice should describe any evaluation procedures that will be conducted. Even though schools may follow the procedures outlined in the law when evaluating children, parents may feel estranged from the process. Simply notifying parents of an evaluation and providing an explanation of the evaluation does not guarantee parental understanding. School personnel need to be committed to assuring that parents understand all facets of the evaluation process. For example, parents can be provided examples of test questions and an explanation in lay terms of the test results.

Read the scenario in Box 8.2. How could the evaluator have better explained the evaluation process to help the parents understand what will occur?

A major reason for involving parents in the evaluation process is to obtain information they have about the child. During the conducting of the evaluation, parents will be asked to provide relevant functional and developmental information concerning their child. This information will be used in determining whether or not the child has a disability. Parental information also may be used in the development of the child's IEP, including the child's participation in the general education curriculum or for preschool children their participation in appropriate preschool activities.

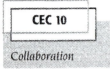

Collaboration

TEACHER TIP 8.4

Parents have access to information that the school personnel might never know; they have been with the child for many years and can add significant informal information that can be crucial in the evaluation of the child.

BOX 8.2   *EXAMPLE OF EXPLANATION FROM SCHOOL EVALUATOR*

Hello Mr. and Mrs. Green. My name is Bob Wright and I am the school's evaluator. I would like to tell you about the assessments that I will be using to try to identify Linda's strengths and needs. First, I will give her an individual intelligence test such as the Wechsler Intelligence Test for Children. This is a norm-referenced instrument and will allow us to determine how Linda is functioning cognitively. After this intelligence test, I will administer a diagnostic achievement test, such as the Woodcock-Johnson Achievement Battery and diagnostic tests in the areas of Reading and Mathematics, to determine Linda's academic strengths and areas of need. Overall, these examinations will give us a very good understanding of her cognitive and academic strengths and any areas of need. As I've given you just a very brief description of the types of assessments I'll be giving to your daughter, do you have any questions at this time? I would like to say, though, that I will be glad to answer any additional questions at a later time, too.

The use of norm-referenced, standardized tests is important in the evaluation process. Anecdotal information gathered from observation during the child's development is also important. Interviews using a guided, open-ended format are an excellent method of gathering information (Hutchins & Renzaglia, 1998). During such an activity, school personnel should ensure that parents feel comfortable and understand the purpose of the process. Such interviews help identify problems experienced by the student, as well as possible solutions to the problems. "The primary advantage of interviews of this type as a source of assessment information is that they provide information about how the child functions in the natural settings of home and school, information that norm-referenced tests neglect" (Witt, Elliott, Daly, Gresham, & Kramer, 1998, p. 50). Shea and Bauer (1991) provide an outline for such an interview (see Table 8.2).

Table 8.2 Outline for interview with parents.

1. Establish rapport with the parents. Sample questions: How was your day? How is your child today?

2. Obtain the parents' description of the behaviors concerning them, including their frequency, intensity, and duration. Sample questions: What exactly does the child do that you find unacceptable or annoying? What exactly makes you say he is hyperactive, nonresponsive, or disobedient? In the course of an hour, how often is he hyperactive, nonresponsive, or disobedient?

3. Obtain the parents' description of the situations and environments in which the behavior occurs and the people present when the behavior occurs. Sample questions: Where does this behavior occur? What happens after your child acts in this way? What is your child doing when this occurs? Who is around when this occurs?

4. Explore the contingencies that may stimulate and sustain the behavior. Sample questions: What happens just before the behavior occurs? What happens just after the behavior occurs? What do you usually do when the child behaves in this way? How do other people indicate to the child that the behavior is unacceptable?

5. Attempt to determine the ratio of positive to negative interactions between the child and the parents. Sample questions: Is your relationship with the child usually pleasant or unpleasant? Do you usually praise his accomplishments? Do you think you praise his successes as much as you reprimand his failures, or do you think you do one more than the other?

6. Explore the parents' methods of behavior control. Sample questions: Do you punish the behavior? How do you punish inappropriate behavior? Who administers the punishment? Do you always use this method of punishment? What other methods do you use?

7. Determine how aware parents are of the way they communicate praise or punishment and its effect on the child's behavior. Sample questions: Can the child tell when you are angry? How? Can he tell when you want him to stop doing something?

(continued)

Table 8.2 *Continued*

8. Explore how parents communicate their expectations to their child. Sample questions: How clearly do you spell out the rules you expect the child to follow? Does he know what you expect him to do?

9. Detect irrational and unrealistic ideas that make it difficult for the parents to understand, accept, or modify the child's behavior. Restate these irrational ideas but avoid reinforcing them. Sample questions: What do you feel is the reason for the behavior? Do you think the behavior can be changed?

10. Conclude the interview by restating the unacceptable behavior and clarifying the desirable behavior.

Note: From *Parents and Teachers of Children with Disabilities* (pp. 151–152), by T. M. Shea and A. M. Bauer, 1991, Boston: Allyn & Bacon.

Eligibility

CEC 1

Foundations

Following the evaluation, a determination is made by the multidisciplinary team that includes the child's parents about the eligibility of the child for special education services under IDEA. Parents are provided a copy of the evaluation report and documentation of eligibility. Psychometrists, counselors, special education staff members, and other school personnel should ensure that the report is clear and understandable so that all persons involved, such as parents and general education teachers, understand the reports and can make informed decisions and participate in program development. Additionally, professionals will need to reduce the use of jargon typically found in psychological reports. Read the excerpts from evaluation reports in Box 8.3 and consider which ones are best for parents.

Parents often voice concerns over the eligibility determination process. In a series of hearings conducted by the National Council on Disability, more than 400 witnesses testified about their concerns regarding IDEA and special education services. Among the findings related to eligibility were:

1. Too many children who need services are not identified and are therefore not provided appropriate services.

2. Too many children from minority backgrounds are identified, resulting in an overidentification of children from these groups.

3. The overall harmful effects that labeling, which is required as part of the eligibility decision, has on children. (National Council on Disability, 1995)

These results indicate that school personnel should make greater efforts to ensure that eligibility decisions are made fairly and with a strong database to support the decision. The entire array of techniques that can be used to lessen discriminatory assessment practices should be employed to prevent overidentification of children from any diverse cultural group. Parental participation is essential in this process.

Box 8.3

Which of these statements would likely be understandable by family members and which ones would not be understandable?

- ❏ She is functioning about two standard deviations below the mean.
- ❏ She is performing about as well as 15% of the students in her age range.
- ❏ He is doing math at the third stanine.
- ❏ Her IQ is 109.
- ❏ She is a little smarter than average children in her class.
- ❏ Her math scores are the equivalent of someone in the 11th grade.
- ❏ She is doing as well in reading as most kids who are in the fourth grade.
- ❏ His adaptive behavior scores are well below the mean.
- ❏ He is performing daily activities about as well as most children in his age group.

If parents do not consent to their child being determined eligible for special education under IDEA, the school may not classify the child as eligible; the school also cannot pursue this decision through due process. The 2004 reauthorization of IDEA notes that children will not be determined eligible for services if their problems result from a lack of appropriate instruction in reading or math, or due to limited English proficiency.

Program Development

After the evaluation has been completed and a decision has been made by the interdisciplinary team that the student is eligible for and in need of special education services, an individualized program is developed. Depending on the age of the individual, this may be an IFSP, an IEP, or an individualized transition plan (ITP).

Individualized Family Service Plan (IFSP)   Part C of IDEA mandates a written document describing the services to be provided for infants and toddlers with disabilities. This document is known as the IFSP (Bruder, 2000). (See Chapter 7 for a description of the IFSP components.) Instead of being focused on educational services for the child as in an individualized education plan (IEP), the IFSP focuses on both the family and the child with a disability. This family-focused document is written to enhance not only the child's needs but to empower the family in its ability to support itself and the child with the disability.

Individualized Education Plan (IEP)   For students determined to be eligible for special education and related services, an IEP must be developed by a team of individuals who are knowledgeable about the child and about services that the child may need. The IEP team must include the child's parents and, whenever appropriate, the child.

When developing the IEP, the team must consider the concerns of the parents for enhancing the education of their child and the results of the initial or most recent

CEC 4

*Instructional
Strategies*

INTASC 7

Planning

PRAXIS 3

*Delivery of Services
to Students with
Disabilities*

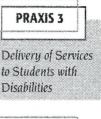

INTASC 7

Planning

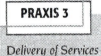

reevaluation including the strengths of the child. Dabkowski (2004) notes, "the most significant venue for exercising the right to parental participation in decision-making is the IEP meeting" (p. 36). Although it is not necessary for the team to include in the IEP everything the parent suggests, close attention should be paid to parental requests. As with evaluation information, parents may have unique insights into the needs of their children and into the non-school environment in which they live. The length and context of the parent-child relationship may provide very useful information for the IEP and for the development of long-term goals. Involving family members in the development and implementation of the IEP is a professionally sound practice and can greatly enhance educational opportunities for students with disabilities (Smith et al., 2004). Family members are better able to support their child's intervention plan if they were involved in developing it (Hutinger, 1996). As participants, parents are more likely to better understand the entire plan and how to implement components of the program at home. The participation of parents gives them an opportunity to become actively involved in their child's educational program. Strategies schools can use to enhance participation by parents in IEP development are discussed in a later section.

TEACHER TIP 8.5

Prior to the IEP meeting, ask parents to write goals for their child and then bring them to the meeting. Early in the IEP meeting, ask parents about their goals for the child. This sends the message that you care about their input. When they give you input, make sure you discuss their information or ideas and give them serious consideration.

Individual educational plans should be reviewed periodically, but not less frequently than annually, by the team that includes the parents. In addition to the annual review, parents may request a review of the IEP at any time. Unfortunately, most parents are unaware of this right, or they lack information concerning the child's program and are hesitant to request such a review. Therefore, when possible, school personnel should periodically ask parents if they are satisfied with the IEP, or discuss with them as to whether they see the need for a formal review. Even though this is not a legal requirement, it indicates to the parents that school personnel are concerned about their input and desire their participation.

Individual Transition Plan (ITP)   Will (1984) notes that parents and professionals have voiced concerns that their children with disabilities were not being successful when they left the school. When reviewing the individualized educational plans that were being developed, it was noted that the IEPs did not identify future goals and were not written to assist the child in the transition from school to work. As a result, in the 1990 reauthorization of IDEA, the concept of transition services was added. Now transition services are to be included in a document known as an individual transition plan (ITP). IDEA 2004 notes that the child's IEP that is in effect when the child turns 16 years of age, must include the transition goals for the child and services needed to assist the child's achievement of those goals. This must be updated at least annually when the child's IEP is updated. Also, beginning no later than 1 year prior to the child reaching majority age, a statement indicating that the child has been informed of his rights and that those rights will be transferred to him when he reaches the age of majority shall be included in the IEP. The parents and the student as members of the team are to be involved in identifying future goals (future planning) and the steps to reach those goals (National Center on Secondary Education and Transition, 2002). This focus on transition planning as the essential goal for the student's educational career is emphasized in the IDEA amendments of 2004, where it states that the student's plan is to facilitate children achieving measurable post-secondary goals. Thus, the ITP has a three-fold emphasis to include: (1) plans for future employment, (2) plans for future education after high school, and (3) plans for independent living (National Information Center for Children and Youth with Disabilities, 2003).

By age 16, the focus of what has been known as the IEP moves to address post-school outcomes and becomes the ITP. As a result, the student, as well as the parents, should participate in the process to develop the ITP. Additionally, representatives from other agencies such as vocational rehabilitation, employment services, mental health services, developmental disabilities services, social security, and so on. should be invited to attend the planning meeting because they will be involved with the person as he/she transitions into the community.

TEACHER TIP 8.6

Parents are often more interested in their child's future as an adult than school personnel. Therefore, make sure that transition goals for the student reflect the parents' and student's desires.

Behavior Intervention Plans (BIP)   Parents should also participate in the development of the behavior intervention plan (BIP). IDEA requires schools to develop BIPs for students with disabilities with behavior problems. Behavior intervention plans are developed following a functional behavior assessment by the school, which is an attempt to determine the function of the child's inappropriate behaviors (Alberto & Troutman, 2003).

Functional assessment, the basis for behavior intervention plans, focuses on trying to understand the interactions between behaviors and events in the environment. From this understanding a behavior intervention plan is developed that specifies actions that attempt to change inappropriate behaviors into appropriate behaviors. Because the core of functional assessment is gathering information to assist in determining relationships, family members are critical in the functional assessment process (Dunlap, Newton, Fox, Benito, & Vaughn, 2001). There appears to be an increasing emphasis on behavior plans that can be implemented in community contexts by family members and other natural intervention agents (Fox, Vaughn, Wyatte, &

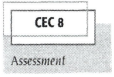

CEC 8

Assessment

Dunlap, 2002). With a renewed emphasis on family-focused interventions, including behavioral interventions, close collaboration between schools and family members is very important (Becker-Cottrill, McFarland, & Anderson, 2003).

Placement Decisions

CEC 5

Learning Environments and Social Interactions

Once the individualized plan is developed based on an analysis of the results of the multidisciplinary evaluation, a decision on the most appropriate site for plan implementation must occur. In other words, the contents of the individualized plan dictate the educational placement for each child. Educational placement options are selected from a continuum of service delivery formats mandated in IDEA (Smith et al., 2004). This model conceptualizes services from the general education classroom seen as the least restrictive option to a residential school or institutional setting seen as the most restrictive option (Sands, Kozleski, & French, 2000). Other service delivery options include itinerant services, resource room services, special class services, and special school services. The selection of the appropriate service delivery option is based on the needs of the child as designed in the IEP. The IEP should always control the decision regarding placement, not the availability or ability to provide the placement options. In other words, placement decisions are to be made *after* the development of a child's IEP

Often, parents have preconceptions concerning the appropriate educational placement for their children. Sometimes this placement is appropriate, whereas at other times, it might be inappropriate. Parents may not have knowledge of the various placement options or understand which placement option would be more appropriate. Parental beliefs and wishes may prevent them from accepting one placement as more appropriate than another option. Regardless, parents have the right to express their opinions and school personnel should attentively listen. Because parents know their child differently than school personnel, the IEP team should strongly consider parental views related to placement.

TEACHER TIP 8.7

Show a sincere interest in the child. Listen to parents. Sometimes parents need to talk. Being a good listener and empathizing will help establish trust. Work to avoid conflict.

During the past several years, the trend in placement decisions has focused on inclusive settings. Inclusion does not mean that every child must be placed in the general education classroom, but it does suggest that all children belong with their nondisabled peers as much as possible. From this perspective, students may be pulled out of classes from time to time for specialized instruction and services, but

Table 8.3 Areas of expectation for children.

Responsibility—Teachers and family members want their children to develop a sense of responsibility.

Independence—Teachers and family members want their children to develop a sense of independence.

Self-management—Teachers and family members want their children to become self-managers.

Self-determination—Teachers and family members want their children to be able to engage in self-determination activities.

Academic Success—Teachers and family members want their children to achieve as high academically as possible.

Social Success—Teachers and family members want their children to be as socially successful as other children.

---

they remain with their nondisabled peers as much as possible. This concept is aligned with the legal requirements of the least restrictive environment (LRE) and the provision of opportunities to participate within the general education curriculum.

Some parents like inclusive placements for their child, but others may have strong reservations (Duhaney & Salend, 2000). Parents may want their children in schools and in classrooms where certain expectations are present. They may have heard that expectations for students placed in certain special education settings are not very high. Teacher expectations could include responsibility and independence, academic and functional literacy, and supportive environments (Lange, Ysseldyke, & Lehr, 1997). Table 8.3 further describes each of these possible areas of expectations.

Parent-School Disagreements

Even though schools and families may try to work together to provide the best possible program and placement decisions for their child with a disability, disagreements do occur. "Conflict is a part of the human condition and is inevitable" (Lake & Billingsley, 2000, p. 241). IDEA provides a two-part process for parents and schools to meet and try to resolve their disputes (Murdick, Gartin, & Crabtree, 2002). Courses of action include mediation, resolution meeting, and due process hearing. These actions were discussed in Chapter 7.

Although conflict may be inevitable, schools should be proactive in avoiding conflict. Lake and Billingsley (2000) identify seven factors that frequently either escalate or de-escalate conflict between schools and parents. A summary of these factors is presented in Table 8.4.

Collaboration

School and
Community
Involvement

Mediation Mediation is a process in which the parents and school representatives meet with a trained, impartial party known as a mediator. At that time both the parents

Table 8.4 Factors causing escalation of conflict.

1. *Discrepant views of the child or the child's needs.* According to Lake and Billingsley's research (2000), parents were concerned that school personnel focused on their child's weaknesses, that is, viewing their child from a deficit perspective.

2. *Parent knowledge.* Professionals believe that one of the escalators of conflict was the "lack of problem-solving knowledge and lack of strategies for communication among school officials and parents" (Lake & Billingsley, p. 245). Parents often feel that when conflicts arise they do not have sufficient knowledge to discuss the problems at a mediation session.

3. *Parents concerned that school personnel seemed to lack knowledge about service delivery and quality of services.* Often parents saw this as indication that there was something wrong with the way their child's services were being delivered, thus escalating the possibility of conflicts instead of collaboration.

4. *Financial constraints on the district.* As a result of schools not being able to use lack of finances as a valid reason for not providing services, school personnel may end meetings early before parent issues can be addressed or the parents are made to feel guilty that their child needs expensive services to the detriment of other children in the school.

5. *Valuation.* What we value as important is where we focus our attention and funds. Parents often feel that they are devalued in the family-school partnership and that their children are also devalued within the school system. In such cases parents may feel upset because they perceive devaluation of their child and as a result may not discuss issues with the school until a conflict arises.

6. *Reciprocal power.* Both parents and school personnel have a power base and use it in what Lake and Billingsley call "interactive power play." This is a form of power base reciprocity wherein as each person escalates their response to a perceived power play, the other interacts and increases the escalation. The use of power plays is very detrimental to all parties involved because "regardless of how the dynamics of power played out in individual cases, parents, school officials, and mediators recognized the human costs of the consequences of such conflicts and uses of power" (Lake & Billingsley, 2000, p. 248).

7. *Communication.* These issues include the frequency of communication, the lack of communication, the lack of follow-up communication, misunderstood communication, and the timing of attempts to clarify communication. Parents noted that communication was hampered when too many people were in the meetings or when they felt as if their feelings and comments were ignored (Lake & Billingsley, 2000).

and the school describe their concerns and the resolution or resolutions that they would like. Through a process of "facilitated negotiation" (Riskin, 1996), the parents and school, with the assistance of the mediator, "seek a mutually satisfying resolution to the problem" (Center for the Study of Dispute Resolution, 1996, p. 6).

The role of the parents during the mediation process is to prepare a clear description of the issue or issues they have with the evaluation, program, or placement of their child. Parents should also prepare in advance a list of options upon which they could agree and be prepared to negotiate in order to reach a feasible solution. The role of school personnel is the same.

TEACHER TIP 8.8

Too often, due process hearings intensify negative feelings among parents and school personnel. Hearings are also stressful and time-consuming. Mediation is often a viable option.

Due Process Hearing   If the parent-school disagreement cannot be resolved either partially or completely by the mediation process, then a due process hearing is an option. The goal of the due process hearing is to provide a legal forum for the parents and the school to present their disagreements to a nonbiased hearing officer or panel of hearing officers. From the hearing a ruling is made that is legally binding on both parties unless they choose to appeal to the court system.

PRAXIS 2

Legal and Societal Issues

Resolution Session   Prior to the opportunity for a due process hearing, the school district must convene a resolution meeting with parents and relevant members of the IEP team. The purpose of this session is to attempt to resolve the dispute prior to a due process hearing. If both parties agree in writing to waive this meeting, then it will not be held. The meeting should be scheduled within 15 days of the school's receipt of the complaint. The school may not have an attorney present unless the parents have an attorney. If a resolution is reached, the agreement becomes a legally binding written document, signed by both parties. Either party can void the agreement within 3 days of its development.

Because the due process hearing is a more adversarial process, parents who have requested a hearing should hire an attorney who is knowledgeable in special education law to represent them. The parents should be prepared to describe their issues, provide basic support information and documentation, provide a timeline of events leading up to the hearing, and identify the decision they would like the hearing officer to make. As Murdick et al. (2002, p. 173) state, ". . . it often is in the best interest of all involved to avoid these adversarial situations. School districts and parents can avoid disputes by focusing on the child and his/her needs." Participating in mediation may eliminate the need for the due process hearing.

STRATEGIES TO INCREASE PARENTAL PARTICIPATION

Despite the requirement that parents are to participate in the development of their child's IFSP, IEP, or ITP, and the commonsense acceptance that parental participation can result in improved programming, too often parental involvement is either limited or nonexistent. The National Council on Disability (1995) reports that:

> in spite of provisions mandating parent participation in decision making, parents in many parts of the country still feel largely left out of the process. Many parents reported that they arrived at the IEP planning meetings only to be presented with a completed plan. (p. 11)

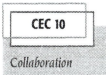

CEC 10

Collaboration

A study by Ryndak, Downing, Morrison, and Williams (1996) concludes that:

> . . the overall unhappiness and frustration that parents expressed about the process used to decide the location in which their child would receive services suggests that parents are not valued members of their child's education team, or that school districts are not sufficiently open to discussing the pros and cons of services in various types of settings. (p. 116)

Many parents are reluctant to participate in the IEP process. Regardless of why some parents are reluctant to participate, school personnel should encourage parental participation because parents represent an incredible source of untapped information about children being served in special education (Harry, Allen, & McLaughlin, 1995).

There are numerous strategies for enhancing parental participation in the education process of their child. Lytle and Bordin (2001) suggest the following when enhancing parental participation during the IEP process:

- Inform parents before the meeting about their local family resource center.
- Provide information about parent groups, both national and local.
- Facilitate parents talking to other parents of students with disabilities.
- Invite parents to spend time in the classroom.
- Make home visits.
- Value what parents have to say.
- Ask parents about some of their needs.
- Keep the number of professionals at the meeting as low as possible.

Many of the strategies described above can dramatically increase parental participation in every phase of the special education process, as well as other school activities. However, despite school efforts to engage parents in educational programs for their children, there will likely be situations where parent participation in IEP development will remain low (Dabkowski, 2004).

When these barriers are present, school personnel must go beyond the typical methods used to increase parental participation. School personnel must attempt to devise methods that will result in more participation by parents. Without parental participation, the ability of schools to meet the needs of children, especially those with disabilities, will be significantly restricted (Smith et al., 2004).

TEACHER TIP 8.9

Arrange for transportation to meetings. Hold meetings in family-friendly locations. Never assume parents have information or skills; instead, be eager and willing to share information in a respectful, nonthreatening manner. Avoid jargon. Have interpreters at meetings when necessary (Parette & Petch-Hogan, 2000).

Sometimes parents face significant problems in their lives that make it very difficult for them to participate in school collaboration (Thompson et al., 1997). Dealing with personal problems may result in parents not having the energy or time to devote to school-related activities. When parents experience these kinds of problems, school social workers or other staff may consider making referrals to appropriate agencies that could provide assistance to families. For example, referrals may be appropriate when parents experience stress due to finances, employment, or domestic issues; when parents are homeless or living in extreme poverty conditions; or when parents are unavailable for long periods of time. School personnel should attempt to ascertain which, if any, of the previously discussed issues are limiting family-school partnerships. Once these have been identified, strategies to circumvent them can be developed and implemented, with the end result hopefully being greater collaboration.

Although there are several different characteristics of successful family-school partnerships, a key feature is that special education programs are "family friendly" (Singh et al., 1997). Family friendly is a commonly used phrase that may mean different things to different people. What might be family friendly to one family may not be family friendly to another. More importantly, just because professionals consider their actions to be family friendly does not mean that families perceive them that way. In order to be truly family friendly, the family must consider the program accessible and supportive; they must feel like schools genuinely want their involvement.

To be family friendly, school personnel must try to understand the position of the parents. They need to try to see things from the family's perspective. Imagine yourself in a doctor's office waiting to receive the results of a comprehensive medical exam for your child who is suspected of having a serious illness. Now, how do you feel while you are sitting around the table with eight medical specialists as they explain their diagnoses and treatment suggestions in their professional terminology? What could these professionals do that might make you feel at ease and that your ideas are credible, important, and even desired? Many parents feel the same sense of incompetence or intimidation when they are listening to school staff discuss educational problems of their children. School staff need to keep this in mind when trying to make their meetings "family friendly." Always remember to put yourself in the position of the parent. It may help reveal ways to make parents feel more at ease and become more involved.

School personnel need to remember that involving families in one component of educational programs can result in increased involvement in other areas. Kay and Fitzgerald (1997) suggest that participation of family members in action research with teachers often leads to their increased participation in other school activities. Teachers can easily involve parents in such activities by having them complete take-home surveys, observe children in the home setting doing specific activities, or collecting simple data related to specific tasks. Many parents just need to be asked to participate. Regardless of the success of intervention programs for students with disabilities, the participation of families is critical to ensure the comprehensiveness of the programs (Kutash & Duchnowski, 1997). The National Agenda for Achieving Better Outcomes for Children and Youth with Serious Emotional Disturbance notes that collaboration between professionals and families is essential for effective educational programs (Kauffman, 1997). Although intervention programs will likely assist students in achieving their IEP goals and objectives, the likelihood that programs will be

CEC 9

Professional and Ethical Practice

Table 8.5   Tips to facilitate parent-teacher collaborations.

- Talk with and treat parents as equals.
- Use terms that parents understand.
- Believe that parents are equal partners in the educational processes of their child, actually they are the senior partners.
- Believe in the uniqueness of each family, but avoid expectations based on race, gender, socioeconomic, or any other characteristic.
- Remember that family members care about their child and their child's education.
- Solicit information from parents that will help in developing and implementing programs.
- Ask parents for their opinions about their child's problems and needs.
- Ask parents what they want for their child.
- Ask parents to help carry out aspects of the child's program at home.
- Arrange for a home visit if families are willing.
- If the family is a non-English-speaking family, have an interpreter present.

better developed and implemented with parental support is strong. School personnel must develop strategies to encourage and reinforce parental involvement.

Felber (1997) suggests several strategies that can result in the development of strengthening partnerships between school and parents. These include:

1. Let parents know that you celebrate their child's individuality.
2. Put yourself in the shoes of the parents of a child with a disability.
3. Provide parents with information about their child's disability.
4. Talk with parents, not at them.
5. Avoid stereotyping students and their families.
6. Reach out to parents to establish and maintain effective communication with them.
7. Warn parents about the media's portrayal of children with disabilities.

Additional examples of ways to facilitate parent-teacher collaborations are listed in Table 8.5.

School personnel must remember that simply inviting parents to participate may meet legal requirements, but additional actions should be taken to secure active participation and meaningful family-school collaboration. Parents are a wonderful source of information and support that can greatly facilitate students with disabilities achieving success in their educational programs. As a result, school personnel need to be creative and willing to go well beyond legal requirements to secure parental participation in the special education process.

SUMMARY

This chapter has focused on how families and school personnel can work together during the special education process. Reasons for involving parents in the education of children with disabilities were discussed and it was noted that without parental participation, the abilities of school personnel to meet the needs of students with disabilities are restricted. Children with disabilities benefit a great deal, in many different ways, when their parents and school personnel collaborate. Specific IDEA requirements for schools during the special education process including referral, assessment, IEP development, and placement issues were described. IDEA legal requirements and ways to implement them were discussed. Finally, the benefits of parental participation were emphasized.

QUESTIONS FOR DISCUSSION

1. The special education process requires that families are involved in a wide variety of decisions about their child. What are some of the reasons parents give for not wanting to be involved? Should schools leave these parents alone and make decisions about the education of children without parental involvement, or go to great lengths to secure such involvement? Why do you believe this?

2. Of all the steps in the special education process that parents are involved (e.g. referral, evaluation, eligibility determination, IEP development, etc.,) which do you think is the most important and why?

3. Getting parents to become more involved in the special education process can be a major challenge for school personnel. Describe some examples of why parents do not want to be involved and specific actions school personnel can take to gain more involvement. When do you think "enough is enough" in your efforts to gain parental involvement? When do you just say "they don't want to be involved so we'll just leave them out of it"? Is it all right, at any time, to give up on parental involvemnt? Why of why not?

REFERENCES

Alberto, P. A., & Troutman, A. C. (2003). *Applied behavior analysis for teachers* (6th ed.). Upper Saddle River, NJ: Prentice Hall.

Becker-Cottrill, B., McFarland, J., & Anderson, V. (2003). A model of positive behavioral support for individuals with autism and their families: The family focus process. *Focus on Autism and Other Developmental Disabilities*, 18, 113–123.

Bruder, M. B. (2000). The individualized family service plan (IFSP). ERIC EC Digest #E605. Retrieved May 26, 2003, from http://ericec.org.

Center for the Study of Dispute Resolution. (1996). *Missouri department of elementary & secondary education: Basic mediation skills training*. Columbia, MO: University of Missouri-Columbia School of Law.

Dabkowski, D. M. (2004). Encouraging active parent participation in IEP team meetings. *Teaching Exceptional Children*, 36, 34–39.

Dowdy, C. A., Patton, J. R., Smith, T. E. C., & Polloway, E. A. (1998). *Attention-deficit/hyperactivity disorder*. Austin, TX: Pro-Ed.

Duhaney, L. M. G., & Salend, J. S. (2000). Parental perceptions of inclusive educational placements. *Remedial and Special Education*, 21, 121–128.

Dunlap, G., Newton, J. S., Fox, L., Benito, N., & Vaughn, B. (2001). Family involvement in functional assessment and positive behavior support. *Focus on Autism and Other Developmental Disabilities*, 16, 215–221.

Felber, S. A. (1997). Strategies for parent partnerships. *Teaching Exceptional Children*, 30, 20–23.

Fox, L., Vaughn, J., Wyatte, M. L., & Dunlap, G. (2002). We can't expect other people to understand: Family perspectives on problem behavior. *Exceptional Children*, 68, 437–450.

Guy, B., Goldberg, M., McDonald, S., & Flom, R. A. (1997). Parental participation in transition systems. *Career Development for Exceptional Individuals*, 20, 165–177

Harry, B., Allen, N., & McLaughlin, M. (1995). Communication versus compliance: African-American parents' involvement in special education. *Exceptional Children*, 61, 364–377.

Hutchins, M. P., & Renzaglia, A. (1998). Interviewing families for effective transition to employment. *Teaching Exceptional Children*, 30, 72–78.

Hutinger, P. L. (1996). Computer applications in programs for young children with disabilities: Recurring themes. *Focus on Autism and Other Developmental Disabilities*, 11, 105–114.

Jayanthi, M., Bursuck, W., Epstein, M. H., & Polloway, E. A. (1997). Strategies for successful homework. *Teaching Exceptional Children*, 30, 4–7

Kauffman, J. W. (1997). Conclusion: A little of everything, a lot of nothing is an agenda for the future. *Journal of Emotional and Behavioral Disorders*, 5, 76–81

Kay, P. J., & Fitzgerald, M. (1997). Parents + teachers + action research = real involvement. *Teaching Exceptional Children*, 30, 8–12.

Kutash, K., & Duchnowski, A. J. (1997). Create comprehensive and collaborative systems. *Journal of Emotional and Behavioral Disorders*, 5, 66–75.

Lake, J., & Billingsley, B. (2000). An analysis of factors that contribute to parent-school conflict in special education. *Remedial and Special Education*, 21, 240–251

Lange, C. M., Ysseldyke, J. E., & Lehr, C. A. (1997). School choice and students with disabilities: Parent perspectives and expectations. *Teaching Exceptional Children*, 30, 14–19.

Lytle, R. K., & Bordin, J. (2001). Enhancing the IEP team: Strategies for parents and professionals. *Teaching Exceptional Children*, 33, 40–44.

Murdick, N. L., Gartin, B. C., & Crabtree, T. (2002). *Special education law*. Upper Saddle River, NJ: Merrill/Prentice Hall.

Murdick, N. L., & Petch-Hogan, B. (1996) Inclusive classroom management: Using preintervention strategies. *Intervention in School and Clinic*, 31(3), 172–176.

Nassar-McMillan, S., & Algozzine, B. (2001). Improving outcomes and future pratices: Family-centered programs and services. In D. J. O'Shea, L. J. O'Shea, R. Algozine, & D. J. Hammitte (Eds.), *Families and teachers of individuals with disabilities* (pp. 273–292). Boston: Allyn & Bacon.

National Center on Secondary Education and Transition (NCSET). (2002). Summarizing recent laws and regulations. *Policy Update*, 1, 1–8.

National Council on Disability. (1995). *Improving the implementation of the Individuals with Disabilities Education Act: Making schools work for all of America's children*. Washington, DC: U.S. Government Printing Office.

National Information Center for Children and Youth with Disabilities. (2003). Creating the transition plan. *The Inclusion Notebook*, 5, 5–8.

Parette, H. P., & Petch-Hogan, B. (2000). Approaching families. *Teaching Exceptional Children*, 34, 4–9.

Riskin, L. L. (1996). *Draft: Mediation training guide*. Columbia, MO: Center for the Study of Dispute Resolution.

Ryndak, D. L., Downing, J. E., Morrison, A. P., & Williams, L. J. (1996). Parents' perceptions of educational settings and services for children with moderate or severe disabilities. *Remedial and Special Education*, 17, 106–118.

Sands, D. J., Kozleski, E. B., & French, N. K. (2000). *Inclusive education for the 21st century*. Belmont, CA: Wadsworth/Thomson Learning.

Shea, T. M., & Bauer, A. M. (1991). *Parents and teachers of children with disabilities*. Boston: Allyn & Bacon.

Singh, N. N., Curtis, W. J., Wechsler, H. A., Ellis, C. R., & Cohen, R. (1997). Family friendliness of community-based services for children and adolescents with emotional and behavioral disorders and their families: An observational study. *Journal of Emotional and Behavioral Disorders*, 5, 82–91.

Smith. T. E. C., Polloway, E. A., Patton, J. R., & Dowdy, C. A. (2004). *Teaching students with special needs in inclusive settings* (4th ed.). Boston: Allyn & Bacon.

Thompson, L., Lobb, C., Elling, R., Herman, S., Jurkiewicz, T., & Hulleza, C. (1997). Pathways to family empowerment: Effects of family-centered delivery of early intervention services. *Exceptional Children*, 64, 99–113

Westling, D. L. (1997). What parents of young children with mental disabilities want: The views of one community. *Focus on Autism and Other Developmental Disabilities*, 12, 67–78.

Will, M. (1984). Let us pause and reflect—but not too long. *Exceptional Children*, 51, 11–16.

Witt, J., Elliott, S., Daly III, E., Gresham, F., & Kramer, J. (1998). *Assessment of at-risk and special needs children* (2nd ed.). Boston: McGraw-Hill.

CHAPTER 9
Working with Families: Ethical and Confidential Considerations

Objectives

After reading this chapter, you will:

- Know the meaning of the terms *ethical* and *confidential* as they apply to working with families
- Understand how ethics impacts education
- Know the basic elements of the codes of ethics of the major teacher organizations

- Understand how ethics affects behavior management programs
- Understand the relationship between ethics and assessment
- Understand the importance of confidentiality
- Know the legal issues impacting confidentiality
- Have a basic understanding of FERPA
- Know strategies that can facilitate confidentiality

The terms *ethical* and *confidential* are terms used when working with children with disabilities and their families. Ethical is from the stem word *ethics*. Ethics is defined as (1) the study and philosophy of human conduct, with emphasis on the determination of right and wrong, (2) the basic principles of right actions, or (3) a work or treatise on morals (*Funk & Wagnalls*, 1997, p. 436). In other words, ". . . ethics is the awareness of what we believe and how we justify our actions" (Gartin & Murdick, 2000, p. 1). Confidential, on the other hand, is defined as (1) a secret or private relationship with someone, (2) a confidence that is a secret such as "confidential information," or (3) a disposition to confide in another (*Funk & Wagnalls*, 1997, p. 274).

Why should educators be concerned about ethical and confidential considerations? A review of these two concepts will provide a basis for working with children with special needs and their families in a confidential, ethical, and professional manner.

ETHICAL CONSIDERATIONS

CEC 9

Professional and Ethical Practice

Ethics is the study of *good* and *bad*, *right* and *wrong*. Currently, in the wake of escalating school violence incidents, teaching children to be "good" is a growing consideration. The introduction of character education to the curriculum, something that would have met with considerable resistance just a few years ago, is increasing. Because children often learn more about ethical behavior by observing the adults in their environment than through posters, slogans, or direct instruction, the way professionals act has taken on more significant meaning (Jones, 1998).

Teachers and other school personnel make judgements on a daily basis. These judgments may impact on students in a classroom, colleagues, school administrators, family members of students, or community members. The range of these judgments varies from deciding what disciplinary measure to use with a student to deciding when and what to tell parents about a student's behavior. Other examples of daily judgments made by school personnel include the following:

- Deciding to send a student to the office for inappropriate behaviors
- Making a determination about passing or failing a student's homework that is near the failure cutoff
- Sending a note home to parents concerning their child
- Ignoring the inappropriate behavior of students
- Deciding to call a new IEP committee meeting, even though it is in the middle of the year, because the student's current IEP is not working and the student likely needs additional services

Judgments such as these have a direct impact on students and their families. When judgments are made that affect people, they reflect the ethics of the individual making those decisions. The values and beliefs of an individual are virtually impossible to exclude from decisions made by that individual. School personnel should learn to identify personal biases that are based on personal beliefs. If they do not do this, then the bias may go unrecognized and impact decision making in all areas of educational programming. This connection of personal beliefs with unidentified biases means that school personnel should ensure that unrecognized bias does not enter into decisions made about students and their families. Some questions that should help focus school personnel on these issues include:

- Who should have the ultimate control over a child's educational program?
- What should I tell parents about their child's performance?
- How much involvement should parents have in developing and implementing children's educational programs?
- Who should have the final say in where a child with a disability is educated?

Read the scenarios in Box 9.1. What biases may have been involved in each of the decisions made? Could self-recognition of those biases have positively affected the decisions?

Box 9.1

Scenario #1

Mr. Jacobson came into his fifth-grade classroom and saw 10 students running around the room throwing paper wads at each other. He immediately asked that Frank, Alex, and Jerry go to the office. Frank, Alex, and Jerry were all African American students. Mr. Jacobson assumed they were the ringleaders of the misbehavior. He assumed the other boys, all Caucasian, were simply following their lead.

Scenario #2

Ms. Jenkins believed that Linda was not trying to learn. She thought that all Linda wanted to do was sit in her chair and doodle, or stare out of the window and daydream. No doubt her parents didn't care much about her; they consistently sent her to school with dirty clothes and a dirty face. Obviously no one in the family cared or valued education.

Scenario #3

Mr. Bates, the elementary school principal, was tired of being stood up by Jimmy Wilson's mother. He had set up three parent conferences during the last 3 weeks, and Ms. Wilson had not bothered to come or even call. Of course, Mr. Bates was pretty sure that Jimmy, his mother, and two sisters lived in a car. Rumor had it that they were homeless. Just what Mr. Bates needed, a family without a great deal of motivation to work and make ends meet. Well, he guessed he would just have to be a little more assertive in the way he dealt with Jimmy. A suspension was probably going to be the next move for him to take.

TEACHER TIP 9.1

Make sure you acknowledge, to yourself, if you have a personal bias against certain children. Recognizing personal prejudices will help you make decisions that are not impacted by the bias.

Ethics is present in all facets of life. A person's ethics affects his or her choices, relationships, behaviors, and judgments. There are several basic ethical principles that help guide the decision making and behaviors of all individuals, including teachers, parents, and students. Kitchner (1984) includes:

- Autonomy. Freedom of action and freedom of choice, including the responsibility to treat others in the same manner.
- Non-malfeasance. Not intentionally hurting or harming others.
- Beneficence. Helping others; doing kind things for others.
- Justice. Treating all individuals alike, or having justification for treating some different.
- Fidelity. Promise keeping, faithfulness, keeping one's word.

Sergiovanni (1992) suggested four additional principles of ethics. These include:

1. Relationships with other people create obligations of various kinds, and these should be honored unless there is a compelling reason not to do so.
2. Certain ideals enhance human life and assist people in fulfilling their obligations to one another.
3. The consequence of some actions benefit people, whereas those of other actions harm people.
4. Circumstances alter cases. (p. 110)

Professional Codes and Standards of Professional Practice

Ethical standards are a component of any profession, including that of lawyers, physicians, psychologists, social workers, and accountants. Most professions adopt and adhere to a professional code of conduct (also known as a code of ethics) that governs the behaviors of individuals in their specific profession. For example, in 1999 the American Educational Research Association (AERA), the American Psychological Association (APA), and the National Council on Measurement in Education (NCME) jointly developed a set of standards for educational psychological testing. These standards were to provide individuals engaged in the assessment of individuals with disabilities a document to guide their practice in an ethical manner. For the same reasons, the National Education Association (NEA), the largest teacher organization in the United States, adopted its Code of Ethics in 1975. This code, depicted in Table 9.1, focuses on two principles: commitment to the student and commitment to the profession. Although a code of ethics provides members of a profession with guidelines for behaviors, these are generally set forth only in broad generalities.

CEC 9

Professional and
Ethical Practice

Table 9.1 NEA Code of Ethics.

Code of Ethics of the Education Profession Preamble

The educator, believing in the worth and dignity of each human being, recognizes the supreme importance of the pursuit of truth, devotion to excellence, and the nurture of the democratic principles. Essential to these goals is the protection of freedom to learn and to teach and the guarantee of equal educational opportunity for all. The educator accepts the responsibility to adhere to the highest ethical standards.

The educator recognizes the magnitude of the responsibility inherent in the teaching process. The desire for the respect and confidence of one's colleagues, of students, of parents, and of the members of the community provides the incentive to attain and maintain the highest possible degree of ethical conduct. The Code of Ethics of the Education Profession indicates the aspiration of all educators and provides standards by which to judge conduct.

The remedies specified by the NEA and/or its affiliates for the violation of any provision of this Code shall be exclusive and no such provision shall be enforceable in any form other than the one specifically designated by the NEA or its affiliates.

PRINCIPLE I: Commitment to the Student

The educator strives to help each student realize his or her potential as a worthy and effective member of society. The educator therefore works to stimulate the spirit of inquiry, the acquisition of knowledge and understanding, and the thoughtful formulation of worthy goals.

In fulfillment of the obligation to the student, the educator—

1. Shall not unreasonably restrain the student from independent action in the pursuit of learning.
2. Shall not unreasonably deny the student's access to varying points of view.
3. Shall not deliberately suppress or distort subject matter relevant to the student's progress.
4. Shall make reasonable effort to protect the student from conditions harmful to learning or to health and safety.
5. Shall not intentionally expose the student to embarrassment or disparagement.
6. Shall not on the basis of race, color, creed, sex, national origin, marital status, political or religious beliefs, family, social or cultural background, or sexual orientation, unfairly—
   a. Exclude any student from participation in any program
   b. Deny benefits to any student
   c. Grant any advantage to any student
7. Shall not use professional relationships with students for private advantage.
8. Shall not disclose information about students obtained in the course of professional service unless disclosure serves a compelling professional purpose or is required by law.

(continued)

Table 9.1 *Continued*

PRINCIPLE II: Commitment to the Profession

The education profession is vested by the public with a trust and responsibility requiring the highest ideals of professional service.

In the belief that the quality of the services of the education profession directly influences the nation and its citizens, the educator shall exert every effort to raise professional standards, to promote a climate that encourages the exercise of professional judgment, to achieve conditions that attract persons worthy of the trust to careers in education, and to assist in preventing the practice of the profession by unqualified persons.

In fulfillment of the obligation to the profession, the educator—

1. Shall not in an application for a professional position deliberately make a false statement or fail to disclose a material fact related to competency and qualifications.

2. Shall not misrepresent his/her professional qualifications.

3. Shall not assist any entry into the profession of a person known to be unqualified in respect to character, education, or other relevant attribute.

4. Shall not knowingly make a false statement concerning the qualifications of a candidate for a professional position.

5. Shall not assist a noneducator in the unauthorized practice of teaching.

6. Shall not disclose information about colleagues obtained in the course of professional service unless disclosure serves a compelling professional purpose or is required by law.

7. Shall not knowingly make false or malicious statements about a colleague.

8. Shall not accept any gratuity, gift, or favor that might impair or appear to influence professional decisions or action.

Note: Adopted by the NEA 1975 Representative Assembly.

Another professional group, the National Association on the Education of Young Children (NAEYC), focuses on children and their families and has also developed a code of ethics or conduct. The NAEYC notes that its standards of ethical behavior are based on their commitments:

- Appreciating childhood as a unique and valuable stage of the human life cycle
- Basing our work with children on knowledge of child development
- Appreciating and supporting the close ties between the child and family
- Recognizing that children are best understood in the context of family, culture, and society
- Respecting the dignity, worth, and uniqueness of each individual (child, family member, and colleague)
- Helping children and adults achieve their full potential in the context of relationships that are based on trust, respect, and positive regard (p. 25)

The NAEYC Code of Ethical Conduct includes four major sections. Section I focuses on ethical responsibilities to children; Section II deals with ethical responsibilities to families; Section III deals with ethical responsibilities to colleagues; and Section IV targets ethical responsibilities to community and society. The fact that one of these four sections emphasizes professional ethical responsibilities to families reveals the importance of families in the education of young children. Section XI of the NAEYC Code of Ethical Conduct includes attention to ideals and principles. For a full version of the NAEYC Code of Ethics, go to its web page at **naeyc.org**.

Many professions expand their code of ethics or conduct into standards for professional practice. Special educators, through their professional organization, the Council for Exceptional Children (CEC), have a code of ethics that focuses on a wide variety of issues related to providing services to children with disabilities (CEC, 2003; FACT, 2003). (See Table 9.2.) The CEC Code of Ethics has been expanded to include a set of performance standards for teachers in the field of special education. These standards focus on the areas of how professionals relate to people with disabilities, their families, and professional employment. See the appendix for the CEC Standards for Professional Practice and note where families and parents have been emphasized (Hanson & Lynch, 1989). As you can see, there are numerous references to parents and families. This reflects the importance of professionals interacting and collaborating with parents and family members when providing services to students with

Table 9.2 CEC Code of Ethics for educators of persons with exceptionalities.

We declare the following principles to be the Code of Ethics for educators of persons with exceptionalities. Members of the special education profession are responsible for upholding and advancing these principles. Members of the Council for Exceptional Children agree to judge and be judged by them in accordance with the spirit and provisions of this Code.

a. Special education professionals are committed to developing the highest educational and quality of life potential of individuals with exceptionalities.

b. Special education professionals promote and maintain a high level of competence and integrity in practicing their profession.

c. Special education professionals engage in professional activities that benefit individuals with exceptionalities, their families, other colleagues, students, or research subjects.

d. Special education professionals exercise objective professional judgment in the practice of their profession.

e. Special education professionals strive to advance their knowledge and skills regarding the education of individuals with exceptionalities.

f. Special education professionals work within the standards and policies of their profession.

g. Special education professionals seek to uphold and improve where necessary the laws, regulations, and policies governing the delivery of special education and related services and the practice of their profession.

h. Special education professionals do not condone or participate in unethical or illegal acts, nor violate professional standards adopted by the Delegate Assembly of CEC.

Note: From *CEC Code of Ethics and Professional Standards* (p. 1), by Council for Exceptional Children, 2003.

special needs. The Code of Ethics underscore the ethical considerations of involving family members. These codes of ethics provide a basis for decision making and actions and help guide individuals in that profession in their interactions with their clientele and with each other. Even though these codes of ethics provide useful directions, there are gaps and even contradictions in many ethical codes. As a result, professionals must have some personal ethical base or basic principles to guide their own individual behaviors, in addition to a general code of ethics (Stanard & Hazler, 1995).

TEACHER TIP 9.2

Make an effort to know the contents of your professional Code of Ethics. If you teach young children, read those of the NAEYC. If you teach students with disabilities, read the CEC Code of Ethics. In your daily professional practice, try to implement the intent of your professional code of ethics.

CEC 9

Professional and Ethical Practice

Whether a part of the curriculum or not, the concept and application of ethics, that is, ethical considerations or ethical behavior, can be found in many different areas of our schools. Morrison (1997) noted the following ways that ethics is found in schools:

- The relationship between teachers and students, colleagues, and parents.
- The manner in which teachers practice their profession.
- The personal choices and classroom behaviors made by teachers.
- The manner in which personal ethics and professional ethics affect educators.

Teachers, though, are not the only educators who should address ethical considerations of their actions. School administrators face significant ethical issues in the management of schools. Rebore (1998) suggests that in the area of personnel management, administrators have responsibilities in three major areas: (1) the school district and its staff, (2) the school personnel profession, and (3) personal responsibilities. The first focuses on concerns related to supporting school staff in achieving their goals and the goals of the district. For example, school administrators have a responsibility to support and implement school policies and support school staff. Related to responsibilities to the school personnel profession, Rebore (1998) suggests that administrators have the responsibility to promote membership in such organizations and professional development activities. Finally, in the third area, personal responsibilities, school administrators have the responsibility to seek consultation from others, when necessary, and exhibit personal characteristics like prudence and honesty and serve as models for others in the district. According to Rebore (2001), the behaviors of a school administrator should follow the code of ethics put forth by the American Association of School Administrators (AASA) and "support the integrity and dignity of professional educators, the value of public education, the centrality of student welfare, and the importance of educational opportunity" (p. 131).

Although there are general ethical standards that teachers and administrators must consider when working with students with special needs and their families, there are also standards associated with specific practices used by professionals. For example, issues arising from the use of the behavior management intervention model have resulted in calls for ethical considerations prior to its implementation. The following questions are proposed to help professionals focus on ethical issues involved in behavior management:

- Is a child free to make choices?
- Should a child be free to make choices?
- Does a child act in accordance with specific principles of behavior that are observable, measurable, and repetitive?
- Can a child's behavior be changed by external forces?
- Can an educator modify a child's behavior?
- Who shall determine whose and which behaviors are to be changed?
- Which interventions shall be applied in the classroom and school to change children's behavior?
- Who will legitimize and monitor the interventions being used to change the behavior of children?
- To what ends will the interventions be applied? (Walker & Shea, 1995, pp. 8–9)

Assessment is another area of special education that is frequently impacted by ethical issues and considerations. Assessing students with special needs often presents unique ethical and confidentiality issues for the evaluator and other individuals who have access to the assessment information. Areas that are related to ethical issues in assessment include: (1) selection of appropriate assessment instruments, (2) consideration of variables that could impact on assessment results, (3) determination with whom to share assessment results, and (4) decisions regarding the presentation of assessment results.

Although nondiscriminatory assessment is a requirement under IDEA (Smith, Polloway, Patton, & Dowdy, 2004), the actual implementation of the principle is difficult. It is, however, the ethical responsibility of individuals involved in the assessment process to utilize nondiscriminatory practices, even if it requires exceeding the minimum assessment requirements of IDEA (Schloss & Henley, 1994). For example, IDEA requires that schools test children in the language that will give most accurate results to ensure nondiscriminatory assessment. Some schools, lacking the services of interpreters for a specific language, might choose to meet this requirement by testing children in English. However, a better solution might be to ensure that test materials are available in the primary language and that language assistance is available. During the assessment meeting, the language factor should be given emphasis in the decision-making process. IDEA 2004 specifically notes that children should not be determined eligible for IDEA services if their problems are due to language issues.

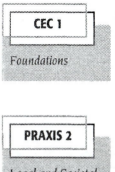

CEC 1

Foundations

PRAXIS 2

Legal and Societal Issues

TEACHER TIP 9.3

When you are involved in the assessment of a student and feel like discrimination has occurred, it is your responsibility to indicate this to the committee. Request a meeting with the assessment team to ensure adequate understanding of the evaluation and to protect the child from possible discrimination.

PRAXIS 2

Legal and Societal Issues

INTASC 10

School and Community Involvement

When working with infants and toddlers with exceptionalities through Part C of IDEA, assessment is twofold with the focus both on the child and on the child's family. IDEA states that at a minimum an assessment under Part C should be "a timely, comprehensive, multidisciplinary evaluation of the functioning of each infant or toddler with a disability in the State, and a family-directed identification of the needs of each family of such an infant or toddler, to assist appropriately in the development of such infant or toddler" (IDEA 2004). Therefore, school personnel should avoid any semblance of discriminatory practices. The simple fact is that if assessment is discriminatory, then it is invalid and may not lead to the development of an appropriate Individualized Family Service Plan (IFSP). Therefore, discriminatory or inappropriate assessment practices could lead to intervention programs that would not meet the unique needs of the infant or toddler, and would therefore be a direct violation of the IDEA requirement that schools providing early intervention services provide "quality" early intervention services (IDEA, Sec. 631 [6]). Again, ethical practice demands knowledge of the law so that decisions can be made based on an accurate perception of what is right or wrong.

When working with families of students with disabilities, ethical concerns and considerations other than assessment also become apparent. Walker and Shea (1995) note that there are three ethical principles that should form the basis of educators in interactions with children and adults. These include the principle of normalization, the principle of fairness, and the principle of respect.

Using the principle of normalization, school personnel should try to ensure that students with special needs and their families have an opportunity to live as normal a life as possible. When interacting with families with students with special needs, school personnel should keep this principle in mind. Parents who have children with special needs not only want their children to have "normal" opportunities, but they also want school personnel to interact with them in the same manner as they interact with other parents.

INTASC 10

School and Community Involvement

The principle of fairness means fundamental fairness, or due process of law. This principle requires that school personnel involve students with special needs and their families in making decisions that will affect the educational programs. Providing notice and securing parental consent prior to implementing specific actions is not only required by law, but is also required as an ethical practice. Regardless of the legal requirement to involve family members of students with disabilities, school personnel can easily circumvent the intent of this requirement and only involve family members superficially. Shea and Bauer (1991) present examples of unfair and therefore unethical practices that include:

- Refusing to provide students with programs that they need
- Refusing to attempt to modify a student's behavior systematically
- Placing students in more restrictive settings without attempting classroom interventions first
- Refusing to seek assistance from specialists because school personnel do not want to be viewed as incompetent

---

TEACHER TIP 9.4

Make sure that you put the child's needs above other issues. If the administration objects to providing a service because it is expensive, but you firmly believe that the service is needed and appropriate, request more information concerning the issue. As a team member, your role is to ensure that information is available so that good decision making can occur. Continue to work toward understanding the needs of the student and a process for obtaining what is necessary to meet those needs. It is the professional and ethical action to take.

Teachers may occasionally find themselves with the dilemma of "doing what is right" or "doing what the administration wants them to do." For example, there may be situations where teachers think that a particular intervention for a child would be appropriate, but they also know that the intervention is expensive and the school may not want them to mention it to family members. As one teacher stated in a focus group on advocacy issues, "they tell you that you have to be careful what you say at a meeting because then the school district will have to pay for it" (Gartin, Murdick, Thompson, & Dyches, 2002, p. 10). Or, they may think that a child really needs special education services, but because the family does not give consent for testing, they are not able to provide such a service. In this situation, if the school does not pursue the issue through due process, then the child does not receive the services. These ethical dilemmas may result in "special educators [who] are often accountable to many bosses which can cause confusion and conflict" (CEC, 1998, p. 3). Read the scenario in Box 9.2. What would be the ethical thing for Ms. Brown to do in this situation? How could Ms. Brown do this and protect her job in the school district?

| CEC 9 |

Professional and Ethical Practice

The principle of respect should always be remembered when working with students and their families. Ways to interact respectfully with families are dependent on cultural norms (Harry, 1992). Here are some examples of ways to implement the principle of respect when interacting with family members:

- Referring to family members as Mr. or Mrs., unless the family member asks that you use first names.
- Referring to family members with their names, not as "Mom" or "Dad," or "Grandma" unless the culture uses a role as a title such as "Aunt" or "Uncle" as a sign of respect.
- Referring to the child with the child's name, not "the student."

Box 9.2

Scenario

Ms. Brown has been concerned with Angela's progress all year. Angela had been diagnosed with a learning disability and placed for 1 hour in a resource room each day. Ms. Brown was pretty sure that Angela had some emotional problems. She was in the seventh grade and was slipping further and further behind her peers. Also, her behavior was getting worse. Although many of her nondisabled peers were beginning to act out in typical teenager fashion, Angela's behaviors were different. She picked on kids smaller and weaker than her, taunted her other peers, and was beginning to get into a lot of fights. Last week, Ms. Brown found a note that Angela had written to her brother, who is currently in a juvenile detention center. In the note, Angela said that she was going to burn down the school and hurt some people. As a result of this note and her other concerns, Ms. Brown went to see Mr. Smith, the school principal. She told Mr. Smith that Angela was likely emotionally disturbed and needed to be in an ED classroom. Mr. Smith reminded Ms. Brown that the school did not have an ED classroom, or any teachers with training to teach children with emotional disturbance. Therefore, Angela could not be classified as having emotional disturbance. And, Mr. Smith noted that he was sure that Angela was just spouting off at the mouth and that she really would not do anything. He said she was probably just trying to get some attention.

- Encouraging and reinforcing input from family members.
- Giving family members an easy way to contact school personnel if they have questions or concerns.
- Making eye contact when interacting with family members.
- Using terminology that is understandable by family members.
- Making sure that family members understand what is being discussed about their child without directly asking questions such as "Do you understand what we are saying here?"
- Taking time to get acquainted with family members before starting the meeting.

These are just a few examples of ethical issues that often confront educators. Without a professional grounding based on a code of ethics with accompanying professional standards, educators may not consider the ramifications (or illegality) of their actions (or inactions) and may fail to meet the needs of children and their families.

TEACHER TIP 9.5

Always treat parents and other family members the way you would want to be treated if the roles were reversed. Remember a time when a loved one was extremely ill and you were meeting with people who used language that you didn't understand and seemed to "talk down" to you. Beware that you do not become one of those people. Respect parents' needs as well as the needs of the student.

CONFIDENTIAL CONSIDERATIONS

Confidential considerations should go hand in hand with ethical considerations of educational practice. Without understanding the importance of confidentiality, educators may actually display unethical behaviors that could result in significant harm to students and their families.

Confidentiality is an important element in many professions, especially those professions that deal with people. For example, according to Stanard and Hazler (1995, p. 397) "confidentiality is an essential component of counseling practice whose original intent was to promote full client disclosure and protect clients from stigmatizing." Similarly, confidentiality is an important component in any educational setting. When working with parents of children with special needs, it should be obvious to school personnel that confidentiality is critical. Parents are more likely to share personal information about their child and their family if they believe that the information will remain confidential and will not be accessible to a wide variety of individuals who do not need to have the information (Remley, Herlihy, & Herlihy, 1997). When parents do not believe that their confidences will be maintained, they will be less likely to share information that could be important in identifying and meeting the needs of a child with special needs. Turnbull, Turnbull, Shank, and Smith (2004) provide an excellent discussion of the need for confidentiality when a student has HIV or other health or medical conditions. In such a case, school personnel should not disclose that fact unless the student or the student's family gives permission or the school is compelled to do so by law. Because students with health impairments often feel helpless, discussing the condition without the student's knowledge or permission may increase the feelings of powerlessness. Therefore, teachers need to ask permission of the student before sharing health-related information (Fleitas, 2003).

In the area of school records, parents, other family members, and individuals with disabilities upon reaching the age of majority have both legal and ethical rights related to confidentiality (Culatta & Tompkins, 1999). These include the right to examine and copy records that the schools maintain, and the right to prevent access to those records to people who do not have a need to see them. The right to access school records that contain information about their children allows parents to hold school personnel accountable for their actions. When parents have the right to review school records, teachers and other school personnel are less likely to include unsubstantiated, unnecessary, and possibly biasing information in student records. Parents also can review the information about their child that the school has identified through assessment, and the programs that have been recommended for the child.

Information such as intelligence test scores, clinical diagnoses, and behavior patterns are examples of some materials found in student records that should not be available to all school personnel. Persons not directly involved in teaching a child have no need to have access to such information. Neither should school personnel have access to sensitive information about a family, such as the family's income or marital status, unless they are directly involved with referrals to other agencies for benefits or services for the child (Turnbull & Turnbull, 2000).

CEC 9

Professional and Ethical Practice

TEACHER TIP 9.6

Never share personal, identifiable, confidential information with individuals who do not have a need to know that particular piece of information. Remember that the information is to be shared only with those who are working directly with the student and only if they NEED to know it. Do not share it with the teachers of the child's siblings. Even if the information is "juicy," just don't do it. If others try to tell you something you do not have a need to know, politely excuse yourself from the conversation.

Legal Issues and Confidentiality

PRAXIS 2

Legal and Societal Issues

CEC 1

Foundations

Confidentiality is not only an ethical consideration and a professional responsibility, but it has legal bases as well. The Individuals with Disabilities Education Act (IDEA) includes the provision that states are eligible for federal funds if they comply with the components of the act, including compliance with confidentiality of student records (Turnbull & Turnbull, 2000). The regulations for Public Law 105–17, originally published in 1977, noted the following safeguards necessary to ensure the confidentiality of student records:

1. One administrative officer should be appointed to monitor the use of student records and to assume overall responsibility for protecting their confidentiality.
2. All persons collecting or using personally identifiable data should receive training regarding the confidentiality and use of student folders.
3. A record of the names and positions of all district professionals who have access to the personal data must be maintained.
4. The records must be made available for public inspection as required.

These safeguards have been included in every reauthorization of the act, including the most recent revision of IDEA in 2004. IDEA, therefore, mandates that the records of students served in special education programs are to be maintained with a strong emphasis on confidentiality. School personnel cannot have access to student information without a need-to-know basis, and family members should have access to all records the school maintains about their child (Lewis & Doorlag, 2003).

Family Educational Rights and Privacy Act (FERPA)   One of the most far-reaching federal acts that clarifies family rights and privacy issues is the Family Educational Rights and Privacy Act (FERPA), also known as the Buckley Amendment. FERPA was passed as part of Public Law 93–380 in 1974, three years before Public Law 94–142, now IDEA, was implemented. FERPA is an extremely strong privacy protection law that primarily gives parents, and children after they reach the age of 18, the right to review and determine the accuracy of any information in their student records (Policy Studies Associates, 1997). It also prohibits schools from releasing information found in a student's records to anyone without parental permission (or student if age 18 or older)

Table 9.3 Basic components of FERPA.

---

1. FERPA applies to public schools and state or local education agencies that receive federal funds.
2. FERPA protects paper and computerized records.
3. Noncompliance could result in loss of all federal education funds.
4. FERPA requires schools and local education agencies to have written policies regarding the release of student records.
5. Written policies should include procedures to explain parent rights under FERPA.
6. Written policies should define what qualifies as directory information (personal information that can be made public).
7. Written policies should explain how to correct erroneous information in records.
8. FERPA rights transfer to students when they reach the age of 18 (age of majority).

Note: From "Protecting the Privacy of Student Education Records," by Policy Studies Associate, 1997, *Journal of Student Health.*

(Surratt, Majestic, & Shelton, 1998). FERPA is very comprehensive. Table 9.3 summarizes the FERPA requirements.

As a result of this broad definition of education records, much of the information schools have on students is covered by FERPA and is, therefore, not accessible by individuals who do not need to know that information. FERPA defines education records as:

> Date and place of birth, parent (s) and/or guardian addresses, and where parents can be contacted in emergencies, grades, test scores, courses taken, academic specialization and activities, and official letters regarding a student's status in school, special education records, disciplinary records, medical and health records that the school creates or collects and maintains documentation of attendance, schools attended, courses taken, awards conferred, and degrees earned, and personal information such as a student's identification code, social security number, picture, or other information that would make it easy to identify or locate a student. (Policy Studies Associates, 1997, p. 139)

As can be seen from the definition above, the information covered by FERPA is extensive. This means that most of the information in the student's cumulative folder, which used to be fairly accessible by all school personnel, should have restricted access.

But there is information about students that is not covered by FERPA, such as personal notes made by a teacher and other school officials that are not shared with others as part of the student record (Policy Studies Associates, 1997). Therefore, teachers and other school personnel, such as counselors, can take notes during observation periods, counseling sessions, or other times, without those becoming a part of the student's records. But it should be understood that if these notes are shared with other school staff, they become part of the official record and are then covered by FERPA.

TEACHER TIP 9.7

Even though some of your notes may not be legally available to parents, don't write things down about a child you would not want the parent to see. You never know who may read your written notes.

The confidentiality regulations included in IDEA conform to the FERPA provisions (Turnbull & Turnbull, 2000). Therefore, school personnel ensuring confidentiality should not be concerned that adherence to one of these federal acts would result in noncompliance for the other (see Table 9.4 for applicable FERPA definitions).

Prior to the passage of federal and state legislation, many records maintained by the schools were not available to parents. In fact, some schools denied parents any level of access to their child's educational records. Some school personnel would even tell parents that their child's records were confidential and were therefore not available. As a result of FERPA and IDEA, schools are required to maintain specific records on children receiving special education services and parents have a right to access this information. Additionally, this access is not limited to information on official forms, such as IEP forms, but is applicable to any items classified as student records. As a result of the Buckley Amendment (FERPA) and IDEA, school personnel are now more cautious in what they include in the child's records. Nothing should be included in students' records that was not validated or justified. Additionally, these two federal acts give parents the right to see records and to copy any information included in their child's records.

Under FERPA, parents and students who have reached the age of majority have the right (1) to be informed about the types and location of education records maintained by the school and the officials responsible for them, and (2) to receive an explanation or interpretation of the records if requested (Underwood & Mead, 1995, p. 267). However, some records are not available to parents. These include:

1. Notes of teachers, counselors, or school administrators made for their personal use and shown to nobody else (except a substitute teacher);
2. Records of school security police when they are kept separate from other school records and used only for law-enforcement purposes throughout the local area, and when security police have no access to any other school files; and
3. Personnel records of school employees. (Anderson, Chitwood, & Hayden, 1990, p. 65)

There have been disagreements concerning what information must be made available to parents under FERPA and what information must be protected. For example, assessment personnel have argued in the past that test protocols should be considered their "notes," and can therefore be withheld from parents. However, the Office of the General Counsel of the U.S. Department of Education has concluded that such information is personally identifiable and should therefore be accessible by

Table 9.4   FERPA definitions applicable to IDEA.

1. *Education records* is defined by inclusion and exclusion.
   a. Included in the term are those records that are
      i. related directly to a student and
      ii. maintained by an LEA or party acting on its behalf.
   b. Excluded from the term, and therefore not assured confidentiality, are the following records:
      i. Records of instructional, supervisory, and administrative and educational personnel ancillary to those persons that are kept in the sole possession of the maker of the record and are not accessible or revealed to any other person except a temporary substitute for the maker of the record—that is an educator's "private" notes about a student.
      ii. Records of a law enforcement unit of an LEA, but only if the education records the LEA maintains are not disclosed to that unit and only if the law-enforcement records are (a) maintained separately from education records, (b) maintained solely for law-enforcement purposes, and (c) disclosed only to law-enforcement officials of the same jurisdiction as LEA (that is, the LEA's city or county or other jurisdiction's law enforcement agency)

2. *Parent* refers to a natural parent, guardian, or individual acting as a parent in the absence of a natural parent or guardian

3. *Student* refers to an individual who is or has been in attendance at an education agency (an LEA or state-operated school or program) and regarding whom the agency maintains education records

4. *Eligible student* refers to a student who has reached 18 years of age

5. *Personally identifiable information* includes, without limitation, the student's name, the name of the student's parent or other family member, the address of the student or student's family, any personal identifier (such as the student's Social Security number or an agency's assigned student number)

6. *Directory information* is information contained in a student's education record that generally would not be considered harmful or an invasion of privacy if disclosed, and includes, without limitations, name, address, telephone listing, date and place of birth, major field of study, participation in officially recognized activities and sports, weight and height, dates of attendance, degrees and awards received, and the most recent previous educational institution attended.

7. *Disclosure* means permitted access to, or the release, transfer, or other communication of, education records or the personally identifiable information contained in those records to any party, by any means, including oral, written, or electronic means.

(34 C.F.R. Part 99.3)

parents. On the other hand, when parents have requested personnel records of their children's teachers, they have been denied access (Anderson, et al., 1990). Personnel records are not considered personal information about the child and are therefore not covered under IDEA or FERPA.

Under both IDEA and FERPA, student records are accessible only to individuals who have a *need* to see those records. As previously noted, before these two acts were passed, many school personnel had access to student records and often, school personnel who did not need to see a student's records had access to them. The need-to-know test was rarely applied. Under the new guidelines, individuals who do not have any reasons to know what is in a student's records simply do not have access to those records (Underwood & Mead, 1995).

Even though there will always be individuals whose need to know is questionable, the following are individuals considered to frequently have a need to know the content of student records:

1. School officials (including teachers) in the same district with a "legitimate educational interest," as defined in the school procedures;

2. School officials in the school district to which a child intends to transfer (but only after the parent has had a chance to request a copy of the records and to challenge their contents);

3. Certain state and national education agencies, if necessary for enforcing federal laws;

4. Anyone to whom a state statute requires the school to report information;

5. Accrediting and research organizations helping the school, provided they guarantee confidentiality;

6. Student financial aid officials;

7. People who have court orders, provided the school makes "reasonable" efforts to notify the parent or student before releasing the records;

8. Appropriate individuals in health and safety emergencies such as doctors, nurses, and fire marshals. (Anderson et al., 1990, pp. 68–69)

Everyone on this list should *not* automatically have access to student records. These are just individuals who frequently have a need to see portions of the student records. Actual access should be determined on a case-by-case basis. For example, the school nurse may have a need to see records of students with health problems, but not students without health problems. Other individuals who may need access, from time to time, may actually not have access. For example, unless a state law was passed prior to November 19, 1974, requiring schools to make student records available to police, probation officers, and employers, these groups may not access student records without parental consent (Anderson et al., 1990).

Both FERPA and IDEA establish standards related to confidentiality of student information. In general, the need-to-know criterion should be used to determine who may see student records. These laws, though not perfect, assist in limiting access to information that is considered personal. School personnel should understand the requirements of these two laws and implement methods for ensuring compliance for the protection of the students and their families.

CEC 9

Professional and Ethical Practice

Ethical Issues and Confidentiality

Confidentiality is also an ethical issue (Remley et al., 1997). Regardless of the legal requirements of FERPA and IDEA, in reality, school personnel control the access to records and information about students. Schools can take steps to limit access, such as maintaining records in a central location, requiring school personnel to sign for access to records, and limiting access to specific people. Unfortunately, these safeguards are not foolproof. In the end, individual school personnel must monitor access. This is much easier with written or computer records than oral information. There is no way to limit access to oral information other than through ethical actions of individuals. Each person must be responsible for limiting access to information on a need to know basis. Read the scenario in Box 9.3. What actions could Ms. Reeves take to limit access to confidential information about Billy? What actions could school personnel take to reduce the likelihood that this will not reoccur?

CEC 9

Professional and Ethical Practice

Practical Suggestions Related to Confidentiality   As noted above, the ultimate control over access to student records rests with individual school personnel. If they want to see records, or if they want to listen or talk about students, there may be little that schools can do to limit such access. Following are a few suggestions that school personnel can employ to limit access of student information by individuals who do not need to have the information:

- Provide staff development at the beginning of each school year about confidentiality issues and expected professional behavior.

Box 9.3

Scenario

Ms. Reeves, the third-grade teacher, was sitting in the teachers' lounge during her preparation period working on her lesson plans for next week. While sitting there, Mr. Brandon and Coach Sewall walked in. They were discussing the actions of Billy Jones, one of Mr. Brandon's students in his biology class. Coach Sewall, the basketball coach, did not have Billy in any classes and did not know much about him. Mr. Brandon was telling Coach Sewall that Brandon was definitely going to get an *F* in his class for the 9-week period because he had not done anything that was required. Mr. Brandon continued talking about Billy, telling Coach Sewall that Billy had already been suspended one time during the year for making obscene comments to one of the girls in his class. Coach Sewall was actively involved in the conversation. He asked Mr. Brandon why he didn't try to get him expelled, and Mr. Brandon replied that it was only a matter of time. Mr. Brandon then began telling Coach Sewall about how bad Billy's parents were. He said that they were basically just welfare junkies who very likely spent all their government money on drugs and booze.

Throughout the entire episode, Ms. Reeves sat quietly, trying not to listen in on the very loud conversation. While attempting to attend to her work, Coach Sewall asked her: "Well, Ms. Reeves, what do you think we should do about kids like Billy and their families? Don't you think that they are just ruining our school?"

- Post information in the teacher's lounge regarding confidentiality issues.
- Maintain a sign-out sheet for student records.
- Keep student records in areas with limited physical access.
- Keep a list of individuals who should have access to student records on the exterior of student folders.
- Remind other school personnel who are openly discussing a student that such behavior is inappropriate.

TEACHER TIP 9.8

If you ever have a question about confidentiality issues, always ask. Don't just decide on your own if you are unsure of the law.

Regardless of legal reasons for maintaining confidentiality, professional and ethical codes should be sufficient for educators to know that they should not be sharing information about students or family members without a just cause. The practice of confidentiality is required of all educators. In the end, it is the individual's responsibility to ensure that he or she practices confidentiality and encourages others to do so as well.

SUMMARY

This chapter has focused on ethical and confidential considerations that impact on the way school personnel interact with family members. It was noted early in the chapter that both of these areas have a major influence on the provision of services to individuals with special needs and their families, as well as to the general treatment of these individuals and their families.

Ethical considerations are derived from the concept of ethics, the study or understanding of what is good and bad, right and wrong. Ethics form the bases for many of our behaviors, including how we deal with families. It affects the way we interact with others, feel about ourselves, treat other people, and carry out our professional responsibilities.

Many organizations, including organizations for teachers, have codes of conduct or ethics to guide professionals in their consideration of what is an ethical action. These codes, however, cannot guarantee that ethics or professional conduct will be a part of a person's everyday actions. As a result, individual teachers and other school personnel should assume the responsibility to establish their own code of ethics and then follow this code. How school personnel interact with family members is an indication of that person's professional and personal ethics.

There are legal reasons for confidentiality, but the most important consideration is ethical in nature. School personnel should establish criteria for access to information about individual students and their families. However, they should also take it upon themselves to limit their access to information. Laws and procedures cannot guarantee confidentiality; individuals must restrict themselves to access to information that they do not have a need to know.

Educators continue to debate the professional nature of their jobs. They like to argue that teaching is a profession, and teachers and others who work with children in schools are indeed professionals. There are strong arguments that support this position. However, if education is indeed a profession, the field of education should address ethical issues. A code of ethics, including the principle of confidentiality, should be viewed as an important component of the profession; otherwise, the field of education will never be fully developed as a profession.

QUESTIONS FOR DISCUSSION

1. Suppose you witness a teacher doing something unethical. What should you do? Let's say you observe a teacher actually signing the name of a parent on a due process special education form that needs to be completed before special education services can be changed. The teacher either does not want to go to the trouble of getting the parent's consent or may not be able to obtain consent. Should you discuss this with the teacher, who just happens to be a senior member of the faculty? Should you act like you did not see the action? What would you do in this situation and why?

2. You are the special education teacher helping write an IEP and the committee feels that the student in question needs physical therapy services. The parent is not present, so school personnel are openly discussing the pros and cons of the needed services. The assistant principal says that the central office has given them specific instructions not to include services on IEPs that the school cannot easily afford. Therefore, she does not want the committee to include PT as a service on the IEP. You feel strongly that if the assessment data indicates that a particular service is needed, that the student should have access to that service. What are your actions in this situation? Do you try to convince the committee to include PT in the IEP, but let the issue drop if you cannot make your case? Do you privately communicate with the parent about the needed service that has not been included and encourage the parent to pursue the issue? Or do you simply bow to the administrative pressure?

3. Confidentiality is a huge issue when dealing with students with disabilities and their families. What should you do if you walk into a teacher's lounge and several of your colleagues are openly discussing confidential issues about a particular child and you know that most of these teachers do not have any need to know or discuss this information? Do you openly state your disagreement that such things should be discussed? Do you exit the room quietly? Do you convey your concerns to your principal? What do you think would be the best course of action and why?

REFERENCES

Anderson, W., Chitwood, S., & Hayden, D. (1990). *Negotiating the special education maze* (2nd ed.). New York: Woodbine House.

Council for Exceptional Children (CEC). (1998, March 12). *Conditions for special education teaching: A prospectus concerning the conditions that inhibit special educators from fully using professional practice standards.* Unpublished document.

Council for Exceptional Children (CEC). (2003). CEC *Code of Ethics and Professional Standards.* Retrieved December 7, 2003, from www.cec.sped.org/ps/code.html

Culatta, R. A., & Tompkins, J. R. (1999). *Fundamentals of special education.* Columbus, OH: Merrill.

FACT: The National Fair Access Coalition on Testing. (2003). CEC *Standards of Practice.* Retrieved December 7, 2003, from www.fairaccess.org/CEC_standards.htm

Fleitas, J. (2003). *Band-Aides and blackboards: When chronic illness goes to school.* Retrieved January 25, 2004, from http://www.faculty.fairfield.edu/fleitas/kids.html

Funk & Wagnalls new international dictionary of the English language. (1997). Chicago, IL: World Publishers.

Gartin, B. C., & Murdick, N. L. (2000). Teaching ethics in special education programs. *Catalyst for Change, 30,* 17–19.

Gartin, B. C., Murdick, N. L., Thompson, J. R., & Dyches, T. T. (2002). Issues and challenges facing educators who advocate for students with disabilities. *Education and Training in Mental Retardation and Developmental Disabilities, 37,* 3–13.

Hanson, M. J., & Lynch, E. W. (1989). *Early intervention: Implementing child and family services for infants and toddlers who are at-risk or disabled.* Austin, TX: Pro-Ed.

Harry, B. (1992). *Cultural diversity, families, and the special education system: Communication and empowerment.* New York: Teachers College Press.

IDEA Practices. (2003). *Laws and regulations.* Downloaded from the Internet, December 7, 2003, at www.ideapractices.org/law/law/index.php

Jones, R. (1998). Looking for goodness. *The American School Board Journal, 185,* 14–19.

Kitchner, K. (1984). Intuition, critical evaluation and ethical principles: The foundation for ethical decisions in counseling psychology. *The Counseling Psychologist, 12,* 43–55.

Lewis, R. B., & Doorlag, D. H. (2003). *Teaching special students in general education classrooms* (6th ed.). Upper Saddle River, NJ: Merrill/Prentice Hall.

Morrison, G. S. (1997). *Teaching in America.* Boston: Allyn & Bacon.

Policy Studies Associates. (1997). Protecting the privacy of student education records. *Journal of School Health, 67,* 139–140.

Rebore, R. W. (1998). *Personnel administration in education.* Boston: Allyn & Bacon.

Rebore, R. W. (2001). *The ethics of educational leadership.* Upper Saddle River, NJ: Merrill/Prentice Hall.

Remley, T. P., Herlihy, B., & Herlihy, S. B. (1997). The U.S. Supreme Court decision in *Jaffee v. Redmond:* Implications for counselors. *Journal of Counseling and Development, 75,* 213–218.

Schloss, P. J., & Henley, J. G. (1994). Ethical issues relating to families of persons with disabilities. In S. K. Alper, P. J. Schloss, & C. N Schloss (Eds.), *Families of students with disabilities.* Boston: Allyn & Bacon.

Sergiovanni, T. J. (1992). *Moral leadership: Getting to the heart of school improvement.* San Francisco: Jossey-Bass.

Shea, T. M., & Bauer, A. M. (1991). *Parents and teachers of children with exceptionalities: A handbook for collaboration.* Boston: Allyn & Bacon.

Smith, T. E. C., Polloway, E. A., Patton, J. R., & Dowdy, C. A. (2004). *Teaching students with special needs in inclusive settings* (4th ed.). Boston: Allyn & Bacon.

Stanard, R., & Hazler, R. (1995). Legal and ethical implications of HIV and duty to warn for counselors: Does *Tarasoff* apply? *Journal of Counseling and Development, 73,* 397–400.

Surratt, J., Majestic, A., & Shelton, S. (1998). Both sides of the story. *The American School Board Journal, 185,* 47–52.

Turnbull, H. R., & Turnbull, A. P. (2000). *Free appropriate public education* (6th ed.). Denver, CO: Love.

Turnbull, R., Turnbull, A., Shank, M. & Smith, S. J. (2004). *Exceptional lives: Special education in today's schools.* Upper Saddle River, NJ: Merrill/Prentice Hall.

Underwood, J. K., & Mead, J. F. (1995). *Legal aspects of special education and pupil services.* Boston: Allyn & Bacon.

Walker, J. E., & Shea, T. M. (1995). *Behavior management: A practical approach for educators* (6th ed.). Upper Saddle River, NJ: Merrill/Prentice Hall.

CHAPTER 10
Working with Families: Supporting Young Children with Disabilities and Their Families

● ○ ○ ○ ○

Objectives

After reading this chapter, you will:

- Understand the need for a family support group
- Understand the array of services available for preschool children with disabilities

- Understand the eligibility criteria for preschool children with disabilities
- Know the components and rationale for the Individual Family Service Plan (IFSP)
- Understand the transition points experienced by children and their families in preschool settings
- Know the types of preschool services available
- Understand the need for a collaborative partnership between professionals and family members

When a child is identified as having a disability, whether it is at birth or early in the child's life and whether families move through acceptance stages in a sequential or cyclical pattern, or not at all, a support system will need to be provided. This support system can be provided in a number of different forms. Those health care professionals who are present at the birth of the child or at the moment when the disability is identified may be the first support system accessed by the parents (Cooley, 1992). Family members who arrive and provide the emotional support needed at this time are the second group usually accessed by the family. Later professionals arrive who will provide the counseling and information concerning other resources specifically available to families and children with needs related to specific disabilities or services.

Most parents, siblings, grandparents, and other family members are not cognizant of the positive and negative characteristics of disability categories, nor are they aware of the types of support available. Therefore, emotional support and informational materials are important support needs. These needs are most often met through interactions with representatives of governmental agencies, service organizations, and professional organizations encountered through the parents' search for answers and services. Often the professionals introduce the family to parent support groups where there are opportunities provided for parents and others to talk and share information. The information and support provided in this venue often assists the parents as they take the first essential steps in coping with the reality of caring for a child with disabilities.

TEACHER TIP 10.1

Teachers of preschool children should develop information packets, written in easy-to-understand language, that describe various disabilities and services for preschool children. Ask parents of preschool children to help prepare the packets.

SERVICES FOR INFANTS AND TODDLERS WITH DISABILITIES

In most cases, early intervention services for infants and toddlers with disabilities and their families were first provided by medical professionals who were aligned with the local hospital or by local parent support groups. Because these services were not mandated by law nor supported financially through federal monies, they were not always available in all areas of the country. In 1986, this changed with the reauthorization of IDEA to include early intervention services for infants and toddlers.

Today many families and their children with disabilities, newborn to age 3, receive early intervention services. Early intervention programs vary; however, they are often home-based services for infants and toddlers. These programs involve the family members in the planning and implementation of the interventions. Typically early intervention services encourage family members to interact with the professional each time services are provided. Where early intervention is offered as a center-based program, parents are often involved in observation and play activities with their children at the center. Further, they have the opportunity to communicate with professionals, often on a daily basis and in some cases receive weekly progress updates (Hadden & Fowler, 1997).

In special education preschools that provide services for 3- to 5-year-old children, the opportunity for communication, although still extensive, may be more limited than in home-based programs. Reduced opportunities for communication between the family and the school may be a result simply of the fact that the program is outside the home setting (Hadden & Fowler, 1997; Hains, Rosenkoetter, & Fowler, 1991). The transition from early intervention services to special education preschools has been shown to be a time of stress for many families (see Hadden & Fowler, 1997, for a summary of this research). However, effective and timely communication can assist in the reduction of stress and frustration for families and set the stage for good educational cooperation.

TEACHER TIP 10.2

Make an extra effort to communicate with family members when children move from Part C programs to preschool programs, especially during the first school term after the move occurs. Home visits are an excellent means of maintaining communication and many parents whose children were served in Part C programs are accustomed to this access to professionals.

ELIGIBILITY AND SERVICES UNDER PART C OF IDEA

Eligibility under Part C of IDEA is not based on categorical eligibility but on the identification of infants and toddlers as having delayed development or who are at risk for delayed development. Although funding and service delivery according to different disability categories was seen as appropriate and effective for school-age students with disability, this was not so for infants and toddlers. The difficulty in identifying young children successfully and the consequences of misidentification supported the move to "noncategorical" service delivery under the rubric of developmental delay.

CEC 1

Foundations

PRAXIS 2

Legal and Societal Issues

CEC 1

Foundations

PRAXIS 2

Legal and Societal Issues

CEC 2

Development and Characteristics of Learners

Part C of IDEA mandated a written document describing services to be provided for infants and toddlers. This document was known as the Individualized Family Service Plan (IFSP; Bruder, 2000). Similar to IEPs, the IFSP must include some specific components. Table 10.1 describes each of the required components of the IFSP.

TEACHER TIP 10.3

Every IFSP should have some outcomes and activities for the family as well as the child. In order to truly provide a family-oriented program, the child's needs must be addressed in the context of the family needs.

Table 10.1 Components of the IFSP.

1. A statement of the infant's or toddler's present levels of physical development, cognitive development, communication development, and adaptive development, based on objective criteria;

2. A statement of the family's resources, priorities, and concerns relating to enhancing the development of the family's infant or toddler with a disability;

3. A statement of the measurable results or outcomes expected to be achieved for the infant or toddler and the family, including preliteracy and language skills, as developmentally appropriate for the child, and the criteria, procedures, and timelines used to determine the degree to which progress toward achieving the results or outcomes is being made and whether modifications or revisions of the results or outcomes or services are necessary;

4. A statement of specific early intervention services based on peer-reviewed research, to the extent practicable, necessary to meet the unique needs of the infant or toddler and the family, including the frequency, intensity, and method of delivering services;

5. A statement of the natural environments in which early intervention services will appropriately be provided, including a justification of the extent, if any, to which the services will not be provided in a natural environment;

6. The projected dates for initiation of services and the anticipated length, duration, and frequency of the services;

7. The identification of the service coordinator from the profession most immediately relevant to the infant's or toddler's or family's needs (or who is otherwise qualified to carry out all applicable responsibilities under this part) who will be responsible for the implementation of the plan and coordination with other agencies and persons, including transition services; and

8. The steps to be taken to support the transition of the toddler with a disability to preschool or other appropriate services.

Note: Adapted from IDEA 2004.

Instead of being focused on educational services for the child as in an Individualized Education Plan (IEP), the IFSP focuses on the child with a disability within the family. It is written to address the child's needs and to empower the family in its ability to support itself and the child with the disability (Fox, Dunlap, & Cushing, 2002). In order for the family and other team members to develop effective IFSPs, the following steps, adapted from Bruder (2000), should be followed.

First, the child within the family as the focus of the process must be continually reinforced. Therefore, the beginning of this program development should be the family; that is, the family's concerns, priorities, and resources should be evaluated. The goal of this first step is to identify the supports and services available to the family in order to enhance their ability to provide the care for their child. This is significantly different from the child-focused and education-focused emphasis of the programs for the school-aged child. As a result, the family is the lead individual with the professionals serving as the supports and assistants in the search for appropriate and useful services.

Young children develop best in their "natural environments," that is, the home, and when involved in the everyday experiences of the family. Thus, the second step is for the family and the team to identify family routines in which the child is or can be involved and that would provide enjoyable learning experiences. In addition to those experiences and settings in the home, activities that could occur in the community should also be noted.

In order to assure that all facets of the needs of the family and child are addressed, a functional assessment should be completed. This assessment will review the child's development in conjunction with the family's goals, concerns, and priorities for their child. This assessment is completed in order to provide "a complete and accurate picture of the child's strengths, needs, preferences for activities, materials, and environments" (Bruder, 2000, p. 2). During this period, parents should begin the development of a recordkeeping system to assist in the retention of documents related to their child and the special education process. The retention of documents will allow for their review of their child's growth and progress. The documents may also be useful at some future date in terms of establishing the need for services and evaluating the effectiveness of programs that have been used with their child.

Once all information from the first three steps is available, then the team should meet to compile and review all the information. It is essential that the family is an active participant in this step. This is the time when the goals for the IFSP are developed, and to be successful this development should focus on the needs of the family to enhance the child's participation in identified activities in the home and community environments. Read the scenario in Box 10.1 and describe some of the family's strengths and how the school can provide family supports.

If the services are to support the goals, then their implementation must not be left to chance. Therefore, all team members must be involved with each member's specific roles and responsibilities identified and accepted. The use of a transdisciplinary model in which all individuals, no matter their area of expertise, work together toward a common goal as defined by the needs of the child and family, not by their

CEC 9

Professional and Ethical Practice

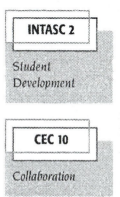

INTASC 2

Student Development

CEC 10

Collaboration

Box 10.1

Debi Jacobs is a single mother. She has three children, ages 11, 8, and 2. The 2-year-old, named Millie, has had difficulties since birth. She was premature, and has been significantly delayed in all of her developmental milestones. Millie was referred for Part C services and was assigned a service coordinator to facilitate her receiving services. Apparently she needs speech/language therapy, physical therapy, and general supports in learning basic developmental skills. Debi is a good mother, but knows very little about raising children with special needs. She has a part-time job, and receives some assistance from welfare. Her part-time job is expanding to full-time, but Debi may not be able to continue because of childcare issues and transportation. Her part-time job enables her to be home when her children are out of school, but if she goes to work full-time, she will have to place her children in childcare. Millie goes to an integrated childcare program in the mornings when Debi goes to work. Debi does not have any extended family in the area, and literally lives from month to month. The service coordinator needs to develop a comprehensive program to meet the needs of Debi and her entire family.

discipline, has been shown to be effective in early intervention. The team decides, based on the needs of the child and family, which individuals will serve as primary implementers of the services and which individuals will serve as supports and consultants.

TEACHER TIP 10.4

Home visits might encourage families to become more involved with the development of the IFSP. Remember that family members have important information concerning the child. It is essential to solicit input and assist in developing the outcomes and activities for the family.

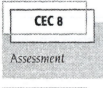

CEC 9

Professional and Ethical Practice

CEC 8

Assessment

PRAXIS 3

Delivery of Services to Students with Disabilities

Once the team members have their assigned roles, then specific strategies to assure success of the plan's implementation should developed and implemented. As opposed to an IEP, an IFSP includes strategies not just to facilitate the child's learning, but to increase opportunities for learning in the home and community, and to identify the most effective teaching strategies and effective reinforcers that will support the child and family. The family needs to be intimately and actively involved in this process, as one of the outcomes of the IFSP process is to assure that families can continue the program and that the child's learning will generalize to other non-identified situations. Additionally, family involvement increases the likelihood that the IFSP will be both coordinated and effective (Fox et al., 2002). According to Bruder (2000) for this process to be ideal, interventions should:

- Be embedded in everyday natural environments.
- Emphasize the acquisition of functional competencies.
- Make it possible to increase a child's participation within the environments.
- Include both social and nonsocial activities.

In order to assure successful programs, evaluations, both ongoing and periodic, should be included in the plan. The format and focus of the evaluations is decided when the team develops the goals and criteria for success. The inclusion of an evaluation component ensures that the focus continues on the stated goal of progress for the child as well as support for the family and that when changes need to be made in the plan they occur in a consistent and timely manner. Additionally, annual evaluations of the IFSP are required. However, the family should receive a review of the plan at least every 6 months, or sooner if necessary. These reviews provide for the sharing of information with the family on a consistent basis as well as assuring that support and collaboration among team members will be encouraged throughout the duration of the plan.

TEACHER TIP 10.5

Involve family members in the evaluation of the program. Family members should be asked about the effectiveness of services, what services were not available that were needed, and how the program should be changed to better meet the needs of their family.

Services provided through Part C to infants and toddlers with disabilities and described in the IFSP can be provided either in the home (home-based services) or in an outside setting (center-based services) or through a combination of both. An increasing number of professionals in the field of early childhood special education, though, have espoused the belief that wherever the services are provided, the most appropriate instruction for young children is one that is offered in the natural environment. The natural environment is described as one that "makes use of typically occurring events, activities, and consequences as a context in which to teach specific skills . . . [and] consists of routine events and everyday activities in a variety of settings" (Warger, 1999). This strategy is known as "embedded learning opportunities" (ELO; Davis, Kilgo, & Gamel-McCormick, 1998). Its use has been supported as a means to provide children with practice within daily activities, can be used in inclusive environments, enhances interest and motivation, is easily available to family members and teachers, and can be incorporated into various curricular models (Bricker, Pretti-Frontczak, & McComas, 1998; Hemmeter & Grisham-Brown, 1997; Sewell, Collins, Hemmeter, & Schuster, 1998).

As stated earlier, the IFSP process focuses on the family and the parents. Parents, therefore, have specific roles and responsibilities in the special education process in order to ensure that the program that is developed meets the needs of the child and his or her family. Indeed, the family is the most important intervention agent (Harrower, Fox, Dunlap, & Kincaid, 2000). According to Knoblauch and McLane (1999), there are specific suggestions that may help the parents to participate as key members in the process. Often parents are unsure of what they can offer in the process to develop an IFSP for their child. They may not understand the importance and amount of information that

CEC 9

Professional and Ethical Practice

they can provide to the professionals with whom they will be working. Parents should be reminded to prepare for meetings concerning their child by listing what they would like for their child to learn and deciding what behaviors the child exhibits that might interfere with his or her learning. It is suggested that parents should collect copies of relevant materials such as medical records, past school records, evaluation results, samples of work, and so on, and keep them in an expandable folder or notebook that they can bring to the IFSP meeting to share. Parents may not be aware that they have information that is not available to the professionals with whom they will be working. If the child is receiving or may receive related services, a description of these should be available for all members of the team. Although it is suggested that parents request information about ways to support their child's program at home, they may not feel comfortable asking to do this. If this is the case, then the professional may wish to provide them with suggested ways to assist at home and offer to work with them. With parental and family support of the skills the child is to learn, the child's progress can often be accelerated.

One of the supporting tenets of IDEA is family involvement. Part C of IDEA expands family involvement by addressing the service needs of young children within the context of the family. The special education process includes all members of the child's family in the hope that such collaboration will ensure "the best possible supports and services for a child with a disability and for the child's entire family" (Cone, 2001, p. 1). When providing these family-centered early intervention services, numerous agencies may be involved, including medical, social, and educational agencies. As a result, a component known as service coordination was included in IDEA and an individual known as a service coordinator (formerly known as a case manager) is selected to ensure that identified services focus on the child as a member of a family and that the family's needs for support are considered.

INTASC 10

School and Community Involvement

TEACHER TIP 10.6

A service coordinator is important when providing services for children with disabilities in the infant/toddler program. It is often difficult to coordinate all of the various services that are needed by the child and family. Because the parents are the ultimate service coordinators, teachers should support them by providing information concerning services whenever the family indicates a need.

CEC 4

Instructional Strategies

Because this is a family-focused intervention, education is not the only area considered. The needs of the "whole" child as a member of a family become the basis for the identification of services to be provided. Thus, service delivery may include family education, family counseling, health care services including physical and occupational therapy, nutritional services, and so on. Thus, the range of services that can be included has been expanded from the narrow educational services view of IDEA.

PRESCHOOL PROGRAMMING

Transitions can be defined as "points of change in services and personnel who coordinate and provide services" (Rice & O'Brien, 1990, p. 2) and as such can and do occur throughout the life of all individuals (Hanson, 1999). The first transition is usually the move from the hospital to the family home and then from that into early intervention services. When infants and toddlers reach the age of 3, they and their families face a major transition time—transition from the family-focused early intervention programs into the child-focused and usually school-based preschool programs (Berry & Hardman, 1998). At this time, the parents' role also changes as they assume the role of service coordinator for their child, become IEP team members, and must begin to collaborate with a new set of professionals. As a result, this may be a time when increased family stress may appear and parents may need additional support and communication with school personnel (Fox et al., 2002). Table 10.2 provides some suggestions for parents to enhance their participation in the special education process.

Table 10.2   Suggestions for parents to enhance participation.

Develop a partnership with the school. Share relevant information about your child's education and development. Your observation can be a valuable resource.

Ask for an explanation of any aspect of the program that you don't understand. Educational terms can be confusing, so do not hesitate to ask.

Make sure the IFSP outcomes and activities are specific and measurable. This will ensure that everyone teaching your child is working toward the same goals. Take the IFSP home to think about it before you sign it. You have 10 school days in which to make a decision.

Make sure your child is included in the regular school activities program as much as is appropriate, including at least lunch, recess, and nonacademic areas such as art, music, and physical education.

Monitor your child's progress and periodically ask for a report. If your child is not progressing, discuss it with the teacher and determine whether the program should be modified. As a parent, you can initiate changes in your child's educational program.

Try to resolve directly with the school any problems that may occur with your child's evaluation, placement, or educational program. Most states have protection and advocacy agencies that can provide you with the guidance you need to resolve a problem.

Keep records. There may be questions about your child that you will want to discuss, as well as meetings and phone conversations you will want to remember. It is easy to forget important information that is not written down.

Join a parent organization. Besides sharing knowledge, experiences, and support, a parent group often can be an effective force on behalf of your child. Parents often find that, as a group, they have the power to bring about needed changes to strengthen special services.

Note: From *Rights and Responsibilities of Parents of Children with Disabilities: Update 1999,* by B. Knoblauch and K. McLane, 1999 (ERIC EC Digest No. E575).

Parent involvement is still an integral part of preschool programs, although the focus on the family as the center of the program development has changed to the more educational-focused programming of the preschool (Smith, 2004). For the preschool teacher, Kraft (2001) has provided some suggestions on ways to assist in integrating the child with a disability into the preschool setting:

CEC 5

Learning Environments and Social Interactions

- Physical environment should be evaluated and monitored to ensure that all children can move safely and easily from one activity to the next.
- Adults with disabilities should be encouraged to participate in the classroom so that role models are available to those students with disabilities.
- All children should be encouraged to play with each other and activities to foster play between children with and without disabilities should be provided.
- A system to communicate with parents consistently and frequently, not just when problems occur, should be developed and used.

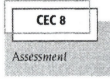

CEC 8

Assessment

Children with disabilities between the ages of 3 and 5 may have their programs developed using either an IFSP or an IEP depending on the specific needs of the child, and may opt to receive services under Part C until they enter kindergarten. Although the IEP can include a family focus, frequently it shifts the focus to the child. The IEP differs from the IFSP in the following ways:

- It focuses on the child more than the family.
- It includes outcomes targeted for the child alone as opposed to outcomes that are targeted on the family along with the child.
- It focuses on the school learning environment as the "least restrictive environment" instead of the "natural environment" of the home and community.
- It no longer focuses on the integration of activities by multiple agencies, but centers its focus on educational services.
- The parent assumes the role of coordinator of the child's services in lieu of a "service coordinator."

The decision of whether services should be written into an IFSP versus an IEP should be made by the family and professionals involved in the programmatic decision making. This decision should be based on the needs of the child and family to be served and not on the format with which the professional is most comfortable.

TEACHER TIP 10.7

The IFSP is written for children below the age of 3 who are at-risk or have a disability. In an effort to provide a more consistent service delivery system, an IFSP can now be written in some states until the age of 6 for preschool children with special learning needs. The use of the IFSP reinforces the role of the family as caregiver and provides support for the child using the family as the focal point. The IEP does not address service coordination and emphasizes the educational needs of the child as opposed to the needs of the child within the family context. If the family of the child has serious family-based issues, it might be better to serve the child and the family through an IFSP rather than an IEP. This decision must be made on an individual family basis.

FAMILY-SCHOOL PARTNERSHIPS

A collaborative partnership of parents and professionals is the most optimal way for services to be identified, developed, and provided for the child with a disability, despite his or her age. Harrower et al. (2000) found that such partnerships increased the likelihood of coordinated and effective interventions. However, for both parents and professionals, the partnership role is not the one with which they relate with great comfort as this is their first experience with this role. When a child is first identified as having a disability, parents are usually unprepared for assuming the role of advocate and for serving as a knowledgeable member of the service delivery team. Without advocacy and partnership training, many families will decide to ignore this role. Dunst, Trivette, and Deal (1994) developed a model, the Family Enablement Project, to use in empowering families to participate in early intervention services. This model incorporates four steps:

INTASC 10

School and
Community
Involvement

CEC 9

Professional and
Ethical Practice

1. Determination by families of the individual priorities and concerns of the family unit.
2. Identification by professionals and family members of the family's coping styles and the facets of the family system that work.
3. Identification by professionals and family members of the potential resources needed by the family to meet the needs and wants identified in step 1.
4. Collaboration of family members and professionals to achieve goals based on the needs and wants identified in step 1.

Not only do collaborative partnerships between parents and professionals provide better programs for a child with a disability and his or her family, they provide the basis for the future involvement of families in the child's education. Thus, the focus of family involvement and collaborative partnerships is to facilitate family empowerment. Therefore, the parent and other family members should be empowered to support and advocate for the services required for their child to be successful in school and subsequently in transition to adulthood. As O'Shea, O'Shea, Algozzine, and Hammitte (2001) have said:

> The ultimate outcome of any empowerment program should be a shift from the role of the professional as the primary leader and decision maker with regard to services for the child and family, to the families assuming the leadership role. In fact, the professional should be seen as assistant to the parent, a provider of a service deemed necessary by the parent.

SUMMARY

When a child is born into a family, the parent and extended family interactions are changed. This is even more apparent when they become aware that their child has a disability. As a result of this, the focus of their lives changes. Some parents and family members have described this process as working through sequential steps similar to those in the grieving process, whereas others disagree. For all parents a supportive network is essential. Early intervention services and preschool programs, once only provided in some locations, are now mandated by federal legislation. Early intervention services focus on families of a child with a disability by acknowledging the strengths of the family as well as its needs. This family-centered focus changes to a student-centered focus when the child transitions into the preschool program. Throughout this process the goal for professionals is to work with the parents and families collaboratively to provide services for the child and his or her family and to empower the family to become lifelong advocates for their child.

QUESTIONS FOR DISCUSSION

1. Services to young children with disabilities focus on the entire family, not just the child. This differs from programs for older children where the focus is on the child. What are some reasons why focusing on the entire family is a good idea for preschool programs? Would it be a good idea for schools to do the same thing even as children get older? Why or why not?

2. One of the requirements for serving young children with disabilities is the designation of a service coordinator. This is not a role found in services for older children. Why is it important to have a service coordinator involved in serving young children with disabilities and not important for serving older children?

3. The assessment process for young children with disabilities differs from the assessment required for older children. What are the components of a good assessment for young children? How do these differ among young children and older children?

REFERENCES

Berry, J. O., & Hardman, M. L. (1998). *Lifespan perspectives on the family and disability.* Boston: Allyn & Bacon.

Bricker, D., Pretti-Frontczak, K., & McComas, N. (1998). *An activity-based approach to early intervention* (2nd ed.). Baltimore, MD: Brookes.

Bruder, M. B. (2000). *The individualized family service plan (IFSP).* (ERIC EC Digest No. E605), retrieved May 26, 2003, from http://ericec.org

Cone, A. A. (2001). *Fact sheet: Person-centered planning.* Retrieved on May 30, 2003, from http://www.aamr.org

Cooley, W. E. (1992). Natural beginnings—unnatural encounters: Events at the outset for families of children with disabilities. In J. Nisbet (Ed.), *Natural supports in school, at work, and in the community for people with severe disabilities* (pp. 87–120). Baltimore, MD: Brookes.

Davis, M. D., Kilgo, J. L., & Gamel-McCormick, M. (1998). *Young children with special needs.* Boston: Allyn & Bacon.

Dunst, C. J., Trivette, C., & Deal, A. G. (1994). Enabling and empowering families. In C. J. Dunst, C. M. Trivette, & A. G. Deal (Eds.), *Supporting and strengthening families* (27–42). Cambridge, MA: Brookline.

Fox, L., Dunlap, G., & Cushing, L. (2002). Early intervention, positive behavior support, and transition to school. *Journal of Emotional and Behavioral Disorders, 10,* 149–158.

Hadden, S., & Fowler, S. A. (1997). Preschool: A new beginning for children and parents. *Teaching Exceptional Children, 30,* 36–39.

Hains, A. H., Rosenkoetter, S. E., & Fowler, S. A. (1991). Transition planning with families in early intervention programs. *Infants and Young Children, 3,* 38–47

Hanson, M. J. (1999). *Early transition for children and families: Transitions from infant/toddler services to preschool education.* (ERIC EC Digest No. E581) retrieved May 26, 2003, from http://ericec.org

Harrower, J. K., Fox, L., Dunlap, G., & Kincaid, D. (2000). Functional assessment and comprehensive early intervention. *Exceptionality, 8,* 189–204.

Hemmeter, M. L., & Grisham-Brown, J. (1997). Teaching language and communication skills in the context of ongoing activities and routines in inclusive preschool classrooms. *Dimensions in Early Childhood Education, 25,* 6–13.

Knoblauch, B., & McLane, K. (1999). *Rights and responsibilities of parents of children with disabilities: Update 1999.* (ERIC EC Digest No. E575), retrieved May 26, 2003, from http://ericec.org

Kraft, S. G. (2001, February). Full early childhood inclusion maximizes kids' potential. *Early Childhood Report, 12,* 1.

O'Shea, D. J., O'Shea, L. J., Algozzine, R., & Hammitte, D. J. (2001). *Families and teachers of individuals with disabilities: Collaborative orientations and responsive practices.* Boston: Allyn & Bacon.

Rice, M. L., & O'Brien, M. (1990). Transitions: Times of change and accommodation. *Topics in Early Childhood Special Education, 9,* 1–14.

Sewell, T. J., Collins, B. C., Hemmeter, M. L., & Schuster, J. W. (1998). Using simultaneous prompting within an activity-based format to teach dressing skills to preschoolers with developmental delays. *Journal of Early Intervention, 21,* 132–145.

Smith, D. D. (2004). *Introduction to special education: Teaching in an age of opportunity* (5th ed.). Boston: Pearson/Allyn & Bacon.

Warger, C. (1999). *Early childhood instruction in the natural environment.* (ERIC/OSEP Digest No. E591), retrieved May 26, 2003, from http://ericec.org

Westling, D. L., & Fox, L. (2000) *Teaching students with severe disabilities* (2nd ed.). Upper Saddle River, NJ: Merrill/Prentice Hall.

CHAPTER 11
Working with Families: Understanding Transitioning and the Transition Process

●●●●●●●●●●●●●●●●●●●●●●●

Objectives

After reading this chapter, you will:

- Understand the different transitions that occur in the lives of children with special needs and their families
- Know the legal requirements for transition services
- Recognize the challenges to effective transition

- Understand the supports necessary to assist children and their families during times of transition
- Know strategies to use in preparing transition plans

Transition can be defined as movement from one service system, grade level, or program to another. The focus of transition, therefore, is change. Change is a constant for most individuals with some changes being daily, expected, and usually smooth, whereas others are unexpected and problematic. Thus, it should not be surprising that changes in school programs may result in concerns for all students. However, students with special needs may have more difficulty because of the nature and complexity of services and supports that are being provided and the number of transitions that occur.

Planning and implementing effective transition programs can assist students in avoiding or overcoming many of the problems during transitions. In all instances, involving family members and students, as appropriate, in transition planning is critical in developing effective programs. Without joint planning, many challenges can develop that may impede the provision of an appropriate educational program, including: (a) lack of parental understanding of the new service system; (b) lack of awareness of the child to changes in the environment, program, and expectations; (c) lack of communication between family and school staff; (d) lack of continuity between services; and (e) change-related stress for families, students, and school personnel (Gottwald & Pardy, 1997; Hanline, 1993).

Many different transitions occur in the lives of children with special needs and their family members. Some of these transitions are vertical transitions, which are generally associated with predictable events such as beginning and exiting school or the movement from one grade level to the next, whereas others are horizontal transitions, such as the movement from situation to situation or setting to setting (Patton & Dunn, 1998). Figure 11.1 depicts possible vertical and horizontal transitions likely to occur during the life of a child with special needs. This figure reflects the complexity of the many different transitions with which children with special needs and their families, and school personnel, must contend.

Children with special needs and their parents have been afforded substantial rights under the Individuals with Disabilities Education Act (IDEA) and Section 504 (Smith & Patton, 1998). These laws provide the opportunity for parents to participate as full members of educational teams that determine appropriate programs for their children. In essence, parents should participate in designing and implementing programs to ease the transition of children from preschool programs through each transition period during their school career and into their post-school experiences. Parents and school personnel should develop partnerships to ensure as smooth a transition as possible and the continuation of appropriate services with minimal disruptions for the child. Although the participation of family members in transition does not guarantee a smooth transition, such participation greatly facilitates it.

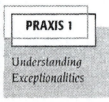

CEC 1

Foundations

PRAXIS 1

Understanding Exceptionalities

PRAXIS 2

Legal and Societal Issues

CEC 1

Foundations

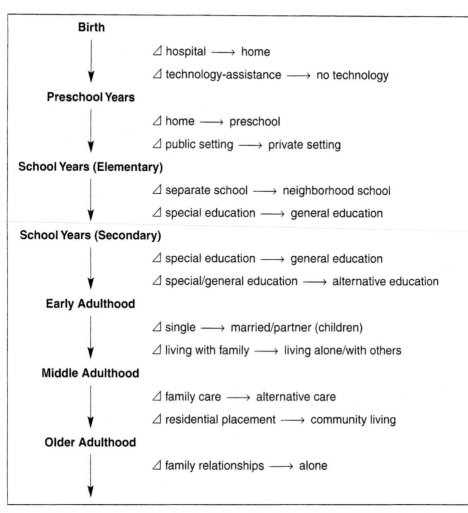

Figure 11.1   *Possible vertical and horizontal transitions during the life of a child with special needs.* Note: *From* Transition from School to Young Adulthood: Basic Concepts and Recommended Practices (p. 2), *by* J. R. Patton *and* C. Dunn, 1998, Austin, TX: Pro-Ed. *Used by permission.*

TEACHER TIP 11.1

Make sure that family members are involved in all transitions by discussing the transition and possible difficulties of the transition before the transition actually occurs.

Even though all of the transitions that affect children with special needs are important, more attention has been paid to transitions that occur at specific points. Since the mid-1980s, the Office of Special Education and Rehabilitative Services (OSERS) of the U.S. Department of Education has emphasized the importance of improving the transition of students with disabilities from high school to post-school environments. IDEA 2004 continues to require schools to plan and implement transition services for students with disabilities.

The primary intent of the transition requirements in IDEA is to promote effective transition programming through a coordinated group of activities leading to positive postsecondary outcomes. This legislative and regulatory emphasis resulted from many different factors, but is primarily a result of follow-up studies of young adults who had been in special education programs during their public school years. Numerous follow-up studies conducted in the early 1980s indicated that young adults with special needs were experiencing significant difficulties in employment, independent living, and social skill areas (Sitlington & Frank, 1998). Many of these students never successfully completed high school; they frequently dropped out, became too old to continue, or received a certificate of attendance (U.S. Department of Education, 2002). Additionally other studies found that among adolescents and young adults with disabilities there were significantly above-average levels of unemployment, significantly above-average levels of underemployment, economic instability, high levels of dependency on family members and friends, social isolation, and extremely low levels of involvement in postsecondary education and training programs. These results were noted in spite of the fact that many of these students had received special education services for years prior to their exit from the public school system. Although such findings would not have been surprising, and may even have been predictable before the major push to expand special education in the early 1980s, these results occurring after the special education mandate had been in effect for several years were disappointing. In response to the follow-up studies, changes were mandated. The 1990 reauthorization of IDEA required schools to develop transition plans for students with disabilities; this requirement was continued in the 1997 and 2004 reauthorizations.

However, change is slow. *The Twenty-fourth Annual Report to Congress on the Implementation of* IDEA (U.S. Department of Education, 2002) noted that during the 1999–2000 school year, more than 85,000 students, aged 14 and older dropped out of high school. This number reflected approximately 29 % of students with disabilities who exited during that school year. During the same time period, approximately 160,000 students received a diploma and nearly 33,000 received a certificate of attendance. Such figures indicate a continuing problem encountered by many students with disabilities in their transition out of the public school system. Table 11.1 shows the number of students with disabilities and the method by which they exited school during 1999–2000.

The concern over the transition of students with disabilities from school to post-school environments has not been matched by attention to other transitions that students with special needs must make. For example, many children and their families experience problems when the child transitions from infant-toddler programs to pre-school programs and from preschool programs to kindergarten to first grade (La Paro,

Table 11.1   Number of students with disabilities and the method by which they exited school during 1999–2000.

Age Group	Graduated with Diploma	Received a Certificate	Reached Maximum Age	No Longer Receives Special Education	Died	Moved, Known to Continue	Moved, Not Known to Continue
14	18	6	1	15,587	208	35,644	11,579
15	19	22	7	15,358	339	33,314	12,738
16	918	221	15	13,974	319	30,121	12,941
17	31,135	3,559	66	11,975	336	23,134	11,663
18	76,982	12,869	899	7,236	242	13,365	7,696
19	40,566	9,508	510	2,198	132	4,783	3,352
20	8,405	3,650	883	553	98	1,735	1,499
21+	4,537	3,154	4,457	405	108	923	1,663
14–21+	162,580	32,989	6,838	67,286	1,782	143,019	63,131

"Dropped out" is defined as the total who were enrolled at some point in the reporting year, were not enrolled at the end of the reporting year, and did not exit through any of the other bases described. This category includes dropouts, runaways, GED recipients, expulsions, status unknown, and other exiters.

Note: From U.S. Department of Education. (2002). *Twenty-Fourth Annual Report to Congress on the Implementation of the Individuals with Disabilities Education Act* (p. A-307), U.S. Department of Education, 2002, Jessup, MD: Education Publications Center.

Pianta, & Cox, 2000). Problems are also apparent in the transition of students from elementary to middle and middle to secondary programs. Whereas IDEA has included requirements to address the concern of school to post-school transitions, limited attention has been focused on these other, earlier transitions, even though they may result in substantial problems for students and their families.

TEACHER TIP 11.2

Although federal regulations do not address many of the transitions that children and their families must experience, schools should identify typical problems that occur during these transitions and have procedures for addressing these problems in place as part of school policy and procedures.

Regardless of the point of transition, it is imperative that parents assume an active role in the transition of their children. Without their active participation, transition efforts will likely be less than optimal. This chapter will provide basic information to assist school personnel in increasing and supporting parental involvement in transition planning.

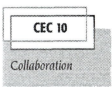

CEC 10

Collaboration

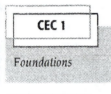

Foundations

Legal and Societal
Issues

LEGAL REQUIREMENTS FOR TRANSITION

As noted earlier, the requirement to provide transition services for students with disabilities began with the 1990 reauthorization of IDEA that required schools to implement transition planning when students reached the age of 16. This was the first legal mandate for such transition programming and resulted from concerns raised by the results of numerous follow-up studies of students who had formerly been in special education programs.

In 2004, IDEA was reauthorized by Congress; it included changes in several areas of the legislation, including transition. The 2004 reauthorization of IDEA defined transition services as:

A coordinated set of activities for a student with a disability that—

A. is designed to be within a results-oriented process, that is focused on improving the academic and functional achievement of the child with a disability to facilitate the child's movement from school to post-school activities, including post-secondary education, vocational education, integrated employment (including supported employment), continuing and adult education, adult services, independent living, or community participation;

B. is based on the individual child's needs taking into account the child's strengths, preferences, and interests; and

C. includes:

    i. instruction

    ii. related services

    iii. community experiences;

    iv. the development of employment and other post-school adult living objectives; and

    v. if appropriate, acquisition of daily living skills and functional vocational evaluation.

In the 2004 reauthorization, schools are to begin transition planning for students at age 16, and annually update the statement of transition service needs included in the IEP to include a statement of needed transition services with a statement of interagency responsibilities and linkages.

TEACHER TIP 11.3

School personnel should consider transition needs of students even before they reach the age of 16. Even though this may be early enough for some students, transition needs may need to be considered before the age of 16 for some students. As soon as students are in junior and middle schools, IEP committees should at least consider if transition issues should be discussed.

Part C of the IDEA requires that the Individual Family Service Plan (IFSP) must contain a description of the appropriate transition services for the infant or toddler (IDEA 2004). Steps that should be included are: (1) discussions with and training of parents regarding future placements and other matters related to transition; (2) development of procedures to prepare the child for changes in service delivery; and (3) with parental consent, transmission of assessment and IFSP information to the local education agency (Bailey & Wolery, 1992, p. 79). IDEA 2004 requires that in the case of a child with a disability ages 3 through 5 (or at the discretion of the state educational agency, a 2-year-old child with a disability who will turn 3 during the school year), the IEP team shall consider the IFSP, which may serve as the child's IEP. It also provides for parents to request the attendance of the Part C service coordinator or other representative at the child's IEP meeting to assist with the transition from Part C to Part B. Although the legal requirements for supporting transition at this level are not nearly as prescriptive as those for the school-to-post-school level, they are equally important and must be addressed by individuals working with children and families.

There are no legal requirements for facilitating transition between grade levels, between different schools within the vertical organization of a school system, or between general and special education programs. However, best practice demands that attention be given to these transitions. Moving from grade level to grade level, one teacher to another, and especially elementary school to middle school and middle school to high school results in significant changes in expectations and daily routines. Without attention to these potential problem areas, students might experience difficulties that could lead to failure, lowered self-concept, behavior problems, and limited success. Having family participation at each of these transition points can facilitate the development of effective transition plans and thus a smoother and less problematic transition time for students with special needs. However, parent participation and family-school collaboration is no guarantee that effective transition will occur.

CHALLENGES TO EFFECTIVE TRANSITION

Despite the legal requirements and the professional rationale to provide effective transition programming for students with disabilities, many challenges to successful transition programming remain. These challenges include attitudes, logistics, and policies and organizational structures. Challenges that are often present and may impede successful transition for children at every level include:

- Natural resistance of professionals to make changes (Winton, 1993)
- Challenges for children in adapting to different physical environments, teachers and school staff, and expectations (Hanline, 1993)
- Challenges for family members in making new relationships with school staff, adapting to different policies and expectations, and understanding different due process procedures from Part C to Part B programs (Hanline, 1993)
- Challenges for professionals in effectively communicating with personnel at the next level, trusting that the next level of professionals will carry out effective

programs, and continuing communication after the transition to facilitate the transition (Hanline, 1993)
- Alienation of family members (Wehmeyer, Morningstar, & Husted, 1999)

If not addressed, these challenges can prove to be a hindrance to students' successful transition. However, if recognized, these challenges can be addressed and do not have to limit the successful transition of students.

Challenges to Transition from Part C to Part B Programs

One of the major challenges to successful transition for young children from Part C programs to Part B programs is the two-part administrative structure established by P.L. 99-457 that established the infant-toddler program (birth to 3 years) and the preschool program (ages 3–5; Winton, 1993). Professionals working in early intervention programs with children age birth to 3 years work under different regulations than do those professionals working in preschool programs with children 3 years of age and older. In addition, these programs are often administered by different organizations. In many states, the Department of Education (DOE), which is always the lead agency for Part B (school-age) programs, is not the lead agency for Part C (preschool) programs; instead, the Department of Health (DOH), Department of Mental Retardation (DMR), or Department of Health and Human Services (DHHS) may serve as the lead agency. Having different lead agencies can easily result in confusion, especially considering that it results in the use of different forms, different programmatic emphases, different personnel, and different training requirements. As a result, ineffective transition may occur even when individuals within each agency are committed to effective transition.

TEACHER TIP 11.4

Interagency coordinating councils or committees are extremely important when different agencies coordinate these two programs. School personnel should be involved in these coordinating councils.

Challenges to Grade-to-Grade Transitions

Moving from Part B preschool programs to kindergarten or first grade often results in additional or different program demands. Differing demands may include (a) a higher child-to-staff ratio, (b) an increased amount of large or whole group instruction, (c) more structured teacher expectations, and (d) changes in the physical and social characteristics of the classroom (La Paro et al., 2000). As a result, transition difficulties may result.

A critical component in the transition is the preparation of the child. First, the child must be able to demonstrate the social, behavioral, and academic skills necessary for success in the next environment. Parents and teachers should be working together to identify the required skills. The instruction of these skills needs to include a plan promoting their maintenance and generalization across environments. Second, the child should be taken on field trips to the new environment. The field trip should allow time in the new cafeteria with, perhaps a snack or lunch, time on the playground playing, and time in the classroom participating in some classroom activities. Pictures can be taken at the new setting and then used to develop a scrapbook with a story about the trip and the new school. The new teacher can come to visit the children in their current setting in an exchange program, with the teacher bringing activities for them to do together. This would allow the children to become better acquainted with the new teacher while in a familiar setting. Third, during instructional time in the current setting, the teacher might read books about "new adventures" or "going to my new school." A play center could be developed for the children to practice "going to my new school." Directed role-playing can also occur using the "new school" center, allowing children to express their concerns about the transitions.

A second component critical to transition is the preparation of the adults, both families and teachers. As the family members and teachers work together to prepare the child for the transition, they will also be preparing themselves for the changes that will occur. Learning about the "new school" and its rules and expectations, meeting teachers and other school personnel, and developing an understanding of the skills that the child will need to be successful in the new environment are essential for transition success.

Families will be determining their level of participation in the transition process. Families might choose to mirror the activities listed earlier or they may choose to limit their participation to meeting and greeting the new teacher. Whatever level the family determines is optimal, communication and collaboration during the transition is important. Educators should provide the family with information concerning the setting and the opportunities for continuing the family-professional partnership that has been established in the early childhood setting.

Challenges for successful grade-to-grade transitions can result from increased or different work demands required of students. Teacher attitudes and knowledge concerning students with disabilities also affect transitions. Students with disabilities may be successful at one level, only to be overwhelmed by the workload and procedures expected at the next grade level. End-of-year IEP conferences, which involve parents, should include a discussion concerning the workload that will be expected in the next grade with appropriate suggestions for supports provided to ensure continued student success. Again, a discussion of the social, behavioral, and academic skills necessary for success in the next environment is essential. A joint discussion of the child's current functioning level and the possible challenges of the next environment can occur with input from the family and the current teacher. The attendance of the receiving teacher would be important at this conference. The receiving teacher's input can assist in determining the level of importance that a skill might have in the

---

Box 11.1   TEACHER'S LOUNGE CONVERSATION

Ms. Jones: Well, all I can say is that I am so glad this year is over, and good luck to you next year with Sammy. He wore me out.

Ms. Smith: I know, I am not looking forward to having him, but since I am the only third-grade teacher, I will definitely have him in class. What do I need to know about him?

Ms. Jones: In one word, he is a nightmare. He never listens, is always out of his seat, picks on other kids, and really defies all of my rules.

Ms. Smith: Oh boy, just what I want. He reminds me of Timmy, whom I had 3 years ago.

Ms. Jones: Well, I don't want to tell you this, but Timmy (I had him the year before you did) is an angel compared to Sammy. Just buckle up your seat belt because he will challenge you.

Ms. Smith: Were Sammy's parents helpful at all?

Ms. Jones: What parents? I only saw them one time, even though I frequently tried to get parent conferences. I don't think they really care about him at all.

Ms. Smith: Too often that's the way it is. The kids whose parents need to be involved are the ones who aren't.

Ms. Jones: If I were you, I would just be prepared to send him to the office every time he messes up. I tried to wait until I thought I had tried disciplining him and it never worked.

Ms. Smith: Guess that will be my strategy. I know if you couldn't handle him, I can't for sure.

Ms. Jones: Just go home for the summer and don't think about it. Maybe he'll move away before the school year starts up.

---

next classroom. With this information, the family and the current teacher can prioritize the instructional needs of the child in preparation for the next setting. Recognition of coming changes and planning for them may reduce the possibility of difficulties and increase the likelihood of success.

See Box 11.1 for a description of a conversation in a teacher's lounge. How are the attitudes of these two teachers likely to impact students moving from one grade to the next?

Challenges to Changes in Service Delivery System

Although professionals and parents generally think of transitions only as those periods when students make grade or school changes, changes in services and supports are also times for transition planning. An example of this type is an increase in time spent in specialized service delivery, such as an increase from 1 hour in the resource room to 2. Likewise, reducing service delivery time from 2 hours in the resource room to only one should also be recognized as a transition. Problems during these periods of change generally result from a lack of planning and communication. As a result, teachers, parents, and students may have limited knowledge about the new service and may not have supports in place as the change occurs.

Challenges in School to Post-School Environments

One of the most difficult transitions faced by everyone is the transition from school to post-school environments. For 12 or more years, students have attended one or more schools where they, teachers, and others have certain roles and certain expectations. Often they may have been provided with extensive supports to increase opportunities for success. Then, often without adequate preparation, they are thrust into vastly different environments that are likely less nurturing, less structured, and with many different expectations. As a result many students face difficulties during this transition. For students with special needs the transitions at this time are even more difficult (Patton & Dunn, 1998; Smith, Polloway, Patton, & Dowdy, 2004).

TEACHER TIP 11.5

Make it a point to become knowledgeable about adult services in your community, including rehabilitation, housing supports, day service programs, and others. Getting to know key professionals in these service agencies can greatly facilitate successful transition.

Challenges to Employment

Employment is an important step for all young adults, including those with special needs. Because many students formerly in special education do not attend college or other postsecondary training, getting and holding a job is a primary goal after exiting the school system. There are many challenges facing young adults with disabilities related to employment (Wehman, 1998).

Limited Experience with Self-Advocacy   Individuals with disabilities typically have few experiences in self-advocacy, resulting in a limited ability to self-advocate. Although this is a limitation during their school years, its impact is minimized because of the due process safeguards included in special education laws and supports provided by school staff. However, in the adult world, limited abilities in self-advocacy can have a significant negative impact.

Health Care Benefits and SSA Policy   Many federal programs designed to provide supports for persons with disabilities result in a disincentive for work. Many individuals with disabilities lose health care and other benefits provided by the Social Security Administration (SSA) when they go to work. As a result, some persons with disabilities who are capable of successful employment choose not to work in order to avoid losing important health care benefits.

Changing Economy   The most important factor related to employment for persons with disabilities is the state of the economy. Employers frequently indicate that the

PRAXIS 1

Understanding Exceptionalities

CEC 2

Development and Characteristics of Learners

reason they do not employ individuals with disabilities is that the economy is not doing well, or that their company is undergoing reorganization and downsizing.

Employer Attitudes　Even when appropriate jobs are available, employer attitudes may prevent many qualified persons with disabilities from securing and maintaining jobs. Professionals cannot overlook the fact that if an employer does not want to employ a person, then that person will probably not be hired, and if hired, will be the first fired.

Vocational Training　Many school personnel who are responsible for preparing students for employment after they leave school lack the necessary skills to properly prepare their students. Often, the curriculum of the school is also not conducive to preparing students for employment or other post-school activities.

Transportation　A lack of available, affordable transportation may impede successful transition, especially for employment opportunities. Individuals with job skills who are employed may not be able to maintain the job because of difficulties securing transportation. Due to limited income or the impact of the disability, some young adults with disabilities may not have access to a privately owned vehicle. In many communities, the availability of public transportation is limited. As a result, a lack of transportation may keep some individuals from working.

Professional Attitudes　Although professionals who work with individuals with disabilities should have positive attitudes concerning their ability to work, many professionals lack confidence in the employability of their students or clients. If such a belief is present, then the likelihood for successful employment is greatly restricted.

Challenges to Independent Living

In addition to employment, difficulties arise for young adults with disabilities who are attempting to transition from home to independent living. Specific challenges include: (a) financial difficulties, (b) limited independent living skills, (c) attitudes of landlords, (d) inadequate social skills, and (e) lack of friends and community supports.

Challenges to effective transition, at every level, are common. Whether these challenges are the result of negative attitudes, different regulations and administrative structures, poor communication, or other factors is only important in that they could impede successful transitions. What is critically important is that school personnel, family members, and students work together to circumvent these challenges. Without a collaborative effort, successful transition may not occur.

NECESSARY SUPPORTS FOR TRANSITION

Transition planning and services can greatly reduce some of these problems related to transition. Although there are no guarantees that implementing well-planned transition services will result in smooth transitions, without them the likelihood is substantially diminished.

Transition Planning

A key to any transition planning is the active participation of the parents, the school personnel, the various individuals involved in services, and, when appropriate, the child. Successful transition requires coordination and collaboration from a wide variety of individuals and agencies. Table 11.2 lists some groups that should be represented in the transition planning and implementation process.

TEACHER TIP 11.6

Many parents decline in their involvement with school meetings and programs as children get older. You must impress upon family members that their involvement in the transition process is critical. Make every effort to secure their full involvement.

Other than family members, who should always be involved in transition, the specific agencies and people involved in a transition plan will depend on the needs and goals of the individual. For example, for children moving from infant-toddler (Part C) programs to preschool programs, agencies that should be involved include representatives from the Part C (infant-toddler) program, any therapists involved in providing services, and representatives from the preschool program. For children moving from a preschool program to a kindergarten, school-based program, individuals who might be involved would be the preschool teacher, any therapists providing services, and the teacher and possibly an administrator from the public school (Blalock & Benz, 1999). For students moving from school to post-school environments, the transition team would include a representative from agencies such as community colleges, 4-year colleges and universities, vocational-technical schools, rehabilitation agencies, adult service agencies, mental health agencies, residential agencies, and social service agencies. Michaels (1998) lists the following

Table 11.2   Groups represented in the transition planning and implementation process.

Student

Parents

Current teachers and other school staff

School psychological examiner

Transition specialist

Community adult service provider(s)

State vocational rehabilitation representative

Representative(s) from community postsecondary education/training programs adult agencies that might be involved in transition planning activities for students moving into the adult service domain:

- State Office of Mental Retardation and Developmental Disabilities
- Social Security Administration
- Local office of independent living
- Representation from local community colleges
- Local vocational training programs
- Supported employment providers

Individuals involved in transition planning for students are not intended to represent all agencies and groups involved in the transition of students with disabilities from one program to another. Rather, they should represent the types of groups and agencies that are involved in providing appropriate services before, during, and after K–12 public school programs. In each school district, transition coordinators or those responsible for individual transition plans should determine on an individual basis who should be invited to participate in the transition planning meeting.

The transition planning process can be enhanced using the person-centered planning model. Person-centered planning describes several different approaches that differ from a more traditional systems-centered approach. In person-centered models, the planning revolves around the needs and desires of the person, not the system. Services are built around a student, rather than fitting a student into available services. Using a person-centered planning model (O'Brien, 1987) or a personal futures planning model (Furney, 1989) for transition planning can facilitate the transition process for individuals with disabilities.

According to O'Brien (1987), the person-centered planning model focuses on everyday activities and puts more emphasis on families and communities than services. Furney (1989) describes a planning tool known as MAPS (Making Action Plans) that is "a planning tool which results in an outline of where a student wants to go, and how he/she will get there" (p. 2). According to Wehmeyer et al. (1999), the MAPS process for transition planning involves a discussion of five questions: (a) What is the student's history? (b) What are the student's dreams for the future? (c) What are the student's fears about the future? (d) Who is the student? and (e) What are the needs now and after high school? MAPS is based on a personal futures planning approach (O'Brien, Forest, Snow, & Hasbury, 1989) that places the focus of the team's planning on the student.

Bassett and Lehmann (2002) developed an agenda for a student-centered planning meeting. The agenda provides an opportunity for developing ideas concerning the future. First, answer "Who is the student?" using positive terms. Next, focus on the person's strengths. Then discuss "hopes and dreams." Next identify the obstacles or nightmares that express one's fears about the future. Then discuss the resources and supports needed for achieving the dreams. Finally, operationalize the discussion by developing an action plan saying who does what and when. As dreams change, the plan is changed. The value of the process is that it allows for the development of a plan by the individual with input from family and friends through a process of empowerment.

Wehmeyer (1995) described another person-centered transition planning model that is student directed and focused on teaching students the skills needed to be meaningfully involved in transition planning. This student-centered planning differs from other forms of program planning in that "its purpose is not to plan for the next IEP or semester, but rather to concretely envision a future filled with a student's hopes and dreams" (Bassett & Lehmann, 2002, p. 14). But, no matter whether the transition planning model used is a person-centered model, a personal futures planning model, or a student-directed planning model, each supports the transition planning process because all focus on specific supports needed by the student.

TEACHER TIP 11.7

Student-centered planning requires school personnel to give up some ownership in the process. School staff must be willing to give up this control to help students learn how to become self-advocates. And, who better to know what is needed for the future than the person who will be living the future?

Coordination of Transition Efforts

Successful transition for students with special needs requires planning and collaboration among different agencies and the family (Cozzens, Dowdy, & Smith, 1999). In fact, "interagency collaboration is the cornerstone of efficient and effective transition process" (Hanline, 1993, p. 142). Without all parties working together, the likelihood of smooth transitions for students with special needs becomes diminished.

Simply inviting individuals from different agencies to participate in transition efforts will not automatically result in effective collaboration or effective transition planning. According to Hanson and Widerstrom (1993), components necessary for effective collaboration among transition planning participants include:

| CEC 10 |

Collaboration

- commitment from the decision makers to agree on transition efforts;
- shared ownership and decision making among all involved participants to make the transition planning a success;
- adequate resources to support planning and coordination of collaboration and the involvement of those who can make decisions on sharing resources across agencies;
- ongoing training and technical assistance for involved professionals;
- ongoing evaluation component to assess effectiveness of the plan; and
- family input and involvement

Coordination and communication are important components of effective transition planning. Schools may need to identify a staff member who will serve as the transition coordinator. This individual can maintain contact among school personnel, preschool service personnel, adult service and community agencies, and family

---

Box 11.2   FAMILY PARTICIPATION IN TRANSITION

Fred and Vicki want the best for their 16-year-old son, Eddie. He has mild mental retardation and is in a vocational program on West Campus. His transition planning meeting will be held tomorrow at the school. Both Fred and Vicki will attend, as well as Eddie. They have talked with Eddie about what he might want to do when he leaves high school. His goals are to live in an apartment by himself and have a job. Ms. Jacobson, the transition coordinator for the high school, has set up the meeting and invited a wide variety of participants she thinks will be helpful. These include representatives from the state vocational rehabilitation agency, local group home for adults with developmental disabilities, and the day service program for individuals with mental retardation. Even though Ms. Jacobson is not particularly interested in Eddie working at a sheltered workshop, she also invited the placement coordinator from the local workshop for his input. Mr. Hanks, Eddie's primary teacher, and Ms. Jordan, the school's psychological examiner, will also be present. She developed the following agenda for the meeting:

- ❏ Introductions
- ❏ A statement from Eddie about what he wants after high school
- ❏ Input from Fred and Vicki about what they want for Eddie after school
- ❏ Input from Eddie's teacher and psychological examiner about his strengths and weaknesses
- ❏ Discussion from all parties about how best to meet Eddie's needs after he leaves school
- ❏ Summary and recommendations

---

members to facilitate communication, planning, and implementation of transition supports. It is important that one person be designated as the individual responsible for transition and given the time and resources necessary to accomplish the activity.

Transition coordinators, whether they are formally recognized in the school or simply the school staff member responsible for a particular student's transition, should facilitate family participation. As noted by Patton and Dunn (1998), "families play a key role in the shared responsibility for preparing their children for dealing successfully with the challenges of life" (p. 16). All school personnel involved in transition programs should understand the importance of family support and participation. Read and reflect on the scenario in Box 11.2.

Communication

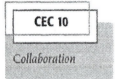

CEC 10

Collaboration

Communication is a critical element in successful transition. Some challenges to effective communication include the use of professional jargon, communication styles used by family members and school personnel, level of rapport between family members and school personnel, limited time to facilitate communication among participants, and a perception by the family that they are being "talked down to" by professionals (Hanline, 1993). Additionally, communication may be difficult because agency professionals with different perspectives, training, and experiences may be involved. For example, vocational rehabilitation counselors work under different regulations, eligibility criteria, and terminology than public schools. The transition coordinator for the district should ensure effective communication among the various parties involved in transition planning. Without such communication, planning and implementing transition supports will be ineffective.

Effective Transition Programs

Effective transition programs require planning, effective communication, collaboration, and commitment. In order to enhance the development of effective transition programs, Patton and Dunn (1998) have identified 12 guiding principles (see Table 11.3). These principles should be considered when teachers, students, and families are engaged in transition planning and programming.

Table 11.3 Guiding principles for transition plan development.

1. Transition efforts should start early and continue until transition occurs. Schools should take a proactive approach to transition. Transition efforts should begin at age 14 and not wait until a student is nearing the end of public school.

2. Planning must be comprehensive. A district must focus on more than just school to post-school environments and services and develop a plan that encompasses transition needs from first grade through high school and provides supports for all students with special needs.

3. The planning process must balance what is ideal with what is possible. Even though it is important for students with special needs, their family members, and school staff to dream about adult opportunities, reality must be a factor in developing and implementing transition plans.

4. Student participation is essential. The one person most affected by transitions is the student with special needs so students and their family members must be involved in the entire process in order to incorporate their dreams, wishes, and ideas.

5. Family involvement is crucial. Family involvement in the transition planning and implementation process is vitally important because family members have information to contribute related to the future of their child.

6. The transition planning process must be sensitive to diversity. Diversity among students and their families must be taken into consideration when developing a transition plan because different cultures expect and desire different outcomes from school.

7. Everyone uses supports and services. All individuals who make changes need supports during transitions but students with special needs may need more extensive supports.

8. Community-based activities are important. Including community-based teaching and training opportunities is an excellent means of easing transition difficulties.

9. Interagency commitment, cooperation, and coordination must be improved. Without the active involvement of all agencies involved in providing services to children and their families, important transition efforts may be overlooked.

10. Timing is crucial if linkages are to be made and a seamless transition to life after high school is to be achieved. Waiting until students have difficulties is too late to provide appropriate support services.

11. The transition planning process should be considered a capacity-building activity.

12. Ranking of transition needs must occur. Part of the transition planning process should be to rank order the transition needs of students.

13. Transition planning is beneficial to all students. Preparing for change is a good way of avoiding pitfalls that often occur when there are changes.

Note: From Transition from school to young adulthood: Basic concepts and recommendation practices, by J. P. Patton & C. Dunn, 1998, Austin, TX: PRO-ED.

ROLE OF PARENTS, STUDENTS, AND SCHOOL PERSONNEL IN TRANSITION PLANNING

Role of Parents

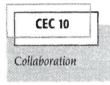

CEC 10

Collaboration

INTASC 10

School and Community Involvement

In all transition planning models used, students, parents, and school personnel should collaborate in order to develop and implement an effective transition program. Parents and students, when appropriate, make the key decisions related to transition. They should be present to assume this role and prepared to participate in transition planning and team meetings as equal partners with school personnel. Wehmeyer et al. (1999) note that in transition, families should:

- be dreamers.
- expect to talk a lot.
- ask school personnel to be specific about what is needed.
- support the student's self-determination/self-advocacy efforts.
- keep the focus on present levels of performance and strengths instead of deficits.
- support the school's efforts to provide career development and job training. (pp. 39–40)

Most parents are eager to participate in their child's education, particularly in transition planning. Although it is important for family members to participate at all levels, it is especially important for family members of young children. Wehmeyer et al. (1999) have listed specific expectations for parents in the transition planning process that will enhance their participation in the process (see Table 11.4).

Role of Students

CEC 2

Development and Characteristics of Learners

For students with special needs, participation in transition planning is critical. Students must be willing to participate in planning for their future. Opportunities should be provided for students to actively participate in transition planning meetings and provide suggestions for identifying and accomplishing goals for the future.

As students mature, their input becomes essential to the decision-making process. However, students would benefit from preparation prior to attending meetings with school personnel and parents. The following suggestions may be helpful in preparing students to actively participate:

- Advise students of meetings early enough for them to work with family members and teachers to formulate questions and statements of concerns or preferences concerning issues that may be discussed.
- Advise students of the purpose of the meeting, the general format of the meeting, and those invited to attend and the reason for their attendance.
- Advise students of the role they will be expected to play and the input that will be sought (for example, why they cannot get their homework done; the type of classroom they prefer; preferred leisure-time activities or club preferences; personal vocational goals; living preferences).
- If appropriate, provide students with information or questions that they may be asked and provide them with the opportunity to prepare answers.

Table 11.4   Parental expectations in the transition planning process.

1. Actively participate in the transition planning process.
2. Work with the student to identify needs and desires.
3. Work with adult service agencies to identify and secure services that might be needed after exiting school.
4. Solicit assistance from advocacy services when necessary.
5. Be willing to compromise regarding transition issues for their child.
6. Involve informal support networks to provide transition services, when appropriate.
7. Consider extended year service needs of students.
8. Work with community college and other postsecondary education agencies when appropriate for their child.
9. Provide natural supports typically provided by parents for children without disabilities.
10. Participate in the community to determine the availability of choices for the child.
11. Join advocacy and parent support groups to learn more about transition services.
12. Dream about their child's future.
13. Share your ideas and thoughts in meetings.
14. Ask school personnel to be specific about issues.
15. Support self-determination and self-advocacy training for the student.
16. Focus on strengths instead of weaknesses.
17. Support school efforts in career development and job training. (Wehmeyer et al., 1999)

- Provide communication skills training specific to the demands of the meeting, including role-playing when appropriate.
- Have discussions prior to the meeting to determine the student's emotional status and stress level and to assist the student in preparing emotionally for the event.

During the meeting, the student may need support and encouragement to ensure and enhance active participation. Opportunities to participate can occur when team members solicit input from the student. To assure that the student understands the discussion, information or explanations should be included throughout the meeting. Student participation should be encouraged during the meeting by acknowledging their comments and recognizing that they should have a strong voice in the activities that affect them. Participation is not only a right, but also an opportunity to practice those skills that will be necessary for their independence as an adult.

Age of Majority

Parent participation in the educational planning for their child changes when the child reaches the age of majority (age 18 in most states). At that time the responsibility and rights the parent has assumed for the development and monitoring of their child's educational program diminishes as those rights transfer to the child. According to IDEA 2004:

> Beginning not less than one year before the student reaches the age of majority, a statement must be included in the student's IEP that he has been informed of his rights and that these rights will be transferred to him upon his reaching the age of majority.

During the year prior to the student's reaching the age of majority, teachers, parents, and the student should work together to understand the ramifications of this change, and to provide self-advocacy training for the student.

In some instances, it may be apparent that the student does not have the ability to assume the responsibilities inherent in this change. According to NCSET (2002, p. 4), "for these students, guardianship, conservatorship, or another form of representation by an advocate may be appropriate." Guardianship is a legal designation in which the individual is rendered legally incompetent and therefore incapable or unable to assume the responsibilities accruing to him/her at the age of majority. If such a designation is made, a guardian, usually a parent, is appointed by the court to assume those legal responsibilities. In some instances, a form of limited guardianship, known as a conservatorship, may be the more appropriate option. The conservator, again usually the parent, is appointed to assume some, but not all, of the responsibilities resulting from the student reaching the age of majority. In this case, the individual retains those rights and responsibilities for which he or she is considered capable of managing.

CEC 2

Development and Characteristics of Learners

TEACHER TIP 11.8

Teaching students to become self-advocates is one of the greatest challenges for school staff. School personnel need to develop and implement curricular opportunities that will help teach students how to take responsibility for their own futures, beginning with transition efforts.

Role of School Personnel as a Partner

Educators are responsible for facilitating the transition process by encouraging parent and student participation and facilitating their participation in transition planning. Specific strategies will depend on the age of the student and the type of transition being planned, and should be directed by the unique needs of each student and family.

Encouraging Family Participation   School personnel have a responsibility to encourage and support family participation in the transition process. Families who are not involved, or are not involved to a significant degree, often list the following reasons for their lack of participation: (a) a lack of understanding why their involvement is important, (b) an inability to attend meetings as a result of work or transportation issues, and (c) a lack of trust in school personnel (*Partnership Series 1: Teachers' Strategies for Involving Hard-to-Reach Families*, 1991). None of these reasons are beyond the control of school personnel. School personnel must circumvent challenges and engage family members in developing and implementing transition programs for their children. Wehmeyer et al. (1999) provide several suggestions for securing meaningful involvement of families in the transition process (see Table 11.5).

CEC 10

Collaboration

Table 11.5   Guidelines for supporting parental participation.

Suggestions for Securing Parental Involvement in the Transition Process. Learning to Listen. The transition process must be centered on the needs of students and their families, not on the needs or perceptions of the school. This requires a person-centered transition planning approach where the student and family members actually take the lead in the transition process. The student and family members must feel like the school personnel are listening to their needs.

Do Not Limit Options. Many students and family members may become frustrated if their options for transition are limited. Within the confines of the school's resources, options must be sufficiently available to meet the needs of the student and family. This might require some creative measures in an attempt to meet the needs of the student and family.

Invite Involvement. Although IDEA requires that schools invite parental participation, and the participation of the student in the transition process, schools can meet the legal requirement of the law without extending an invitation that family members and students feel is a *real* invitation for involvement. Because many parents may become cynical about the school's desire that they are involved, it may take a major effort from the school to extend an invitation that family members think is a true effort to secure their involvement. Get parents together to discuss different transition options, purposes, and activities so that they feel the school is truly interested in their involvement.

Set a Positive Tone for Meetings. School personnel must set the tone of the meeting to ensure that family members are comfortable and feel like their input is valued. This will require school personnel to plan effectively and develop strategies for family participation at the meetings.

Decide Goals. Make sure that the goals and components of the transition plan are developed at the meeting with real involvement of family members. Coming to the meeting with a pre-developed transition plan does not give family members a feeling that their involvement is really necessary. Though it is definitely appropriate to come to the meeting with some general ideas, make sure that family members do not get the impression that the plan has already been developed without their involvement.

Allow Students to Lead the Meeting. One of the best ways to promote family involvement is to support students' leading the transition meeting. This creates an atmosphere that reflects a true openness of school personnel, gives the student an opportunity to develop self-promoting skills, and creates an atmosphere that family members and the student are truly equal partners in the process.

Note: Adapted from: M.L. Wehmeyer, M. Morningstar, and D. Husted, 1999, *Family involvement in transition planning and implementation*. Austin: Pro-Ed.

If families are not involved, school personnel should discover how to involve them. This includes determining different "ways that families feel comfortable and capable of contributing" (Wehmeyer et al., 1999, p. 41). There are specific actions that school personnel can take to improve family-school partnerships. The National Center for Clinical Infant Programs recommended the following actions of school personnel when planning for the transition of young children from one program to another:

1. Inform parents of all of the choices currently available to them in their community (e.g., private preschool education, Head Start, integrated preschool) and of their parental rights and responsibilities.
2. Provide this information up to a year before transitioning to a new program because some programs have extended waiting lists and early application is required for acceptance.
3. Arrange opportunities for parents to visit potential sites, if they choose.
4. Arrange opportunities for parents to meet parents of children enrolled in the potential sites, if they choose.
5. Assist parents in evaluating programs for appropriate placement.
6. Assist parents in completing forms, applications, and compiling records, at the parent's request.
7. Assist the family in gaining access to the new program (e.g., securing transportation, funding).
8. Accompany parents to case conference meetings, IEP meetings, or other intake meetings, upon the family's request.
9. Provide consultation (e.g., physical, occupational, and speech therapies as needed) to the new program provider during the transition period.
10. Arrange for coordination of follow-up services from other community agencies currently involved.
11. Assist the family in advocating for the most appropriate program and services for the child.
12. Remain as a resource for the family if any future need should arise. This should include periodic follow-up with the family. (Zeitlin & Williamson, 1994, p. 191)

Although these actions were specifically identified for planning transitions for young children, most also apply to the transition of older children.

TEACHER TIP 11.9

Do not give up on getting families involved in transition planning. Even though the easiest thing to do may be to ignore family members who are not "at the table," the success of transition for the student demands that schools make every effort to secure family involvement.

Facilitating Transition Planning

The ultimate role for school personnel in the area of transition is to facilitate smooth transitions, regardless of the level. This means not only increasing the participation of family members, students, and other agency personnel, but also coordinating the activities of all parties, and providing follow-up to transition activities to determine how future transitions can be more successful. Cook, Tessier, and Klein (1996) suggested the following eight steps that can assist in making the transition planning meeting and the transition itself successful:

1. Discuss the objectives of the transition and the roles and responsibilities of each member of the child's team.
2. Develop a transition timeline so that transitions proceed in a timely, step-by-step manner.
3. Accompany family members as they view and evaluate program options.
4. Discuss program options with family members.
5. Encourage the family to select a program.
6. Arrange for the exchange of all pertinent records and paperwork in a timely manner.
7. Assist the child and family in making the transition.
8. Encourage reciprocal follow-up between sending and receiving programs. (pp. 169–170)

One of the most effective ways for school personnel and family members to become active in the transition planning process is to review sample transition plans. As parents and school personnel review these plans, they should note trends in the transition process and types of services that have been suggested for some students. An example of a transition plan is provided in Figure 11.2. See Wehman (1995, 1998) for additional examples of transition plans.

> **PRAXIS 3**
>
> *Delivery of Services to Students with Disabilities*

> **CEC 10**
>
> *Collaboration*

TEACHER TIP 11.10

Have sample plans available for family members to review. These sample plans can reflect various needs of students so that family members can see plans that might be appropriate for their own child.

Even though the transition plans presented by Wehman focus on school to work, some plans focus on school to postsecondary educational opportunities. For families with students who are planning on attending college or other postsecondary education or training program, school staff could assist with decisions related to school choice and program of study (Webb, 2000). Figure 11.3 provides an example of a college exploration worksheet that school personnel could use with students and family members when helping to plan for specific postsecondary programs.

Individualized Transition Plan

Student's Name: _____ Kory _____

Last	**First**	**M.I.**

Birthdate: _____   **School:** Marietta _____

Student's I.D. #: _____   **ITP Conference Date:** _____

Participants

Name	**Position**
Kory/Ann-Marie	student/mother
Margaret	transition coordinator
Jim	case manager
Paul	vocational rehabilitation counselor
Angela	employer
Elise	group home director
Kathleen	physical therapist
Jean	occupational therapist

	Date Initiated	Date Completed
1. Referral to Vocational Rehabilitation Services	_____	_____
2. SSI/SSDI	_____	_____
3. Medical/Medicine	_____	_____
4. Referral Local Social Services	_____	_____
5. Application for Special Transportation	_____	_____
6. Referral to Residential Services for Housing Placement	_____	_____
7. Referral to Center for Independent Living (CIL)	_____	_____
8. Referral to Rehabilitation Engineering Services	_____	_____
9. Referral to MH/MR Case Management Services	_____	_____

Figure 11.2 *Sample Transition Plan*

Note: *Reprinted from Wehman, P. (1998). Developing transition plans (pp. 40–43). Austin, TX: Pro-Ed. Used with permission.*

I. Career and Economic Self-Sufficiency	
1. Employment Goal	Full-time competitive employment in food service industry with support.
Level of Present Performance:	Kory works 15 hours per week as a salad preparation associate trainee in the school's transition program.
Steps Needed to Accomplish Goal:	(1) Increase work hours to 35 by June, 1995; and (2) increase job responsibilities by June, 1995.
Date of Completion:	June, 1995
Person(s) Responsible for Implementation:	Kory and employer
2. Vocational Education/Training Goal	Kory will expand number of independent work skills by June, 1995.
Level of Present Performance:	Kory currently has a one-to-one job coach. His occupational and physical therapists and the Engineering College at the University of Virginia are working closely to develop adaptive portable equipment to aid Kory's independent skill acquisition.
Steps Needed to Accomplish Goal:	(1) Develop appropriate adaptive tools so that Kory may chop lettuce, slice tomatoes, and seal plastic containers by January, 1995; and (2) decrease support by April, 1995.
Date of Completion:	April, 1995
Person(s) Responsible for Implementation:	Kory, occupational therapist, physical therapist, and Dr. Smith of Engineering School
3. Postsecondary Education Goal	N/A
Level of Present Performance:	
Steps Needed to Accomplish Goal:	
Date of Completion:	
Person(s) Responsible for Implementation:	
4. Financial/Income Needs Goal	Kory will invest his inheritance with support.
Level of Present Performance:	Kory will inherit a small trust fund by March, 30, 1995, from his paternal grandparents. He is anxious to feel financially secure. He receives SSDI and SSI.

(continued)

Steps Needed to Accomplish Goal:	(1) Kory and his mother will meet with family attorney for advice by June 30, 1994; (2) Kory will name an accountant by August 31, 1994; and (3) Kory will have a financial portfolio in place by his 21st birthday.
Date of Completion:	September, 1994
Person(s) Responsible for Implementation:	Kory, mother, and attorney

II. Community Integration and Participation

5. Independent Living Goal	Kory will develop a repertoire of cooking skills for dinner and lunch.
Level of Present Performance:	Kory independently makes breakfast meal only. He also makes ample sandwiches. He has recently learned to operate a microwave.
Steps Needed to Accomplish Goal:	(1) Kory will make two dinners per week independently by December 31, 1994; and (2) Kory will incrementally increase his cooking skills by April, 1995.
Date of Completion:	April, 1995
Person(s) Responsible for Implementation:	Kory and group home director
6. Transportation Mobility/Goal	Kory will join a carpool at work.
Level of Present Performance:	Kory currently depends on group home staff for transportation. His manager at Morrison's encourages carpooling among employees.
Steps Needed to Accomplish Goal:	(1) Develop an agenda for the July Morrison's staff meeting regarding carpooling plan (with support); (2) develop reasonable rate of reimbursement for coworkers; and (3) join a carpool by September, 1994.
Date of Completion:	February, 1995
Person(s) Responsible for Implementation:	Kory, employer, transition coordinator, and vocational rehabilitation counselor
7. Social Relationship Goal	Kory will increase social activities within and outside the group home.
Level of Present Performance:	Kory lived with his mom in a trailer for several years. He rarely ventured out of his home except for school-related attendance. Kory is somewhat apprehensive to leave home.

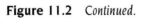

Figure 11.2 *Continued.*

Steps Needed to Accomplish Goal:	(1) Kory will participate in (modified) bowling activity, once a week by August, 1994; (2) Kory will attend weekly excursion to a local mall by October, 1994; and (3) Kory will choose a third activity by December, 1994.
Date of Completion:	December, 1994
Person(s) Responsible for Implementation:	Kory and group home director
8. Recreation/Leisure Goal:	Kory will join a local baseball cap club by July, 1994.
Level of Present Performance:	Kory collects baseball caps (has 116). He has recently become aware of a collector's club through a church contact (Mr. Weaver).
Steps Needed to Accomplish Goal:	(1) Accompany Mr. Weaver to a monthly meeting by June 30, 1994; (2) complete application form with support, and submit by July 15, 1994; and (3) arrange transportation to and from meetings by September 1, 1994.
Date of Completion:	June, 1994
Person(s) Responsible for Implementation:	Kory, group home director, mother
III. Personal Competence	
9. Health/Safety Goal	Kory will maintain personal exercise/therapy program to maintain range of motion in lower limbs.
Level of Present Performance:	Kory has been resistant to maintaining his exercise program, claiming it "hurts." Kory has had a lifelong aversion to his physical therapy.
Steps Needed to Accomplish Goal:	(1) Rule out all physiological causes of pain (neurological) by August, 1994; (2) incrementally develop a planned schedule, with Kory, of physical therapy exercises, by September, 1994; and (3) Kory will develop/maintain therapy by December, 1994.
Date of Completion:	December, 1994
Person(s) Responsible for Implementation:	Kory, physical therapist, and mother

(continued)

10. **Self-Advocacy/Future Planning**	Kory will access community agencies independently.
Level of Present Performance:	Kory currently requests assistance from family or group home staff only.
Steps Needed to Accomplish Goal:	(1) Develop a menu of personally appropriate resources (physician, BMR, Voc. Rehab., etc.) and tape next to telephone in Kory's room; (2) supervise all contacts for 3 months; and (3) Kory will independently contact appropriate resources by December, 1994.
Date of Completion:	December, 1994
Person(s) Responsible for Implementation:	Kory, group home director, transition coordinator
Student Career Preference:	Work in food service industry.
Student Major Transition Needs:	1. Increase independent work skills
	2. Financial portfolio
	3. Increase social activities
	4. Increase working skills
	5. Maintain physical therapy
	6.
	7.
	8.
	9.
	10.

Figure 11.2 *Continued.*

Characteristics of Postsecondary Institutions										
Mark each item Y for yes N for no Make additional notes on a separate page	4-year state college/university	4-year private college/university	2-year college	Community college	Technical institute	Vocational school	Military school	Apprenticeship	Home study	Adult education
Entrance exams required (e.g., SAT, ACT)										
Open admission										
Housing on campus										
Program for students with learning disabilities										
Bachelor's degree granted										
Work experiences or internships										
Remedial or developmental classes										
Average class size (write in number)										
Average tuition/costs for 1 year (write in number)										

Figure 11.3 *College exploration work sheet.*

Note: *Reprinted from* Transition to Postsecondary Education (P.A.) *by K. W. Webb, 2002, Austin: Pro-Ed. p. 19. Reprinted with permission.*

SUMMARY

This chapter has focused on transition services and the role of school personnel and family members in the transition planning process. The Individuals with Disabilities Education Act (IDEA) began requiring schools to plan transition supports for students in 1990, with the most recent reauthorization of the legislation in 2004.

Although IDEA focuses on transitions from high school to post-school environments and from infant-toddler programs to preschool programs, other transitions are often overlooked because no legal mandates are in place. Although all students undergo transitions, students with special needs often experience more difficulties than most other students. Challenges that may impede successful transitions for students with disabilities were discussed, with various strategies presented to circumvent these challenges. Finally, elements for successful transitions were described including transition planning; participation of family members, school personnel, and other agency personnel; and the importance of involving all stakeholders in each step of the transition process.

QUESTIONS FOR DISCUSSION

1. How would you define transition? Describe some of the transitions you have gone through and some of the difficulties associated with them. Would it have been helpful if you had different kinds of supports during these transition times? If so, what kinds of supports would have been useful?

2. What barriers to successful transition are most difficult to overcome between early childhood programs and elementary school programs? What makes these barriers difficult and what are some strategies that could facilitate a successful transition for children and families?

3. Transition from high school to post high school activities can be difficult for many students. What issues do students with disabilities face that exacerbate these difficulties? How can school personnel, family members, and adult agency personnel help make this transition more successful?

REFERENCES

Bailey, D. B., & Wolery, M. (1992). *Teaching infants and preschoolers with disabilities.* Columbus, OH Merrill.

Bassett, D. S., & Lehmann, J. (2002). *Student-focused conferencing and planning* (Transition Series). Austin, TX: Pro-Ed.

Blalock, G., & Benz, M. R. (1999). *Using community transition teams to improve transition services.* Austin, TX: Pro-Ed.

Cook, R. E., Tessier, A., & Klein, M. D. (1996). *Adapting early childhood curricula for children in inclusive settings* (4th ed.).Upper Saddle River, NJ: Merrill/Prentice Hall.

Cozzens, G., Dowdy, C. A., & Smith, T. E. C. (1999). *Adult agencies: Linkages for adolescents in transition.* Austin, TX: Pro-Ed.

Furney, K. (1989). *Making dreams happen: How to facilitate the MAPS process.* Burlington, VT: Vermont's Transition Systems Change Project.

Gottwald, S. R., & Pardy, P. A. (1997). Public schools. In S. K. Thurman, J. R. Cornwell, & S. R. Gottwald (Eds.), *Contexts of early intervention.* Baltimore: Brookes.

Hanline, M. F. (1993). Facilitating integrated preschool service delivery transitions for child, families, and professionals. In C. A. Peck, S. L. Odom, & D. D. Bricker (Eds.), *Integrating young children with disabilities into community programs.* Baltimore: Brookes.

Hanson, M. J., & Widerstrom, A. H. (1993). Consultation and collaboration. In C. A. Peck, S. L. Odom, & D. D. Bricker (Eds.), *Integrating young children with disabilities into community programs.* Baltimore: Brookes.

La Paro, K. M., Pianta, R. C., & Cox, M. J. (2000). Teachers' reported transition practices for children transitioning into kindergarten and first grade. *Exceptional Children, 67,* 7–20.

Michaels, C. A. (1998). *Transition to employment.* Austin, TX: Pro-Ed.

National Center on Secondary Education and Transition (NCSET). (2002). *Parent brief: Age of majority.* Minneapolis, MN: PACER Center.

O'Brien, J. (1987). A guide to life planning. In B. Wilcox & G. T. Bellamy (Eds.), *A comprehensive guide to alternative curriculum for youth and adults with severe disabilities.* Baltimore: Paul H. Brookes.

O'Brien, J., Forest, M., Snow, J., & Hasbury, D. (1989). *Action for inclusion.* Toronto, CN: Frontier College Press.

Parent Education Advocacy Training Center. *The Partnership Series,* Workshop I. PEATC, 1991.

Patton, J. R., & Dunn, C. (1998). *Transition from school to young adulthood: Basic concepts and recommended practices.* Austin, TX: Pro-Ed.

Sitlington, P. L., & Frank, A. R. (1998). *Follow-up studies: A practitioner's handbook.* Austin, TX: Pro-Ed.

Smith, T. E. C., & Patton, J. R. (1998). *Section 504 and public schools: A practical guide.* Austin, TX: Pro-Ed.

Smith, T. E. C., Polloway, E. A., Patton, J. R., & Dowdy, C. A. (2004). *Teaching students with special needs in inclusive settings* (4th ed.). Boston: Allyn & Bacon.

U. S. Department of Education. (2002). *Twenty-fourth annual report to Congress on the implementation of the Individuals with Disabilities Education Act.* Washington, DC: U.S. Government Printing Office.

Webb, K. W. (2000). *Transition to postsecondary education: Strategies for students with disabilities.* Austin, TX: Pro-Ed.

Wehman, P. (1995). *Individual transition plans: The teacher's curriculum guide for helping youth with special needs* (pp. 139–144). Austin, TX: Pro-Ed.

Wehman, P. (1998). *Developing transition plans.* Austin, TX: Pro-Ed.

Wehmeyer, M. (1995). *Whose future is it anyway? A student-directed transition planning process.* Arlington, TX: The ARC.

Wehmeyer, M. L., Morningstar, M., & Husted, D. (1999). *Family involvement in transition planning and implementation* (Transition Series). Austin, TX: Pro-Ed.

Winton, P. J. (1993). Providing family support in integrated settings: Research and recommendations. In C. A. Peck, S. L. Odom, & D. D. Bricker (Eds.), *Integrating young children with disabilities into community programs.* Baltimore: Brookes.

Zeitlin, S., & Williamson, G.G. (1994). *Coping in young children: Early intervention practices to enhance adaptive behavior and resilience.* Baltimore: Paul H. Brookes.

Appendix

● ○ ○ ○ ○

CEC STANDARDS (COMMON CORE)

Standard 1: Foundations

Special educators understand the field as an evolving and changing discipline based on philosophies, evidence-based principles and theories, relevant laws and policies, diverse and historical points of view, and human issues that have historically influenced and continue to influence the field of special education and the education and treatment of individuals with exceptional needs both in school and society. Special educators understand how these influence professional practice, including assessment, instructional planning, implementation, and program evaluation. Special educators understand how issues of human diversity can impact families, cultures, and schools, and how these complex human issues can interact with issues in the delivery of special education services. They understand the relationships of organizations of special education to the organizations and functions of schools, school systems, and other agencies. Special educators use this knowledge as a ground upon which to construct their own personal understandings and philosophies of special education.

Beginning special educators demonstrate their mastery of this standard through the mastery of the CEC Common Core Knowledge and Skills, as well as through the appropriate CEC Specialty Area(s) Knowledge and Skills for which the program is preparing candidates.

Standard 2: Development and Characteristics of Learners

Special educators know and demonstrate respect for their students first as unique human beings. Special educators understand the similarities and differences in human development and the characteristics between and among individuals with and without exceptional learning needs (ELN).[1] Moreover, special educators understand

---

[1] "Individual with exceptional learning needs" is used throughout to include individuals with disabilities and individuals with exceptional gifts and talents.

how exceptional conditions can interact with the domains of human development and they use this knowledge to respond to the varying abilities and behaviors of individual's with ELN. Special educators understand how the experiences of individuals with ELN can impact families, as well as the individual's ability to learn, interact socially, and live as fulfilled contributing members of the community.

Beginning special educators demonstrate their mastery of this standard through the mastery of the CEC Common Core Knowledge and Skills, as well as through the appropriate CEC Specialty Area(s) Knowledge and Skills for which the program is preparing candidates.

Standard 3: Individual Learning Differences

Special educators understand the effects that an exceptional condition[2] can have on an individual's learning in school and throughout life. Special educators understand that the beliefs, traditions, and values across and within cultures can affect relationships among and between students, their families, and the school community. Moreover, special educators are active and resourceful in seeking to understand how primary language, culture, and familial backgrounds interact with the individual's exceptional condition to impact the individual's academic and social abilities, attitudes, values, interests, and career options. The understanding of these learning differences and their possible interactions provide the foundation upon which special educators individualize instruction to provide meaningful and challenging learning for individuals with ELN.

Beginning special educators demonstrate their mastery of this standard through the mastery of the CEC Common Core Knowledge and Skills, as well as through the appropriate CEC Specialty Area(s) Knowledge and Skills for which the program is preparing candidates.

Standard 4: Instructional Strategies

Special educators possess a repertoire of evidence-based instructional strategies to individualize instruction for individuals with ELN. Special educators select, adapt, and use these instructional strategies to promote challenging learning results in general and special curricula[3] and to appropriately modify learning environments for individuals with ELN. They enhance the learning of critical thinking, problem solving, and performance skills of individuals with ELN, and increase their self-awareness, self-management, self-control, self-reliance, and self-esteem. Moreover, special educators emphasize the development, maintenance, and generalization of knowledge and skills across environments, settings, and the lifespan.

---

[2]"Exceptional condition" is used throughout to include both single and coexisting conditions. These may be two or more disabling conditions or exceptional gifts or talents coexisting with one or more disabling condition.
[3]"Special curricula" is used throughout.

Beginning special educators demonstrate their mastery of this standard through the mastery of the CEC Common Core Knowledge and Skills, as well as through the appropriate CEC Specialty Area(s) Knowledge and Skills for which the program is preparing candidates.

Standard 5: Learning Environments and Social Interactions

Special educators actively create learning environments for individuals with ELN that foster cultural understanding, safety and emotional well-being, positive social interactions, and active engagement of individuals with ELN. In addition, special educators foster environments in which diversity is valued and individuals are taught to live harmoniously and productively in a culturally diverse world. Special educators shape environments to encourage the independence, self-motivation, self-direction, personal empowerment, and self-advocacy of individuals with ELN. Special educators help their general education colleagues integrate individuals with ELN in regular environments and engage them in meaningful learning activities and interactions. Special educators use direct motivational and instructional interventions with individuals with ELN to teach them to respond effectively to current expectations. When necessary, special educators can safely intervene with individuals with ELN in crisis. Special educators coordinate all these efforts and provide guidance and direction to para-educators and others, such as classroom volunteers and tutors.

Beginning special educators demonstrate their mastery of this standard through the mastery of the CEC Common Core Knowledge and Skills, as well as through the appropriate CEC Specialty Area(s) Knowledge and Skills for which the program is preparing candidates.

Standard 6: Language

Special educators understand typical and atypical language development and the ways in which exceptional conditions can interact with an individual's experience with and use of language. Special educators use individualized strategies to enhance language development and teach communication skills to individuals with ELN. Special educators are familiar with augmentative, alternative, and assistive technologies to support and enhance communication of individuals with exceptional needs. Special educators match their communication methods to an individual's language proficiency and cultural and linguistic differences. Special educators provide effective language models, and they use communication strategies and resources to facilitate understanding of subject matter of individuals with ELN whose primary language is not English.

Beginning special educators demonstrate their mastery of language for and with individuals with ELN through the mastery of the CEC Common Core Knowledge and Skills, as well as through the appropriate CEC Specialty Area(s) Knowledge and Skills for which the program is preparing candidates.

Standard 7: Instructional Planning

Individualized decision making and instruction is at the center of special education practice. Special educators develop long-range individualized instructional plans anchored in both general and special curricula. In addition, special educators systematically translate these individualized plans into carefully selected shorter-range goals and objectives taking into consideration an individual's abilities and needs, the learning environment, and a myriad of cultural and linguistic factors. Individualized instructional plans emphasize explicit modeling and efficient guided practice to assure acquisition and fluency through maintenance and generalization. Understanding of these factors, as well as the implications of an individual's exceptional condition, guides the special educator's selection, adaptation, and creation of materials, and the use of powerful instructional variables. Instructional plans are modified based on ongoing analysis of the individual's learning progress. Moreover, special educators facilitate this instructional planning in a collaborative context including the individuals with exceptionalities, families, professional colleagues, and personnel from other agencies as appropriate. Special educators also develop a variety of individualized transition plans, such as transitions from preschool to elementary school and from secondary settings to a variety of postsecondary work and learning contexts. Special educators are comfortable using appropriate technologies to support instructional planning and individualized instruction.

Beginning special educators demonstrate their mastery of this standard through the mastery of the CEC Common Core Knowledge and Skills, as well as through the appropriate CEC Specialty Area(s) Knowledge and Skills for which the program is preparing candidates.

Standard 8: Assessment

Assessment is integral to the decision making and teaching of special educators and special educators use multiple types of assessment information for a variety of educational decisions. Special educators use the results of assessments to help identify exceptional learning needs and to develop and implement individualized instructional programs, as well as to adjust instruction in response to ongoing learning progress. Special educators understand the legal policies and ethical principles of measurement and assessment related to referral, eligibility, program planning, instruction, and placement for individuals with ELN, including those from culturally and linguistically diverse backgrounds. Special educators understand measurement theory and practices for addressing issues of validity, reliability, norms, bias, and interpretation of assessment results. In addition, special educators understand the appropriate use and limitations of various types of assessments. Special educators collaborate with families and other colleagues to assure non-biased, meaningful assessments and decision making. Special educators conduct formal and informal assessments of behavior, learning, achievement, and environments to design learning experiences that support the growth and development of individuals with ELN. Special educators use assessment information to identify supports and adaptations required for individuals with ELN to access the general curriculum and to participate in school, system, and statewide assessment programs. Special educators regularly monitor the progress of individuals with ELN in general and special curricula. Special educators use appropriate technologies to support their assessments.

Beginning special educators demonstrate their mastery of this standard through the mastery of the CEC Common Core Knowledge and Skills, as well as through the appropriate CEC Specialty Area(s) Knowledge and Skills for which the program is preparing candidates.

Standard 9: Professional and Ethical Practice

Special educators are guided by the profession's ethical and professional practice standards. Special educators practice in multiple roles and complex situations across wide age and developmental ranges. Their practice requires ongoing attention to legal matters along with serious professional and ethical considerations. Special educators engage in professional activities and participate in learning communities that benefit individuals with ELN, their families, colleagues, and their own professional growth. Special educators view themselves as lifelong learners and regularly reflect on and adjust their practice. Special educators are aware of how their own and others' attitudes, behaviors, and ways of communicating can influence their practice. Special educators understand that culture and language can interact with exceptionalities, and are sensitive to the many aspects of diversity of individuals with ELN and their families. Special educators actively plan and engage in activities that foster their professional growth and keep them current with evidence-based best practices. Special educators know their own limits of practice and practice within them.

Beginning special educators demonstrate their mastery of this standard through the mastery of the CEC Common Core Knowledge and Skills, as well as through the appropriate CEC Specialty Area(s) Knowledge and Skills for which the program is preparing candidates.

Standard 10: Collaboration

Special educators routinely and effectively collaborate with families, other educators, related service providers, and personnel from community agencies in culturally responsive ways. This collaboration assures that the needs of individuals with ELN are addressed throughout schooling. Moreover, special educators embrace their special role as advocate for individuals with ELN. Special educators promote and advocate the learning and well-being of individuals with ELN across a wide range of settings and a range of different learning experiences. Special educators are viewed as specialists by a myriad of people who actively seek their collaboration to effectively include and teach individuals with ELN. Special educators are a resource to their colleagues in understanding the laws and policies relevant to individuals with ELN. Special educators use collaboration to facilitate the successful transitions of individuals with ELN across settings and services.

Beginning special educators demonstrate their mastery of this standard through the mastery of the CEC Common Core Knowledge and Skills, as well as through the appropriate CEC Specialty Area(s) Knowledge and Skills for which the program is preparing candidates.

INTASC PRINCIPLES

Principle 1: The teacher understands the central concepts, tools of inquiry, and structures of the discipline(s) he or she teaches and can create learning experiences that make these aspects of subject matter meaningful for students.

Principle 2: The teacher understands how children learn and develop, and can provide learning opportunities that support the intellectual, social, and personal development of each learner.

Principle 3: The teacher understands how students differ in their approaches to learning and creates instructional opportunities that are adapted to diverse learners.

Principle 4: The teacher understands and uses a variety of instructional strategies to encourage students' development of critical thinking, problem solving, and performance skills.

Principle 5: The teacher uses an understanding of individual and group motivation and behavior to create a learning environment that encourages positive social interaction, active engagement in learning, and self-motivation.

Principle 6: The teacher uses knowledge of effective verbal, nonverbal, and media communication technologies to foster active inquiry, collaboration, and supportive interaction in the classroom.

Principle 7: The teacher plans instruction based on knowledge of subject matter, students, the community, and curriculum goals.

Principle 8: The teacher understands and uses formal and informal assessment strategies to evaluate and ensure the continuous intellectual, social, and physical development of the learner.

Principle 9: The teacher is a reflective practitioner who continually evaluates the effects of his/her choices and actions on others (students, parents, and other professionals in the learning community) and who actively seeks out opportunities to grow professionally.

Principle 10: The teacher fosters relationships with school colleagues, families, and agencies in the larger community to support students' learning and well-being.

PRAXIS CATEGORIES: SPECIAL EDUCATION KNOWLEDGE-BASED CORE PRINCIPLES

i.   Understanding Exceptionalities

ii.   Legal and Societal Issues

iii.   Delivery of Services to Students with Disabilities

I.   *Understanding Exceptionalities*

- Theories and principles of human development and learning, including research and theories related to human development; theories of learning; social and emotional development; language development; cognitive development; and physical development, including motor and sensory

- Characteristics of students with disabilities, including medical/physical; educational; social; and psychological

- Basic concepts in special education, including definitions of all major categories and specific disabilities; causation and prevention of disability; the nature of behaviors, including frequency, duration, intensity, and degrees of severity; and classification of students with disabilities, including classifications as represented in IDEA and labeling of students

II.   *Legal and Societal Issues*

- Federal laws and landmark legal cases related to special education (for example, P.L. 94–142, P.L. 101–476 [IDEA], Section 504, ADA, Rowley re: program appropriateness, Tatro re: related services, Honig re: discipline)

- Issues related to school, family, and/or community, such as teacher advocacy for students and families, including advocating for educational change and developing student self-advocacy; family participation and support systems; public attitudes toward individuals with disabilities; and cultural and community influences

III.   *Delivery of Services to Students with Disabilities*

- Conceptual approaches underlying the delivery of services to students with disabilities (for example, medical, psychodynamic, behavioral, cognitive, sociological, eclectic)

- Professional roles and responsibilities of teachers of students with disabilities (for example, teacher as a collaborator with other teachers, parents, community groups, and outside agencies); teacher as a multidisciplinary team member; teacher's role in selecting appropriate environments and providing appropriate services to students; knowledge and use of professional literature, research (including classroom research), and professional organizations and associations; and reflecting on one's own teaching

- Assessment, including how to modify, construct, or select and conduct nondiscriminatory and appropriate informal and formal assessment procedures; how to interpret standardized and specialized assessment results; how to use evaluation results for various purposes, including monitoring instruction and IEP/ITP development; and how to prepare written reports and communicate findings to others

- Placement and program issues (including continuum of services; mainstreaming; integration; inclusion; least restrictive environment; non-categorical, categorical, and cross-categorical programs; related services; early intervention; community-based training; transition of students into and within special education placements; post-school transitions; and access to assistive technology)

- Curriculum and instruction, including the IEP/ITP process; instructional development and implementation (for example, instructional activities, curricular materials, resources and equipment, working with classroom personnel, tutoring and the use of technology); teaching strategies and methods (for example, direct instruction, cooperative learning, diagnostic-prescriptive method); instructional format and components (for example, individualized instruction, small- and large-group instruction, modeling, drill and practice); and areas of instruction (such as academics; study and learning skills; social, self-care, and vocational skills)

- Management of the learning environment, including behavior management (for example, behavior analysis—identification and definition of antecedents, target behavior, and consequent events, data-gathering procedures, selecting and using behavioral interventions); classroom organization/management (for example, providing the appropriate physical-social environment for learning—expectations, rules, consequences, consistency, attitudes, lighting, seating, access, and strategies for positive interactions, transitions between lessons and activities); grouping of students; and effective and efficient documentation (such as parent-teacher contacts and legal records)

Index